Memories

Edited by Mihaela GLIGOR

# MEMORIES OF TERROR

## Essays on Recent Histories

CEEOLPRESS 2021

Typesetting: CEEOL GmbH, Frankfurt am Main
Layout: Alexander Neroslavsky

ISBN: 978-3-946993-88-9
E-ISBN-13: 978-3-946993-87-2

# Contents

# Foreword

The idea of the current volume came to me in July 2019, on a warm Sunday morning, while visiting the Jewish Cemetery on Okopowa Street in Warsaw. I had been residing in Warsaw for a couple of months already, as a Senior Fellow at the Polish Institute of Advanced Studies, within the Polish Academy of Sciences, working on *(In)Tolerance: Cultural and Political Interactions in Interwar Europe*. My research took me to many places that told the (hi)story of the Jewish community, including POLIN Museum of the History of Polish Jews, Muzeum Polaków Ratujących Żydów/The Markowa Ulma-Family Museum of Poles Who Saved Jews in World War II, the Auschwitz-Birkenau Memorial and Museum, the State Museum at Majdanek, and other places where terrible things happened.

My visit to the Jewish Cemetery – which was established in 1806 and it is the resting place of over 200,000 persons, including spiritual leaders, political activists, creators of Jewish culture, eminent contributors to Polish cultural, economic and social life, and also thousands of nameless victims of the ghetto – was a lesson on remembrance and cultural memory. The Cemetery is a unique landmark of Warsaw, being visited by tens of thousands of tourists every year. While visiting it, I learned that it had been included in the register of historical buildings and monuments in 1973 and has remained under the protection of the Office of Historic Preservation of the Capital City of Warsaw ever since.

What impressed me the most were the many carefully restored funeral stones, some even rebuilt, by members of the family, scattered all over the world (details of the surviving relatives taking care of the restoration process were placed next to the tombs). Those made me think about how surviving family members take care and preserve the memory of ancestors. When memory lives, the departed live, too, but when memory dies, their departure is irrevocable. So I wondered: What should we do to keep their memory alive? In the Jewish Cemetery on Okopowa Street, monuments that look like works of art tell the stories of rich and famous Jews, while near them (or across the alley) there is a nameless mass grave. Here lie some of the victims of the Holocaust. Others did not have mass graves. They are the ash underneath our feet when we visit Auschwitz-Birkenau.

We are our memory. Our own history is nothing else but another type of cultural memory. The relationship between cultural memory, remembrance, and culture itself has emerged globally as an issue of interdisciplinary research. Philosophy, theology, cultural history, psychology, literature and art, or sociology, are all involved in defining and explaining what cultural memory is and why this concept is so important for the humanities.

Stories dealing with the post-Holocaust life of survivors are as important as the stories of the Holocaust itself. I invited several researchers who work on Holocaust and memory studies to join me in this project dealing with memories of terror. I am grateful to those who accepted my invitation: Dr. Sonia Catrina, from the Elie Wiesel National Institute for the Study of the Holocaust in Romania; Dr. Katharina Friedla, from the Fondation pour la Mémoire de la Shoah, Paris; Professor Tuvia Friling, from Ben-Gurion University of the Negev, Israel; Professor Arleen Ionescu, from Shanghai Jiao Tong University; Eugenia Mihalcea, researcher and PhD student at University of Haifa, Israel; and Olga Ștefan, who managed to set up *The Future of Memory* platform, where stories about Holocaust survivors can be found.

The contributors to this volume worked independently, not knowing what the others were writing, or even who the other collaborators were. Thus, it is absolutely remarkable that their works complete one another and create a wonderful volume that covers the vast area of humanities and offer new documents regarding the situation of Holocaust survivors in Europe and beyond. Each chapter includes a well-documented bibliography, thorough notes, and thought-provoking analyses, making the volume indispensable for both the academic community (professors, students, researchers) focusing on Holocaust and memory studies, World

War II, and related topics, and also for those readers interested in Jewish history, in general. I thank all the contributors to this volume for their inspiring research papers and wonderful collaboration, as well as for their constructive discussions and openness.

I am very grateful to Professor Raphael Vago, from Tel Aviv University, Israel, for his willingness to write such a wonderful Introduction to this volume. Since 2014, we have met almost every year, in Tel Aviv, during my annual inter-academic exchange trips to Israel, or in Cluj-Napoca and Brașov, when he travels to Romania for conferences or lectures at summer schools, and I have always cherished his encouraging words and support for my academic trajectory. I am just as grateful to Professor Przemysław Urbańczyk, the director of the Polish Institute of Advanced Studies in Warsaw, Poland, for his warm support during my stay there and for his inspiring words regarding this collection.

In the end, I owe a debt of gratitude to all those who have helped me in various ways in this endeavor: Iulian Țanea, from CEEOL (Central and Eastern European Online Library), for suggesting the publishing house to me; Krisztina Kós, the director of CEEOL Press, for accepting this volume for publication and for the entire collaboration that transformed the manuscript into a precious book; Camelia Crăciun, from the University of Bucharest, for her insightful suggestions; and Professor Marius Turda, from Oxford Brookes University, for his wonderful words about this volume. In addition, I would like to thank my family for their support and unconditional love.

I am confident that this volume will inspire many researchers in the vast area of humanities and in Holocaust studies, in particular. The memory of all those who suffered and perished will live forever. My hope is that this volume will enhance the reader's appreciation of and sensitivity to different points of view regarding the persistence of memory in our post-Holocaust world.

Cluj-Napoca, August 1, 2020

# Introduction

*Raphael Vago*

"How do you know that we are interested in keeping you alive?" This is how Captain Burădescu, the commanding officer on duty in the Vapniarka concentration camp in Transnistria, replied to a delegation of three inmate physicians who complained on the terrible situation in the camp (in Ștefan's chapter in this volume).

This volume introduces us to different perspectives and multi-disciplinary aspects of memories of terror in the eyes of survivors as presented and analyzed by the various authors. If there were any dialogues between the perpetrators and victims, the words of Captain Burădescu ran through most of the studies in the volume.

Although there are several studies focusing on Romania (Mihaela Gligor, Sonia Catrina, Eugenia Mihalcea, Olga Ștefan), three of them focusing on the Holocaust in Romania in the killing fields of Transnistria, the other studies offer a wide perspective both in terms of the geographical, topical, and analytical approaches: Katharina Friedla on the less-researched aspects of religious and social life of Polish Jews in the USSR during World War II; Tuvia Friling on the strange life, death, and after-life of Eliezer Gruenbaum/Leon Berger in Auschwitz-Birkenau, a study dealing as a test case "with the complicated, entangled, and fragile 'relations' between history, memory, and politics" (a definition that could be applied to some of the other studies in the volume); and Arleen Ionescu's analysis of Kathy Kacer's *Shanghai Escape*, a book aimed at a younger readership.

While each of the contributors worked separately and unaware of who the other authors were and what they were writing, the theoretical-contextual apparatus with ample and updated bibliography is common between all the studies. As Mihaela Gligor wrote in her analysis of Saul Steinberg's view of the world from Palas Street, her topic is one of "cultural memory" and the role

11

of the "places of memory" (*les lieux de mémoire*), such places figure in various forms in all the studies in the volume. "Memories are delicate", wrote Gligor in her chapter, but, as is seen in most of the case studies presented in this volume, they are also traumatic. In fact, Saul Steinberg's case as the emigrant artist is different, because he did not suffer direct trauma, he succeeded in evading it in face of rising danger of anti-Semitism, extremism, fascism, but the memory of Palas Street in Bucharest pursued him in his artistic representation. Gligor analyzes some of Steinberg's works as related to the "places of memory" by answering the question of how the artist processed the memories of his childhood, of the center of his world – Palas Street in Bucharest – in his works of art.

The politics of memory is evident in several of the studies. The sociopolitical context is very essential in order to understand the memories and aftermath of terror and trauma. Thus, Tuvia Friling's study, based on his well-known Hebrew and English version of his work on Eliezer Gruenbaum/Leon Berger, the *kapo* from Auschwitz-Birkenau, traces the political implications of this enigmatic story, including his death in battle, or perhaps execution, in Israel's War of Independence, on the polemics in Israeli society and in the political spectrum linked to Eliezer Gruenbaum's father, Yitzhak Gruenbaum, the most important secular leader of interwar Poland's Jewish community and a prominent Israeli politician. The life and death story of Eliezer Gruenbaum, alias Leon Berger, is a fascinating and tragic story. The hero's road as a communist, anti-Zionist, secularist to his role as a *kapo*, the legacy and the arguments around his behavior and performance there, which is a tragedy in itself on the role and place of the *kapo* in Holocaust historiography, his postwar trial, all present one of the more enigmatic stories of the Holocaust and its memory.

In this category of the politics of memory and the memory of terror belongs Eugenia Mihalcea's study based on seven interviews conducted between 1983 and 1984 in Israel with children survivors from Transnistria, while it also belongs to the Romanian themes of the volume. In her theoretical discussion she emphasizes, following Kangisser-Cohen, that survivors changed their stories as individual memory is a continuous negotiation and dialogue in time influenced by the sociopolitical context in which the interviewees lived. She is looking in her research at several questions, also evident in Sonia Catrina's study of Miriam Korber-Bercovici firsthand account of her plight and dehumanization in Transnistria.

Among other essential questions Mihalcea is asking are: "How do they recall the Holocaust? How do they choose to talk about Transnistria? How do they identify themselves as survivors of the Holocaust?" The important part of her study is that they were no longer children when they testified, and that their perception of their own past is in close connection with their experiences over the years that have passed. And in the case of her study, the interviews conducted in 1983 and 1984 reflected the "conspiracy of silence" that existed through the years Israeli society was busy nation building and creating the "new Jew," so that these stories were not heard and people were not interested in hearing them. Mihalcea traces the developing attitudes to the Holocaust in Israel through its various stages, including the shifting of attention to the Holocaust during the Eichmann trial in 1961, which is seen as a turning point in the attitudes in Israel toward the Holocaust. Thus, in her analysis the memories of the trauma are reflected through the personal development and the fate of the survivors in Israel against a background of the shifting shapes of the politics of memory in the young state of Israel.

Sonia Catrina focuses on the diary of Miriam Korber-Bercovici, published in Romania in 1995. Like the other authors of the volume, she provides an ample theoretical introduction on the question of trauma. Korber-Bercovici's diary, like so many diaries and memoirs of the Holocaust, highlights the contrast between life before the tragedy and the trauma of the deportation and its aftermath, the process of dehumanization, and the rapid change from the vanished past into the tragic present. The analysis of the diary provides a picture of the social and human conditions in her native town, the social categories, the growing radicalization of Romanian society and politics. The vivid descriptions of life before the beginning of the deportations are in the sharpest contrast with the rapid process of dislocation, terror, and dehumanization that the young girl and her family underwent, as she felt that "I was not a human being any more." The feeling of terror, anxiety, and trauma accompanied the terrible sights she has seen in the various station and locations of her deportation.

Transnistria, the killing field of the Romanian Holocaust, also figures in Olga Ștefan's study of Vapniarka, one of the most notorious camps in Transnistria. The camp was directly administered by the Ministry of Internal Affairs (and not by the authorities of the Transnistria region) and was intended for political prisoners, most of them Jewish. Ștefan analyzes in depth several memoirs written by former inmates and compares the various approaches to the memory of terror conveyed by those former inmates. Most of the inmates were either members of the underground communist movement or leftist activists. What is very clear from the testimonies is the high degree of internal discipline, organization, hierarchy, solidarity, and cooperation that existed between the inmates, which helped enable their survival. Their spiritual well-being was also bolstered by various social activities. The study also reflects, as other studies and testimonies from Transnistria have indicated, the differentiation in the behavior of the Romanian officers and staff, including the camp commanders. In the case of the Vapniarka inmates, as also in other cases, this differentiation was helped via "negotiations" by the inmates with the authorities. At Vapniarka, for example, this involved the inmate physicians and leaders of the inmates. The study also reflects on the memory of Vapniarka in communist historiography, which diminished or ignored the Jewish origins of most of the inmates. There is no doubt that Ștefan's study adds another compelling aspect to the "Romanian side" of the present volume.

Among the interdisciplinary approaches in the various studies in the volume, Arleen Ionescu's chapter stands out as it combines psychoanalysis and memory and trauma studies, amply quoted and presented in various parts of the text, in order to "explore the traces of the protagonist's memory." Ionescu analyzes Kathy Kacer's *Shanghai Escape*, a book written to be accessible to readers of a younger age. It is a saga of displacement and terror set in the Shanghai Ghetto as seen through the eyes of a young girl from Vienna, Lily Toufar. The story that starts when Lily's family leaves Vienna on the eve of the Kristallnacht, November 8, 1938. From Vienna to Shanghai, and there from one place to another and finally to Toronto, the journey is also one of memories of terror, like that of the Japanese invaders' brutality toward the Chinese people. As Ionescu writes, "she had learned to master her fears of mice and bugs and, in a world in which she witnessed the obliteration of individuals every day and in which death was always present, her fear of death." Based on a true story, *Shanghai Escape* was very well received, and undoubtedly Ionescu's analysis has added a provoking interpretation of young Lily's repression of memory but also of the ways in which she mastered her fears.

Another chapter in the volume that focuses on dislocation and almost impossible journeys is that of Katharina Friedla on the religious and social life of Polish Jews in the USSR during World War II. It aims to "present the trajectories of lives of Polish Jews who remained faithful to their religion in the face of persecution and mass violence in the Soviet Union during World War II." Jewish fate brought Polish Jews as the Szczukowski and Bankir families to baking *matzah* for the Passover holiday, somewhere between Tashkent and Samarkand, after having been exiles by the NKVD to Siberia and then drifted to the Central Asia republics. The saga of religious Polish-Jewish families, running away from the Nazis, for a time persecuted by the Soviet authorities' antireligious policy, is a story of keeping Jewish life and traditions, and developing strategies of not only physical survival but also spiritual one, a topic that that was not very much researched, as the author pointed out. The preservation and keeping forms of national-religious and social identity is presented in this chapter as a case study in forms of Jewish fate during the war years, as those Polish-Jewish refugees fled from the Nazis, encountered for a time Soviet hostility, many of them ultimately creating in Samarkand a "vibrant center of Jewish religious life."

As Mihaela Gligor, the editor of the present volume, wrote in her essay on Saul Steinberg, "The manner in which a community relates to the past involves different actions such as connectivity, storage, retrieval, transmission, and (re)interpretation."

The essays in this volume indeed reflect the various aspects of memories of terror – and of remembering and learning from the past.

Tel Aviv, June 8, 2020

# 1. Dehumanization, the Metaphor of Jewish Errant Life, and the Sense of Self in Miriam Korber–Bercovici's Firsthand Accounts

*Sonia Catrina*

*Definition of the Research Problem*

Considering that the depth of children's Holocaust experiences is by no means subsidiary to that of adults, but, on the contrary, their firsthand accounts make an important contribution to understanding and historicizing their trauma during World War II, we decided to undertake a study of children's responses to the genocidal violence having challenged their existence. Moreover, we have adopted a gendered standpoint of war experiences, in this manner allowing for a specificity that needs to be taken into account when approaching childhood and adolescence during the Holocaust.

By situating the topic of our study within the emerging field created at the intersection of Jewish studies, memory studies, and gender studies, the objective of this chapter is to ethnographically study Miriam Korber's personal experience during the Holocaust. Miriam Korber (later Bercovici) was born in 1923, to a Jewish family of masters from Câmpulung Moldovenesc (henceforth Câmpulung). In October 1941, several days after having turned eighteen, she was deported along with her family from her hometown to Transnistria, a territory under the Romanian authority during the Second Word War. Before the deportation from the Câmpulung railway station, a friend offered her a journal as a gift. She used it to put into writing her experience of various ghettos: Atachi (Basarabia), where she would only pass through, Moghilev (Ukraine), where she would lose her grandparents on her father's side, and Djurin (Ukraine), where she would spend three years with her family. Miriam Korber-Bercovici's *Jurnal de ghetou* [Ghetto journal], first published in 1992, is based on the diary she kept during her deportation to Transnistria. The original diary has been given to the Holocaust Memorial Museum in Washington, DC, and an important part of it has been published in English in Alexandra Zapruder, ed., *Salvaged Pages: Young Writers' Diaries of the Holocaust* (2002).

While Miriam's *Ghetto Journal* "echoes many of the experiences of Jews from Eastern Europe,"[1] at the same time it offers a window into the history of the Holocaust, as lived by a Jewish girl of Romanian origin, at the time of transition from adolescence to adulthood. More specifically, the *Ghetto Journal* foregrounds Miriam's Holocaust experience, as an adolescent Jewish girl from Câmpulung Moldovenesc (a town situated in the southern part of the Romanian province of Bukovina), at the time when she was interned in the Djurin Ghetto, Romania (present-day Moldova). Through the daily notes recorded in her *Ghetto Journal* from October 1941 until her liberation in May 1944, sometimes with large gaps and silences, the author gives the reader insights into the multifaceted issue of deportation in a confined space where she lived with her family and other deported Jews, practically without any means of subsistence other than those brought by her family to Transnistria. Unlike other diaries written during deportation in which there are indications about perpetrators, Miriam does not give detailed information about the authorities from Câmpulung, Moghilev, or Djurin. Peripheral to her deportation are also records of moments when the attitude toward Jews

---

1   Facing History and Ourselves, "*Teaching Salvaged Pages.*"

from Bukovina had dramatically changed, along with other imposed restrictions, in the prewar period up to the deportation. Instead, Miriam focuses especially on her personal experiences in moments of companionship and on her social relationships with other Jews and non-Jews. In this regard, Miriam has explained that her diary contains her innermost feelings that she could not transmit to anyone else.[2]

The choice of this case study clearly shows that our research is relevant for at least three reasons: first, it contributes to the discussion of genocide on the Romanian territories; second, it focuses on a social category underrepresented in the discipline of Holocaust and genocide studies, thus accounting for an overlooked perspective of the Holocaust; third, it raises issues relevant to the discipline, addressing children's daily routines and ways of coping with deportation.

Because of the nature of the firsthand information recollected, revealing especially personal feelings, attitudes and behaviors in respect to the social world of deportation, the author has questioned both the literary aspects of her writings, as well as the usefulness of their presentation in the public space. In the Afterword of the book, Miriam has offered some clues about what prompted her to publish her autobiographical text, half a century after the Holocaust had occurred. From her personal standpoint, "the existence of ghettos and camps is either totally denied" or considered "an unpleasant incident that we should forget about and of which, anyway, only the Germans were guilty" (Korber-Bercovici, Afterword, 125, hereafter Afterword). Positioning herself against these assumptions that deny or minimize the existence of the Holocaust, Miriam declares that "everyone must assume the past as it was, including the deportations and crimes in Transnistria" (Afterword, 125-126) and she passes on to the reader her belief in the importance of knowing the past. From this reflective perspective regarding the contemporaneous attitudes toward

---

2    Florian, "Foreword," 12.

"the turning point in history" that was the Holocaust, her *Ghetto Journal* is deemed by historian Alexandru Florian as "an open message to society."[3]

Another important aspect of her "self-revealing," "self-reflective" and "self-assessing"[4] writing that makes her *Ghetto Journal* so special to our study is to understand her "despair about the purpose of writing,"[5] clearly expressed on July 15, 1942:

> I know that all my writing is meaningless. Nobody will read my journal and, as for me, should I escape alive from here, I will throw into the fire everything that will remind me of the damned time spent in Djurin. And still, I write.
> (Korber-Bercovici, *Jurnal de ghetou*, 87, hereafter *Journal*)

Miriam's mental turmoil caused by the necessity of writing down her Holocaust experience resembles that experienced by Elsa Binder, a Jewish girl from Poland, imprisoned in the Stanisławów Ghetto, who also stated the need to express her feelings. It was "near the end of her teen years when war disrupted [Elsa]'s life,"[6] after the pogrom on October 12, 1941, that "killed ten thousand Jews in the town," when Elsa and the other surviving Jews of Stanisławów "were forced into the newly formed ghetto, where they lived with the constant fear of deportation and death."[7] Although the two girls had different social and cultural backgrounds, and they were captive in ghettos in different countries, their similar emotional states while confronting violence and oppression make their Holocaust experiences comparable. In their diaries, Miriam and Elsa unfolded their families' daily struggles against hunger and bitter cold. Both described in great detail their frustrations, fears, dreams, and constant hope for lib-

---

3   Florian, "Foreword," 5.
4   Adelman. "Self, Other, and Community," 117.
5   "Miriam Korber – Transnistria," 243.
6   Holocaust Memorial Resource & Education Center of Florida, "The Diary of Elsa Binder."
7   Facing History and Ourselves, "Elsa Binder."

eration. While struggling with the reality of what was happening in the confined space of their ghettos, both showed hints of hope. Like Miriam, considering that she is young and she has "a right to fight and to demand everything from life,"[8] on December 24, 1941, Elsa wrote:

> I have to admit to myself that I personally don't believe in an early liberation. I want it and I fear it. From today's perspective a free tomorrow seems to be extremely bright. In my dreams I expect so much from it. [...] But desiring it so much, I fear it. I realize that under the circumstances such thoughts are irrational, but.... Never mind. What really matters is liberation.[9]

Despite the hope for liberation, Elsa was aware that "the atmosphere of continual crisis was distorting her normal attitudes and emotions."[10] Moreover, struggling with the reality of Stanisławów Ghetto, Elsa wondered why she was condemned to suffering:

> Now, when my youth is blooming – and this happens only once for each human being – I am to die without having experienced anything good in life? Why? Was it a sin to be born to a Jewish mother? Have I ever hurt anybody? Why is a man, who is my peer and whom I see for the first time in my life, my deadly enemy, why can he kill hundreds of thousands of innocent people?[11]

Eventually, entirely demoralized by the harsh reality of the ghetto, on June 9, 1942, Elsa confessed that her "whole scribbling doesn't make any sense. It is a fact we are not going to survive. The world will know about everything even without my wise notes."[12] Indeed, it is believed that Elsa and her family per-

---

8    BHEC, "Elsa Binder – Stanislawow, Poland."
9    BHEC, "Elsa Binder – Stanislawow, Poland."
10   Holocaust Memorial Resource & Education Center of Florida, "The Diary of Elsa Binder.".
11   BHEC, "Elsa Binder – Stanislawow, Poland."
12   "Elsa Binder – Stanisławów, Poland," 327.

ished later on, in February 1943, at the Stanisławów Ghetto execution site, "although the exact circumstances of their deaths are not known."[13] Her diary was found "in a ditch on the side of the road leading to the cemetery, which was the execution site for the Stanislawow Jews."[14]

As for Miriam, the meaningless of her writing is given by her disappointment of not being able to escape from the horrendous reality of the ghetto and return home. In fact, being aware of her imprisonment, Miriam has also confessed that she spoke to her diary, she quarreled with herself or "with life, with God, with everyone," in hoping for a return, but the following day she was once more disappointed about it. From this perspective, it is interesting to explore Miriam's "self-conscious" emotions at play in identity settings.

However, apart from the exploration of the cognitive, affective, and behavioral aspects of Miriam's deportation to Transnistria, our interest in her journal is also raised by the poignant life experience the adolescent girl draws using daily details of her survival in the Djurin Ghetto, which she described as a "good" one (Afterword, 122). While recounting her psychological reactions to the experience of the Djurin Ghetto, Miriam has also described her perceptions of social ruptures in the Transnistrian social setting imposed by the Romanian authorities. At the same time, Miriam has examined the behavior of the displaced Jews at various times of deportation, occasioned by the "loss of connection with the civilized world" (Afterword, 122), being shocked that the deported Jews were "insensitive to the sufferings of those around them and even to the mystery of death" (Afterword, 123).

Given these primary elements, we ask whether the physical and psychological dissolution of the deported Jews is related to their dehumanization. How does Miriam explain the psychological reactions of the Jews to the experience of the ghetto? What

---

13   BHEC, "Elsa Binder – Stanislawow, Poland."; Facing History and Ourselves, "Elsa Binder."

14   Facing History and Ourselves, "Elsa Binder."

about hers? To delve into these questions, we turn to scholars who conceptualized trauma in relationship with stigma.

## Theoretical Background of the Research

The present chapter explores stereotypes and prejudice as racial boundaries of stigmatization internalized by the Jewish minority deported to Transnistria, prevailing in Miriam Korber-Bercovici's firsthand accounts. We integrate into our perspective the phenomena of stigma as an inferiority complex and specifically look at the extent to which anti-Semitic persecution affected the Jewish young people of the war generation and how extreme moral and physical trauma was inflicted on them. Thus, from a methodological stance, our approach combines psychological with sociological and trauma studies.

The starting point is the definition of ethnic groups as "social categories which provide a basis for status ascription."[15] While considering ethnic and racial boundaries as relational constructs and interethnic relations organized with reference to statuses that are ascribed to an ethnic group, at the same time we deem identity as a "dynamic process that changes during the whole life, being marked by ruptures and crises."[16] With this in mind, and concurrently considering that individuals are victims of social normative judgments, we argue that the individual's encapsulation in a specific category leads to a stigma-based social identity. In Erving Goffman's view, "stigma" is a deeply discrediting attribute that differentiates and separates "them" from "us," disqualifying and preventing individuals in the first category from being fully accepted.[17] Relying on the assumption that "a person with a stigma is not quite human," the stigmatizer "exercise[s] varieties of discrimination,"[18] thus reducing the stigmatized person's life chances. Goffman added that "[w]e construct a stig-

---

15    Eidheim, "When Ethnic Identity Is a Social Stigma," 39.
16    Stets and Burke, "Identity Theory," 234.
17    Goffman, *Stigma*, 3–4.
18    Goffman, *Stigma*, 5.

ma-theory, an ideology to explain his inferiority and account for the danger he represents."[19] Referring to the social identity of a stigmatized person, Crocker, Major and Steele explained that when "the person is devalued, spoiled, or flawed in the eyes of others" this "calls into question his or her full humanity."[20] By further elaborating on Goffman's interactionist perspective of identity, we take into account the contextual and dynamic nature of stigma which involves a combination of negative stereotyped beliefs, prejudiced attitudes, and discriminatory behavior toward individuals pertaining to an ethnic group. By agreeing that stigmata does not exist in itself, but, conversely, emerges when the relations between personal attributes and stereotypes are established, we think that the stigmatization process contains a form of racial violence exerted on the stigmatized ethnic group.

By examining Miriam Korber-Bercovici's experiences during the Holocaust, this study attempts to address the question of trauma caused by reification of anti-Semitic stereotypes and dehumanization at play in identity settings and personal empowerment. In this endeavor, we cross-examine her published *Ghetto Journal* in conjunction with her other personal confessions recollected through oral history interviews.[21] The use of a qualitative methodology to explore psychological dehumanization in the context of the deportation of the Jews to Transnistria allows us to investigate aspects of personal and social identity against the political, ideological, and social background of growing anti-Semitic, racist, and xenophobic attitudes which led to state-spon-

---

19   Goffman, *Stigma*, 5.
20   Crocker, Major, and Steele, "Social Stigma," 504.
21   We have used as primary sources the interview with Miriam Korber-Bercovici carried out by Cosmina Gușu on October 31, 2009, for the Elie Wiesel National Institute for the Study of the Holocaust in Romania ("Interviu Miriam Korber-Bercovici"), as well as the interview carried out by Maria Andrieș for Libertatea, posted online on July 19, 2019, ("Lecția de viață a lui Mirjam Bercovici"). We have complemented our primary sources with the August 2003 interview carried out by Ana-Maria Hincu for Centropa ("Miriam Bercovici, Bucharest, Romania).

sored genocidal actions during World War II within the territories under Romanian authority. Therefore, our perspective reflects a functionalist view of negative emotions at play in identity settings and provides evidence for the experience of grief associated with ongoing moral and physical pain.

The chapter is organized into three sections: the first one unveils Miriam's family values and behaviors in conjunction with social emotions and state discrimination up to deportation. The second one delves into the social world of deportation in Transnistria, in an attempt to disclose Miriam's self-conscious feelings and their implications for her identity. The third section discloses Miriam's efforts to overcome dehumanization and recraft her fractured self in the aftermath of World War II.

### Family Values, Social Emotions, and State Discrimination up to Deportation

Miriam's childhood memories were mainly focused on her relationship with her maternal and paternal grandparents and their attitudes, behaviors, and values, as well as on the social and cultural life in her native city.

Miriam had "a very close relationship" with her maternal grandparents from Botoşani, whom she would visit "each year, at least twice." Their image seems to reverberate in Miriam's memory especially because, as a child, she spent a while in Botoşani where she would go "before the autumn celebrations" and "for the Christmas holydays." Moreover, her mother used to bring from Botoşani "some things which, for Câmpulung, were delicacies, for it was a smaller town." The affective connection with her maternal grandparents is evident in the way she talks about her two grandmothers after whom she was named:

> I was named Miriam after my grandmother, who died when my mother was eleven. I was given the name Lya after my [other] grandmother. I am Miriam Lya Bercovici. So I have the names of the mothers my mother has loved. I made a connection. I don't know if it has any significance

25

apart from a romantic one. ("Interviu Miriam Korber-Bercovici," hereafter "Interview")

Moreover, about her maternal grandparents, who died in 1945, she remembers that "they were an average family that sometimes had some financial trouble," "with an education level specific to merchants. They could read and my real grandmother, my mother used to say, was from a respectable family," "a rich family even." Miriam describes them as wearing

> not religious clothes, but German clothes – as they used to say back in those days. Grandmother did not wear a wig [and she] tended to be elegant. My grandfather used to wear a winter fur overcoat and a hat. He did not shave. Jews trimmed their beard, a beard very close to the modern ones, like nowadays – not drawn, but a small beard and a moustache. Grandmother wore a hair-loop, but she also dressed her hair. Grandfather would go to the Jewish theater and Grandmother to the cinema. I don't know if Grandfather would go, too. ("Interview")

More to the point, her maternal grandparents

> respected the Sabbath and the other holidays. Grandfather, as he grew old, used to go to the synagogue, where he was a vestryman. It was also a meeting place; it served as a club, too, especially in the case of the Jewish synagogues, where one could speak, where one did not have to stay quiet, where anyone could say their prayers. Grandmother did not go to the synagogue on Saturdays, only on holidays, when the women go. She knew how to read religious books, too. My second grandmother was more cultivated, it seems, than the usual women, and she would dominate Grandfather. [...] Grandfather was in the Committee for the Jewish Community. I have a photograph of him with all the important members who were active in the community. ("Interview")

About one of their dwellings in Botoşani she remembers that "it was on a higher floor. It was furnished in a civilized manner. They had maids, housemaids, as they used to call them." Their second house was "somewhat nicer. There were three rooms. When I came from Transnistria, they conceded one room for me and my father, but with great parsimony, with a lot of restraint." Miriam recalls that in the dwelling there were Romanian carpets, while in the kitchen the carpets were those that one could buy by the meter and were woven from cloth scraps. These carpets "weren't Oltenian carpets, but they were carpets still. Not Persian, like the rich people had." "Now they would be considered very elegant, but then they were used in the kitchen." The high living standard her family had is also visible in the description of the manner in which her grandparents organized their daily life. For example, they valued cleanliness, both for themselves and for their domestic situation:

> It was very clean. They would starch the clothes. [My grandparents] wore nightgowns, not pajamas, as was usual for most people, especially due to their social status. They would change their clothes on Saturdays and the sheets and bedding were changed every three weeks. On Saturdays, Grandfather would change all his clothes. I don't know if he went to the mikvah, but I know that he would go to the steam bath. There probably was a mikvah, too. I don't know, but I know that on Fridays Grandfather would go to the steam bath. He would come back and say: "I had an extraordinary steam bath!" He would be very satisfied. Grandmother did not talk about this thing. It was a personal matter and a civilized person does not talk about going to the bath. ("Interview")

However, the grandparents to whom Miriam had been "essentially tied" and whom she mentions in her *Ghetto Journal* are the ones on her father's side, from Câmpulung. They were "very good and warm," but "certainly poorer" and "simpler" than her grandparents on her mother's side from Botoșani. Their house had only one room, but later they built on another room to be their bedroom, "because otherwise they would all have to sleep in the same room. It is interesting that in one room there was an upright piano." The modest house of her paternal grandparents "which in the beginning was formed of a single room" was later extended so that "from the room one could pass into the kitchen, from the kitchen into the workshop, from the workshop into the glass shop." As in Câmpulung, "there was no sewerage back then. The toilet was a latrine that was cleaned and washed once a week. But it was a latrine." Miriam's grandparents had the same in their home. They "would take a bath on Fridays, in a bathtub. Husband and wife would use the same water." Unlike her maternal grandparents, her paternal ones did not have a housemaid ("Interview").

Because she spent her childhood living next to these grandparents, her memory is full of warm recollections, like the "permanent come and go" between the two homes. The home of her paternal grandparents was her refuge every time an unpleasant event took place in her life. This way she was able to avoid being scolded by her parents: "If I got a bad mark, [...] I would go to my grandparents and I would cry and I would not go home. And if my parents scolded me, I would run away to my grandparents." She still remembers how often she used to visit them up to the deportation: "I used to come from school first to my grandparents and then I would go home. And there was no day that I was not at my grandparents in the evenings." ("Interview")

Although she was not born in her grandparents' house, but "in a house that does not exist anymore in Câmpulung, on the shore of the Moldova River, at a watermill," Miriam had known them since she was born. The customs in her grandparents' kitchen followed the Jewish traditions to a great measure, as the meat "was kosher for everyone. The meat was bought from a kosher butcher and we would take the birds to the hakam to kill them." However, compared to her grandparents, she remembers that her family was not "so religious" and did not always eat kosher: "We, for example, used to eat ham, which was not kosher, but did keep it on a separate plate." At the same time, Miriam emphasizes that "the more religious families would not buy milk from the peasants, as my mother did," but only from "Jews who kept cows and sold milk." Moreover, Miriam recounts some culinary customs that distinguished her mother's cooking from that of her grandparents':

> At Grandmother's I ate very simple things, mostly dishes with lots of potatoes, like the Germans. She made them better than my mother. One could add an egg, or not add one either, some pepper maybe and then they were made into meatballs. Those meatballs were wonderful!

Asked about the type of clothes her paternal grandparents used to wear – Western or religious – Miriam recalls that "my grandfather used to wear a somewhat longer coat, more Jewish-like. With a small beard, too. He would go twice a day to the synagogue," while "Grandmother was always modestly dressed. Maybe on Saturdays she was more smartly dressed. In 1936 she had cataract surgery, but she got progressively blind. However, she knew where everything was, blind as she was" ("Interview").

Her "very good and warm" maternal grandparents, whom Miriam cherished so much and whose image obsessively reverberated in her memory, were modestly schooled: "Grandfather knew how to read, but my grandmother did not. She was illiterate. [...] She knew Romanian, of course. But at home she would speak Yiddish or German." This aspect did not hinder them in transmitting knowledge, familial behaviors, and social norms. Despite not being able to read, her grandmother told Miriam "the most wonderful stories in the world." Not only did her grandmother know how to tell stories that "probably she had heard and then adapted," but "she wanted me to tell her stories, too." From "a family story that has passed down for generations," Miriam recalls her grandfather's efforts to overcome his poor social situation at the time when he already had three children, "probably during the great Romanian emigration." Apparently, he went to Gura Humorului (which is not far from Câmpulung) to buy merchandise for his shop, but then "he disappeared for two and a half or three years." He had gone to America. "Then he came back with enough money to build the house I found them living in." Referring to this family story, Miriam would keep asking him: "'What's it like in America, Grandfather? Tell me!' and he would say: 'I do not know America. I only saw America from rooftops. I built roofs'" ("Interview").

Comparing the financial situation of her grandparents ("quite precarious") to the trades their seven children eventually followed, Miriam's conclusion is that her "grandparents had been very good parents," because, despite their "modest" incomes they established their children in useful trades or professions. Of the seven children, "only one went to the superior school, and he was a doctor. He left to study in Vienna and all the other children worked so that he could study." This son was the eldest. He "had a car – among the few ones," which "he would change every two years." In addition, Miriam's uncle "used to go to Vienna every two years to renew his knowledge in medicine." These details are evidence of the high social status he earned as a result of his parents' efforts to enable their children to achieve better social standings than they managed to have.

Unlike her uncle, Miriam's father "did not study much. He only finished seven years of primary school." Then "he went to a master's school in Vienna to get his certificate as a tinsmith. Grandfather gave him a worker's certificate – that's how it was back then with the guilds – and he obtained his certificate as a tinsmith and glazier."

In search of autonomy, Miriam's father "separated from my grandfather and opened his own shop, becoming a competitor with him." Miriam interprets this episode in the life of her family as a great "disaster," one that she explains through her grandfather's inability to run the shop, faced with his son's search for financial autonomy, which he earned through his qualification as a glazier, an occupation that would bring him a hefty income: "Of course, my father brought in better merchandise. He did not do tinsmithing so much; he was a glazier more than anything else." Not only could her father achieve a prosperous situation from being a glazier, but also a good reputation: "My father's name is even now on the roofs of the two churches in Câmpulung," because "he put his name on his jobs, like a painter." Her father had also won a competition with her grandfather to get the contract for installing the windows on a big job. When "they built the hunting castle in Valea Putnei, the royal castle," her father was selected to install the windows. Under these conditions, "slowly, Grandfather's shop declined" and Miriam's aunt "had to take care of it because Grandfather could not do it anymore. [Then] she went to live with her daughter, who had had a baby, and my grandparents were left alone and so I took care of them," which explains Miriam's "unusual" connection to her paternal grandparents. About her mother, Miriam recounts that "she attended only four years of primary school, but had an unusual penchant for reading. After arriving in Câmpulung, she quickly learned to speak German and at home they would speak German." More to the point, both parents spoke German, and her father "spoke splendid German, Austrian German."

Asked about her father's political convictions, Miriam remembers that "he liked the National Peasants more than the Liberals." However, she remarks that he was not an ideologue, being neither a member of any party, nor an "activist on Jewish lands." She finds this aspect unusual because her grandmother, whom Miriam was named after, was called Maria in her identification papers. When she asked why Miriam, she found out that "it was a Zionist name somehow, Hebrew": "They called me Miriam because it was a name that sounded Hebrew and father wished very much to emigrate. In 1938 I kept hearing whispers around the house that father would go to Palestine […], but he never got to leave" ("Interview").

On the other hand, about her mother, she relates that "she was active in the Wizo Association [where] the Jewish women were," explaining that this affiliation was a manner of formal and informal education among the Jewish community, in the sense that it was where children were transmitted sociocultural values, such as learning Hebrew and participating in the Jewish religious holidays. "What so I mean by active? They enrolled me in kindergarten from age three to age five, where they taught Hebrew. On Purim they would stage some historical shows with Haman and Esther." She also remembers that in the shop there were two boxes: "a blue one with the Star of David, which was called Keren Kayemet [Jewish National Fund] – it was for Israel – and a charity box for the poor. I don't know if daily, but mother and father would always put money in there."

About her father, Miriam also recounts that had "fixed ideas," which were actually stereotypes with no sound basis, and this is why Miriam kept contesting them:

> Father [...] had his opinions. I would tell him that he has fixed ideas, that one cannot say what type of people the Polish are or the Bosnians. He would say: "May God protect you from Bosnians. They would cut your throat. It's good to have business with the Italians. *Die Katzerlfressel* – they eat cats and you can buy them for a song. With the Polish you ought to pray to God." That's what he would say.

But diligence was one of her father's qualities: "Father was a very hard-working man and this is what saved him in Transnistria. Although he was older than the usual people they would take for work, they took father for labor, because he was extremely hard-working and extremely skilled." Moreover,

> He could make anything from nothing. He was good with electricity; he could sew a patch on a coat, mend a shoe, and take a hammer to the wall. And there, where he ended up – near Odessa – some Germans asked for him and he worked for them. Because he could speak German per-

fectly, he had blue eyes, and was very blond – not reddish like me, because I had bright red hair – the Germans grew fond of him. Well, not really fond. They gave him food. He came home full of lice. But they did not kill him because he worked diligently. And I can say is that I was marked by his diligence.

Moreover, he was very punctual and more often than not, this quality was doubled by severity:

It was unimaginable not to respect meal times. If he said two o'clock, then it was not one minute before or after. He was severely punctual and extremely clean. The first question was if one washed their hands and it was forbidden to come to eat dirty, with a dirty apron. We would go to Câmpulung wearing German clothes: a little skirt, a little white blouse with baggy sleeves, with a velvet vest and white apron [...] a kind of German *sarafan* [pinafore]. One must have a spotless white apron. If it got dirty, it needed to be changed. One ought to be perfectly clean while at the table. It did not do to contradict Father, but I did contradict him and he beat me a lot of the time. Mother saved me several times. Father was the severe one, but Mother managed doing everything. She was the brains. ("Interview")

Fairness and proclivity for work were values transmitted to Miriam from her parents. Given that they never had employees, their parents always counted on both children to help "in the glazing shop." When father left to work outside the house, she, a school pupil, and her sister, a high school student, would take care of the shop, "loading and unloading merchandise," or "delivering packages to clients." They never took a penny from the till while working in the shop, without father giving it to them.

Her parents' social status is also clear in the description of the house in which she grew up, which had two rooms in total: "We had a very big room that my parents split in two with a wooden wall, so that they were separated: a bedroom and, for the two of us, two small couches and a table. The kitchen was big, it was immense. That's where the housemaid would sleep."

In the kitchen there was a stove, an oven, where her parents "would bake bread two times a week: on Fridays and Mondays. On Fridays there was white bread, and on Mondays there was rye bread, or black bread, as we called it." They would also bake homemade sweets or buy delicacies: "A guy used to pass by selling ten buns for seven lei." Miriam's family shared a big yard with two other families, "starting from one end, a German shoemaker, a family of Jews, and us." And in this yard there was "the wood stockpiled for the winter, although there was a storeroom, too. The toilets were here, too, on the side." The same can be said about the manner in which some family chores were done. For example, when washing the clothes they "would take water from a pump, from a richer neighbor." They washed the clothes in the tub and then rinse them at a spring not very far from their house, at the chute, and some of the clothes they would "lay down and starch them up and they looked beautiful, they would smell so nice, better than with today's detergents." Anyway, Miriam recalls that she did not wash the clothes, but that "there was someone else to do it."

Although her family was not necessarily rich, as Miriam characterizes their financial situation as "medium to small," she confesses that she benefited from a select education, as when she was six, she started having piano lessons with a teacher at her upright piano up to the time of her deportation. She also learned English. Because the housemaid was German, she first spoke German and then Romanian. She knew Yiddish, but she did not speak it, and from the age of five she started learning Hebrew: "I had a Hebrew teacher coming to our house three times a week. Twice a week we did the Hebrew language and once a week the Torah Hebrew, just like the boys." It was mother who wanted both of her daughters to learn: "'I don't have boys, but girls need to learn, too. What I learned, my girls need to learn, too.' Thus, I studied all the five Torah books and I can understand them – I can read

Hebrew." According to Miriam, her parents "did everything in their power to have us go to high school. Back then one had to pay for high school. As time went by, we had books in the house, too."

Miriam talked as well about the cultural peculiarities of Câmpulung: "There was only one cinema that was open three days a week: on Friday, Saturday, and Sunday." Miriam used to go to the cinema with her sister on Saturday afternoons if she was able to earn her cinema money through work. There was no theater, "only traveling theaters. The Jewish traveling theater used to come quite often and where did they play? In the German house, because there was no other room." What about coffee houses? Miriam thinks there were some, but they never went to one. There was a public pool where she learned how to swim, but she would rather go to the bank of the Moldova River, because it did not cost anything: "The pool had a fee and my parents would not give me money for it." Electricity was available and they had it in their home, her grandparents, too. Although she cannot state exactly the number of Jewish people living in Câmpulung, she recalls that "there were no Jewish schools." Instead, there were three synagogues: "The Old Synagogue, the Talmud-Torah Synagogue, next to the old one, and the New Synagogue. My father was at the New Synagogue, where the less faithful would go."

About the Jews in Câmpulung who formed a "serious community," she remembers they used to practice various trades, being

> in part clerks, not superior clerks, but, for example, head of the railway station, most part of the medics, lawyers (quite a lot, but not all of them), tinsmiths, glaziers, carpenters, painters, shoemakers, tailors, pub keepers (not many, as there were non-Jewish pubs). ("Interview")

The social structure inside the Jewish community was, thus, stratified: alongside the Jews practicing a trade and living either in Jewish or mixed neighborhoods, there were also very poor Jews who more often than not were socially isolated, like in Botoșani, where "there was a neighborhood, not a ghetto, which was called 'Paupers.'" In this isolated neighborhood, there was "cruel poverty." Miriam draws attention to the fact that there was a certain stigma around the poor Jews living in the Paupers. Yet, the socially disadvantaged Jews who lived "from one day to the next" existed all over the Romanian territory. In most cases, the Jewish community would take care of them, offering help. As "there weren't any beggars from Câmpulung per se," quite often, poor Jews from Maramureș would come to beg here, but among the people in the community there were offertories and the beggars were helped. Recalling the pogrom in Borşa, "around 1928–1929," where the mob set fire to a synagogue, Miriam recounts that there were "a lot of people from Borşa who came to beg and the community went to offer supplementary help. There really was serious mutual aid." The social condition generated by the specificity of the practiced trades also determined the physical structure of Câmpulung town: "The ones who had stores were interested in being close to their shops, if they weren't living there already."

Following the social model that intertwines professional and family life, Miriam's father had his shop positioned in the street, "on the corner, next to a Lipovan's cellar – where you could eat Lipovan food and especially drink – and two colonial shops, then came the yard." As everything was very close, "[a]t noon, between one and three o'clock, the shops were closed. Father came home to eat and sent us to watch the shop as he would take a nap sometimes. There was a shop of a German who sold ham nearby." The neighborhood where Miriam grew up "was not a separate neighborhood, but there were quite a lot of Germans." This specificity determines Miriam to affirm that this is "the way in which Austro-Hungary designed its conquest method, to colonize Bucovina." To support her statement, she describes the mosaic of its inhabitants and their social status:

> The local population was formed from the peasants living outside the city, in the villages around. As time went by,

they became the clerks replacing the German clerks. So it was like coming in from the outside. They brought Jews from Poland; they came from Russia to become masters and merchants. And they lived where they would earn their bread and, thus, without being a ghetto, by way of their work, there was a separation. ("Interview")

Despite being a mixed, cosmopolitan neighborhood, relationships with the neighbors of other ethnic origin were good and respectful, based on exchange and mutual aid, as it was the case for the German shoemaker who lived there – they were like his own children to him. As Miriam's family did not have a Christmas tree (as she would later on), at Christmastime they would visit their German neighbor. In turn, he would visit Miriam's family to eat with them on Purim. When they wanted "something good," they "went to him to eat a frankfurter or something like that." Her conclusion is that they had "the best relationship, absolutely the best relationship." Reflecting on her father's relationship with people of other social and ethnic origins, Miriam recounts that her father's best friend "was a German who was a Nichtstuer, a man who did nothing, but had resources to live on. He would come and talk to father." On the other hand, Miriam's father had a tense relationship with a Romanian man:

I remember there was a pub keeper, Toderan, next to the railway, who went to primary school with Father. […] And when Toderan would get drunk in his own pub, he would come and tell Father: "Hey, you, kike, remember when we fought in primary school?" And the German would defend Father, because if Father got angry, he would have gravely beaten Toderan, because Father was very quick to anger. ("Interview")

From Miriam's perspective, the relations between Jews and Romanians were "very good" and "normal," but there was a certain envy brought about by various life circumstances. One poignant example occurred when Miriam was applying for high school, after she had finished the fourth grade in primary school in Câmpulung. She was a good student, but it was suggested to her to make sure not to earn the highest mark in the class so as not to shame the other students, who were part of the majoritarian population:

> A teacher – her son was sitting the exam, too – told me: "You are a very good student, [but] it would be best if you did not come first." And I said: "But my mother said I should come first." And she said: "You will make everybody else look bad." ("Interview")

According to Miriam's explanations, the teacher, knowing how the majoritarian population felt about the Jews, wanted to give her friendly advice, to not come at the top: "The Jew must not come first, so they don't see it as meddling." However, she did come first, "without making an effort," because she was "a quick learner" who "could easily impress the teachers" because she knew "when the right moment was to be brilliant." For Miriam, these were the first signs of anti-Semitism that triggered reflections about herself, what she calls "schizophrenia." At that moment, she asked herself: "Should I be [first] or not? How should I be?" Besides this episode of clear anti-Semitism, she recalls that in the Câmpulung primary school where "half of us were Jews and the other half Romanians and other nationalities," the pupils were all friends, irrespective of their ethnicity. They were dressed alike in the same uniform and acted the same. More to the point, the fact that she was top of the class did not hinder her in becoming the head of the unit, although, she was "a Jew and time went by."

In addition to the malevolent or envious attitudes and feelings her fellow students sometimes had, Miriam also remarks on the gradual manner in which the rights and freedoms of Jews were encroached upon. She argues that, as a child, she had more freedom: "In primary school, we were allowed not to come to school on Saturdays, because we were Jews. But only in primary school. We were allowed to skip school legally on the Jewish holidays."

However, despite the fact that Jews were allowed some freedoms and some of their rights were respected, "you could feel the tension in the air."

Miriam clearly remembers the events from 1929 in Borşa, about which she found out from the newspapers of that time:

> I can tell you I was reading newspapers even when I was little. In Câmpulung there wasn't a town newspaper. There was one in Botoşani, though – *The Bell*. But in Câmpulung, the newspapers came from Cernăuţi [...] and were Jewish-German that is to say the *Allgemeine Zeitung Tagelblatt und Ostjüddische Zeitung* – the eastern Jewish newspaper. They were [...] newspapers from before 1918. And, reading the newspapers, I looked at the Romanian papers, too. [...] Reading to my grandfather, I found out very quickly what was happening in Germany. ("Interview")

Related to this event, she confessed that she did not know "the size of the disaster, although there was an accumulating tension" that they could feel. About the political climate of the period, she declared that she had some knowledge gained from the newspapers as well:

> I was in Botoşani for the Christmas holiday when the Goga-Cuza government came into being. I had heard about the teacher [A.C.] Cuza, but I hadn't known he was also the theoretician professor. Afterward, the legionnaires had their theoreticians, but this I found out in Botoşani. And when the Goga-Cuza government came – which only lasted until the end of February – I was prepared by what I read in the papers. The single party that formed then during the king's time and the blue uniforms sounded really bad in my mind. ("Interview")

Miriam confessed in the oral history interview she gave to Cosmina Guşu that there was tension among the population, but, in the beginning the radicalization of the political climate did not affect her relationships with her fellow high school students as she was on good terms with the non-Jewish students. On the advice of the principal of her high school, she actually tutored two fellow students who "were bad at studying" and she earned money for it. Yet, although she was friends with them, she confesses that she "hanged around with Jewish people." However, she admits that there was reticence on both sides regarding marriages between Jews and non-Jews. Miriam experienced it herself and came to know that she could not have a relationship with a non-Jew as the interdiction would come from both families. Her aunt had waylaid letters Miriam and a non-Jewish boy wrote to each other when she was in Botoşani,22 so she understood that "there was reticence on the part of my family" about the relationship and, therefore "separation came from both sides."

Miriam confessed that the situation of the Jews radically changed in "as little as two years." They received "new identity cards just like everybody else, only they mentioned 'Jew.'" At the same time new administrative-juridical measures were imposed to limit the number of places allowed for Jews in schools: "In 1940 the *numerus clausus* was instituted. I was left among the three Jewish girls in the class, and we were seated separately. Three days later it was *numerus nullus*. What atmosphere was this?! [...] And after three days they expelled us" ("Interview").

Miriam was taken aback by the decision to expel all Jews from the school, especially because – referring to a Jewish colleague's situation – "her father was a World War I hero." Miriam recalled that the Romanian authorities also introduced the yellow badge as a sign to stigmatize and humiliate Jews in public and to segregate them from the rest of the population, thus reinforcing their inferior status: "As soon as the war started we were very quickly given the Star of David to wear. And I would ostentatiously wear it in Câmpulung." At the same time, other restrictions were imposed around 1940–1941: "They put a curfew in place for going

---

22   In 1938 she left for Botoşani.

outside the house. We would make bread at home. [...] We had flour and we made bread at home. I mean, I did not directly feel the food restrictions, because my folks were rather well-off" ("Interview").

Regarding the curfew on movement, Miriam recollects that, along with others, "during the hours that we were allowed to walk outside, we would walk around the street." Asked whether "there were any invective, harsh words, or other manifestations from her fellow students in Botoșani," Miriam recalled the behavior of one student of Romanian origin at the Dragoș Vodă High School, who "not only acknowledged us, but walked with us on the street, with me and other students. Ostentatiously!" There was also the son of a first-year teacher, Mrs. Aurite, who was an adult, ten years older than them, and who "did not leave his Jewish friends with whom he played cards." This solidarity with the Jews coming from a part of the majoritarian population that "manifestly tried to keep a civilized atmosphere" was, however, counterbalanced by the hostile attitudes from other people, like her father's old acquaintance, the one who had the pub and who called Jews "kikes" wherever he met them and, when he could, punched them, saying: "Just you wait and see!" This was almost normal – it was becoming normality" ("Interview"). The word "kike" (*jidan* in Romanian) and its derivations, used with intent to offend, are a clear expression of racism, voicing hatred toward Jews.

Miriam admits that she could not have anticipated what was about to happen to the Jews when the legionnaires came to power on September 6, 1940, because they had only read "bits and pieces" about Marshal Ion Antonescu in the papers. Miriam acknowledges that they knew about Hitler, but they didn't know "how the situation might evolve," and what was interesting, in her opinion, was that the Jews "who lived in the Austro-Hungarian Empire could not imagine how Germany could get by without Jews." Hence, they thought "just as many other Jews in Germany did, [thinking to themselves], 'It will be fine, we are

Germans!'" She remembers that, despite the fact that they were "quite enlightened people," they could not imagine "what might happen," and when they realized the gravity of the situation, "it was too late," as they could not even communicate anymore. The prosperity her family enjoyed even with all the restrictions, but especially not knowing the extent of the anti-Semitic actions and the genocidal intentions of the government, made them stay put in Câmpulung: "I had no idea about it. I mean, who could have imagined how far such a thing could go? Businesses were going on, I was learning: 'Look how well I know English.' With that small amount of English I can get by even today" ("Interview").

The one who opened her eyes in regards to many aspects concerning the anti-Jewish violence was her fiancé, a lieutenant medic from near Câmpulung who had been demobilized from the army. As his family had been banished from the village, her fiancé and his family came and lived in her grandparents' yard, along with the cow and everything: "His mother and elder sister lived with the grandparents and he lived with us. And then we got engaged. I liked him because he was an officer, a beautiful boy and he was older."

About the legionnaire uprising she recollects that "by word of mouth, in the community, they told us to close all the shops, the Jews not to get out and stay inside as much as possible." Jews were also told to "pull the curtains so the light would not be visible, because the head of the legionnaires in Câmpulung had said he did not want killings in Câmpulung. And no Jew was killed. But some Jews were thrown out of the train" ("Interview").

About the pogroms in Dorohoi or Iași in summer 1941, Miriam declared that she knew from the newspapers that "500 Jewish provocateurs were killed, that's what I knew," but she was persuaded that it was "a terrible challenge" as far as "Jews were hiding in basements rather than signaling the Russian armies." From rare cases of aggression toward the Jews, the worsening of the anti-Jewish legislative measures was concomitant to the aggravation of their general situation: "They took our bikes, our radio; we did not have a telephone anyway. That was the general situation from then on." The deportation on October 12, 1941, was preceded by searches in the Jewish homes made on Yom Kippur, and "there was no Jewish house that escaped a search party. What they were looking for we did not know." Miriam was disappointed by some friends taking part in the Legionnaire movement, friends whom she saw when they did "that search of everybody" in September 1941: "A gendarme and two former fellow students of mine came into our house," "dressed in legionnaire shirts." One was the son of Saghin the lawyer, "one of the good lawyers in Câmpulung, but he was known to be anti-Semitic" and "his boy did what he learned from his father." The other one was "the son of a priest."

### Social World of Deportation and Self-conscious Feelings

Uncertainty is one of the feelings that Miriam Korber-Bercovici felt from the moment when the events start unraveling, with the announcement that all Jews in Câmpulung were to be deported, except one of the two Jewish pharmacists, the youngest one to be held back until he was replaced by a Romanian whom the local authorities "brought to Câmpulung": "All our family from Câmpulung was deported: parents, my sister, my grandparents, aunts – sisters of Grandmother's – and their families. Anyway, any beating heart that was Jewish: poor, rich, including the village lunatic" ("Interview").

Rumors about the deportation to "somewhere in Russia, Ukraine" had started two or three days before the baneful event, when "there was nowhere to go, but to some friends, and that would endanger their lives." The deportation was announced in Câmpulung by posters and with a drummer:

> The posters appeared on Friday and the drummer toward noon on Friday, too. There was only one drummer and a soldier with a gun who read the poster that was on the wall: "In the name of Marshal Antonescu, all kikes…", not Jews, all 'kikes'" ("Interview")

Miriam confessed that on hearing the word "kike" instead of Jew, written in an official document and enunciated as such in public, she felt that ethnic origin was a reason for denigration and degradation. Acknowledging that Jewish people were officially despised because of their origin, she felt belittled:

> In that moment I fell apart. And when they did the search, my friends were close, too. But in the moment when we saw it written on the wall … without any embarrassment, intentionally. We were kikes, we were not normal human beings anymore, we were not Jews or, as we had thought, Romanian citizens of Mosaic religion. That's what we were called since the Austro-Hungarian times. No, we were kikes. That was on Friday, toward noon. On Sunday morning all Jews would be at the Eastern Railway. ("Interview")

The "kike" appellative, obviously aimed to dishonor, used by an authority in the public space "without any embarrassment, intentionally," revealed the anti-Semitic feelings leading to the implementation of the extermination policy.

They were forbidden from taking too much luggage: "They were not allowed to bring any money. Money was to be left at the National Bank. No kind of jewels. And the luggage must be at most 30 kilograms per person, because that is how much a human can carry on his back." The short time left until the deportation is characterized by Miriam as "a chase," because "no one knew what to do first." Consequently, the uncertainty and disquiet were doubled by "evacuation fever": "Cries, laments, packing, boiling, everything in everything, no start or end to anything. We had not realized what was expecting us. It was a dream – that's what we thought – we did not realize what was going to happen." Miriam recounts that on Saturday all shops were closed and clandestine selling and gifting started: "Peasants, townspeople, neighbors, and strangers came like vultures and in a morning we emptied our house of our most beautiful things." Even though after the legionnaires came to power Miriam's family had managed to keep the shop, which "hadn't been Romanianized," and even though business had been going very well, at the moment of the deportation they were forced to leave everything behind, just like all the other Jews. They left leaving everything as it was: the shop, the storeroom with merchandise, "a lot of merchandise." They were to hand over the keys at the rail station, leave without papers, and, "theoretically, with no money or any kind of jewels," "theoretically because each of us had devised a method around it." For example, her father, who "was very inventive," used enamel milk jugs with a simple lid to hide some money: "Father made a double bottom; he divided the money between the two mugs, a lot of money, and poured in jam. He put in a metal bottom, then another bottom and poured in jam again."

This way, while attempting to use up some of the merchandise in the shop and to put away some of the things they hoped they would find when they came back, the time until the deportation flew by in great agitation: "Father started giving away the merchandise in the shop [...] and people came ostentatiously. They did not steal; we gave it to them." At the same time they left at a neighbor mother's house a sewing machine and at another house the upright piano. As for the rest of it, they threw away the identity cards and they didn't even give in the keys "because they didn't ask for them," instead "they talked about the money, but nobody asked us to go to the National Bank." Among the things Miriam took with her was a journal she had received for her birthday, on September 11, from Bondy, a boy she had met during the summer of 1941, "when the householders, the more select people in Câmpulung, were kept hostages." Bondy was a student, one or two years older than her, whose father was a teacher of Hebrew from Maramureş. According to Miriam, Bondy was "a bit lower on the social ladder," but they "befriended each other very well," as he "was a man of sterling worth." In her luggage, besides the "new, pristine" journal and "Ciprian Porumbescu's ballad, transcribed for piano" – something she considered an act of patriotism – Miriam only took "new things":

Where did I get the new things? I had been engaged for a few months that year and my mother thought that I would be getting married so she bought a kind of trousseau. That's how I had absolutely new things, not worn, and these would keep me warm, or I could sell them easily. Some things I did not even get to wear at all. I put in some dresses I loved and I had the smallest bag. It was quite a big backpack, but smaller than those of the others, because my task – we divided the tasks among us – was to take care of my grandparents. ("Interview")

As a matter of fact, to be able to survive, some of the new clothes she had packed were to be sold or exchanged in "exile," as Miriam calls deportation in her *Ghetto Journal*, although she admitted that "with every item they let go," they "gave away a part of themselves." At the moment of departure she did not imagine how much she would miss "home" being deported, but for her grandparents she recalls that "it was terrible" to part with the house.

The deportation was not organized, but chaotic: "They were totally unprepared. The only organized things were the social actions of the community which, with the help of a baker, handed bread to the Jews in the railway station." As the deportation took place on a Sunday, Jews were put in "cattle cars that the people had cleaned. They had been full of horse and cow manure. They cleaned it with straw [...] in front of everybody and it took about three to four hours." This allowed Miriam to observe the hostile reaction, the contempt and hatred felt for the Jews, of the local population, which manifested while they assisted the boarding process: "On Sundays, people from the countryside were there. It wasn't a fair day, but many of them came for the dance" at a special place near her grandparents' home. "The people coming from the church looked at us as if we were monsters and even the neighbors who were used to us did not refrain from spitting on us: 'Look, the kikes! They deserve it! It's because of them there's a war!'" ("Interview").

Miriam talks about the moment of the boarding in the deportation trains as being full of chaos resulting not only from a lack of order but also from the fact that no one knew the destination:

> There was no order whatsoever. Each person did what they could. We were about 40 in a car. It was quite crowded. There were 40 people in there! There was a grated window, but the door remained open. All along the way, the doors remained open. I had my grandparents sit on the suitcases. I happened to be in the same car with Bondy and his family [a sister, a brother, and his parents], but also with the village lunatic, a disabled child in a wheelchair. And it was so loud! At the beginning there was terrible confusion. We had taken tea, food, lemons – in case somebody got sick – sugar and some salami. Everybody had packed their [provisions]. But for how long can you pack provisions? "Where are we going?" Nobody had told us where we were going. Nobody. ("Interview")

Besides the authorities using the term "kike" in public, a name also used by the local population who despised Jewish people, or, even by the neighbors with whom, up until the deportation, they had had no conflicts, another dehumanizing instance was related to not being able to take care of one's physiological needs in front of everybody else. The trip from Câmpulung to Cernăuți – the first stop – would usually take four hours, but the train went so slowly that a four-hour journey took a whole day: "Come to think of it, the train did not stop at all. Which way was it going? Forward, backward? Both ways? Even now I don't know." At first it was "horrible": she became "truly aware of the gravity of the situation" when she wanted "to pee for the first time":

> How? Men, women, Bondy, Father, Mother, my grandparents were there. My grandparents wanted to go, too. My parents had brought a chamber pot for my grandparents. But how to use it? Grandmother said, "I don't want to." But eventually.... Men went to the car door and they could

47

do it as the train went along. But the women? And then shame disappeared. From then on I wasn't a human being anymore. Not because I am shy. It's not about being shy, but think about it. I had seen how women came from the countryside bringing milk. They might have a mishap, an emergency. They crouched next to a fence to go. A lot of people didn't wear underwear. They would just do it on the side of the road. But here? One couldn't even do it on the side of the road. But where? With people around? Where? In a jar? One could miss the opening. In my grandparents' chamber pot? Yes, in my grandparents' chamber pot. Yes, but to do this one has to pull down their underwear. And then I ate, I urinated, I did all the human needs in the same place for the whole three days of train traveling. At the Cernăuți stop, where we stood for a long while – I do not remember exactly how long – I climbed down and I did it next to the train. Afterward they made up climb back up into the train. ("Interview")

Compared to her birthplace, each of the destinations of the Câmpulung Jewish convoy – Atachi, Moghilev, and Djurin – appeared to be devastated to Miriam, because all the dwellings were destroyed and the landscape did not seem friendly at all. For example, Atachi, the first destination, was a locality situated "on the banks of the Nistru River, opposite Moghilev," and it was "completely destroyed, with houses without roofs, with no walls, some with three walls, others with two. The walls were spattered with blood, and there were no fences." In Atachi, where she spent several days, the mud and cold were two of the elements that would strongly contrast the memory of the beautiful days spent on Romanian lands:

> Bessarabia was renowned for its mud. There was so much mud when we climbed down onto the bank of the Nistru River! And it was cold, too. Everybody searched as well as they could for shelter between three walls. At least the

48

wind was not blowing. We looked for shelter as everybody else did.

The place was horrifying. "In that mess" "one would go behind a wall to do one's needs, and on the other side one would eat what was brought from home, not too far someone else was making polenta on three firewood." More to the point, "human misery" – reflected in the dehumanization of the deported Jews who lived in animalistic physical conditions – become engrafted onto the mind of the adolescent girl during her first night in Atachi:

> I saw what human misery looked like. I saw people with-out a human face, children with swollen eyes, frozen feet, helpless hands: mothers with dead children in their arms, old and young people wrapped in rags. They were the Jews in the Edineț concentration camp. They were being chased away, infected with typhus, full of lice, half dead from hunger. They barged into Atachi, without the right to set-tle down. (*Journal*, 18)

At the next destination, Moghilev, which they would reach by way of "a bridge with pontoons," Miriam took shelter in "a school, a library of sorts," with her family and "30 other fami-lies from Câmpulung" ("Interview"). The extreme overcrowding there forced many people to share the same room. In the absence of adequate clothing and heating fuel, staying warm was difficult for Miriam, her family, and all the deported Jews: "It was a big room, with no fire, nothing. It was October. All we had were our clothes. You can imagine we were all full of lice. No light. Mother had some candles, as well as some other families" ("Interview").

Here, Miriam's family is forced to part with her grandparents, whom they had left "in a kind of an old age care [home], with doctors from Câmpulung, Gura Humorului, and Vatra Dornei, doctors who were renowned to be good people" ("Interview"). As her connection to her grandparents was very strong, parting with them was very difficult for Miriam: "I had a very heavy heart. [...] We had to find a way to leave. [...] And then, after giving them money, setting them up in the so-called hospital, in the care of the doctors from Câmpulung, we left them" ("Interview").

However, she found out later on that the medics "benefitted hand over fist from this arrangement, because they used all the goods that were left for the elderly" and "they took those things for themselves, to put it in a polite way," Miriam said. Thus, the regret she felt for having left her grandparents to die haunts Miriam's thoughts obsessively:

> And if there's something I reproach to myself, even today, it is that I left them there. I remember the last tea I gave to my grandparents. We could only give them tea with bread. [...] And in my dreams and my nightmares, my grandparents appear even today and they call out to me: "Where are you, Mimi? Where are you? Where are you?" I am on a narrow road and they are somewhere down it and they call out to me. ("Interview")

The memory of the warm times of childhood, "dear to me, but also painful by their beauty," where "Grandfather and Grandmother are foremost," with Miriam "spending the most priceless hours of that young age" (*Journal*, 55), comes back painfully in the thoughts of the adolescent girl: "Grandfather was always busy, either with the shop, or in the workshop, but always with a smile and a good word for his Mimica, his red-haired and freckled little granddaughter, who would run around his things and get in his way" (*Journal*, 55–56). Grandmother was the "mistress of delicious foods, fried potatoes, and kihalăch with or without poppy seeds. Many times Grandmother saved me from a beating or protected me from being scolded. She was always kind and nice to everybody" (*Journal*, 56).

Delightfully pleased by the stories told by her grandmother, Miriam would never forget the pampering and caring moments spent in her lap:

> "Who comes to Grandmother?" "Who wants a story?" Grandmother was a master of stories. She would make up

stories andtell them with a special talent. Sisi and I, with our heads in her lap, would listen attentively, attention that later on we could not muster in school or on other significant occasions. Stories about dragons, Prince Charming, fairies, fantastic birds, good mothers, and bad people. (*Journal*, 56)

Miriam noticed that despite her age and illness – eventually, she went blind – Grandmother kept all her qualities:

Years passed by, Grandmother got old, got thinner, her sight became weaker and weaker until she went completely blind. She could not work anymore, but she persisted in keeping everything clean. She would rustle around the house all day and she did not want anybody to help her because she was ashamed of her weakness. She could recognize people by their voice; she could recognize us, the children, by our walk. Mimica, that's how she called me dearly; she knew when I was in, what dress I was wearing, what I had done, and what was new. (*Journal*, 56)

The pain of leaving her grandparents was sharp, especially because Miriam could not be with them on their last journey, to support them just as they had done for her so many times in her childhood:

They died in silence, just as they had lived: quiet people who had worked hard all their lives and raised their children with the sweat of their brow and made people out of them. And now, they died in the care of strangers, far from the children they had worked for. Only one daughter was with them, Aunt Roza. They died and no one knew. (*Journal*, 55)

Miriam could not accept the thought that they had to die "so alone" and she wonders: "What was left of their lives? What did they work for? For what sins did they need to die in such loneliness? What sins did they have to make amends for and whose sins were they?" (*Journal*, 56). Relating the idea of sin to that of punishment because her grandparents "had always worked and always thought about and remembered God" (*Journal*, 56), Miriam does not understand the absurdity of their death "in Moghilev, far from their home, from their clean bed, from their work of decades of everything they had to leave behind at the mercy of fate" (*Journal*, 55), without the dear ones to be able to offer them "the honor they deserved" (*Journal*, 57). The tragedy of her grandparents' sad death, similar to that of many other Jews, could not find a plausible explanation in Miriam's thoughts, while the idea of deserved punishment for their sin or others' was beyond her comprehension.

Miriam and her family finally reached the new destination – Djurin – by the "good will" of some German soldiers:

> Leaving from Moghilev had to be [...] absolutely in secret, because we were not allowed to leave. Father, because he could speak German very well, found a couple of German soldiers who, for money, were persuaded to take fifteen people in a truck with a tarpaulin to – where? To Ukraine, where, somehow, we needed to arrive with the convoy, or by foot, or not make it at all.

Thus, they arrived in Djurin, in "the so-called center of the town where the Jews used to live," a ghetto that was, however, not surrounded by a wall. Miriam's family would initially dwell in a small room with other three families:

> Three families meant about twelve to fourteen people. Then we were only two families, because one managed to move to another location. Bondy and his family lived in the room one entered first. [...] Anyone who opened the door had to pass through their room. [...] And it was already almost November.

In an attempt to find a less crowded living space, Miriam's family tried renting at some point "a room without a stove or anything else, in fact. In three days, father built a stove out of nothing. Then began the search for firewood. I sometimes dream even nowadays that I'm stealing firewood. We did steal some firewood."

Even though deportees, Jews still tried to recreate forms of organizing that would allow them to survive. Without questioning the utility of those measures, however, Miriam observed that they allowed some of the Jews who were in leadership positions to profit from the social status it would confer on them:

> A community was organized, with a community president. There were the Rădăuți Jews who were the richest. They did not lose materially – they lived better than us – but they did not have the strength to take some of the responsibilities upon themselves. When you take up responsibilities, you also have more rights. The family of the president lived alone in a single room. There were richer people. They made a canteen for the poorer ones who lived in the so-called synagogue, where they would die like flies. They would die there of the epidemic fever.

On the other hand, Miriam remarked that some of the Jews collaborated with the perpetrators in order to survive:

> A hospital was built, with a medic from Vatra Dornei, who had a daughter. And this daughter was kind of like Esther, if you remember the story of Esther. She was the friend of the only gendarme that usually guarded the ghetto, Costică. This Costică had a dog, a whip, and Gherda, that girl. And if you wanted something, you went to Gherda, the Jewish girl.

Apart from this aspect of Jews forming a community in the Djurin Ghetto, which shows a social hierarchy among the deportees, Miriam also met "good, simple people who tried to help, unlike other, wealthier but bad" (*Journal*, 79). As for the locals, she noticed a difference between the Ukrainian and the Romanian peasants:

53

> Our peasant is totally different, closer to us, to our way of being. [...] The Ukrainian peasant is very dirty [...] and more backward than the Romanian. [...] The life they generally lived was unconceivable to our mind. Not that I or my folks lived in luxury, [...] but we did not live like cattle either. (*Journal*, 30)

Although the locals did not seem very talkative or open to helping the deported, Miriam reflects on the help received from a Ukrainian woman in whose house she lived at a certain point:

> The Ukrainian woman helped us a lot. When Mother got us out of the ghetto, she [the Ukrainian woman] promised hand over fist, but she would not take money. [In exchange for what she gave us], I tutored her children in English, and Mother showed them how to hand-sew clothes, because she knew how to sew. She [the Ukrainian woman] took me to dig potatoes with her several times. [But] I did not know how to do it. [...] I made a mess. Anyway, she gave us potatoes so as to not call it for nothing. ("Interview")

In the ghetto, the Jews had to ration their food, because help from the country, from their families or the community, was quite difficult to get, if any. However, "there were families who lived from the money they received, because money was sent quite often" ("Interview"). Reflecting upon the situation of her family, which was envied by some "who did not have the little we did" (*Journal*, 28), Miriam declared that she had the luck to come by some help from the country: "I received a telegram and one time I received money, although more was sent to us. [...] Our folks sent money requiring a signature for delivery. But the money did not get to us. We only received money one time."

That is the reason why they had to watch "the Romanian money," which they managed to live on "for three years," even if "[i]t wasn't that much, because we had to change this money into Deutsche marks and it was worse than the stock exchange." Uncertainty in the Djurin Ghetto was generated not only by the material shortages – which brought people to despair – but also disease. Miriam noticed the frequency of deaths caused by them: "A lot of them die unknown to anybody and when they are to go back home, maybe less than half will go back, because typhus and hunger are devastating the deported" (*Journal*, 73).

Hunger was one of the daily tortures for the deported Jews living on the Ukrainian steppe: "I would really like to eat something good! Another wish next to all the others that I have, because there are so many. First, I want to go home and escape the hell I am in" (*Journal*, 85). "People were desperate for fear of hunger" (*Journal*, 29) and thus, the lack of food deepened their dehumanization, depriving people of their human qualities: "[W]e are not human anymore. Everybody is so sad. We are all lost people" (*Journal*, 29). The adolescent girl often compares the comfort at home with the degrading situation of being deported: "If we could only forget all of this! It's so difficult when you remember the times when it was warm in the house and you weren't hungry!" (*Journal*, 41).

Her personal thoughts about food, heat, comfort, and cleanliness at home compared to her life within the confines of the Djurin Ghetto erased her individuality and humanity, as well as that of the others, who suffer because of poverty, filth, the grueling heat of summer, and the whipping cold of winter. Robbed of the full complexity of their lives, Jews were reduced to a less-than-human state as their behavior had become similar to that of animals: "Yes, we are adapting to the environment. Man is an animal, everything is in the habits. We get used to the bad, but we can remember the good times and this hurts the most!" (*Journal*, 41). The thought of the dreadful living conditions of the Jews compared to the warmth of a family home determines Miriam to emphasize her grief:

> When I see my mother I feel like yelling in pain. I remember what she used to do at home before Easter. I don't need to write it down here to remember it. It was all so

clean, so tidy. And now, six days before Easter, we haven't cleaned up yet; there is still time to finish "the bedroom," "the saloon," "the kitchen," "the firewood storeroom" and "our closet," because all together they are just one room here. And it's not even just ours, but also [belongs] to those with whom we live. (*Journal*, 66)

The holidays spent at home are nothing like the ones in exile: "Oh, holidays of yesteryear! What they would bring to me once. The house was clean as a mirror, the food so plentiful that it was needless to speak about it and a blissful peace that lightens the soul" (*Journal*, 62).

In contrast to the clean home in Câmpulung, Miriam repeatedly talked about the filthy ghetto with its poor sanitation:

We are still in Ukraine here. Far away from my dear mountains, from the beloved grass, from the tall pines, here everything is sad, even if the sun shines. When I take a look from here, up [on the hill], everything seem cleaner, whiter, but from close up it is horrible, chaos is everywhere, filth is all over the place. (*Journal*, 63)

Because of the extremely poor living conditions, Miriam grew conscious about her moral degradation:

This is how I lived those three years. I don't even know if I lived, if that's the right word. Here, too, the dehumanization continued: no toilets, houses with no water. There was a single place where the entire ghetto got water. From a single place, 4,800 souls took water and only at certain hour. And there was ice on that hill! I slipped I don't know how many times. I would get there with the bucket of water and then slip on the way back. I would lose the water and have to borrow that day. ("Interview")

Their fundamental physical needs being refused, including the need for food, water, shelter, and health care, the impact on the deported Jews had cognitive and emotional consequences. In addition, the failure to care for their psychological needs such as relatedness to other humans led to disengagement; this is how we explain Miriam's inability to speak: "I simply fell mute. I would not speak. Mother would say: 'This girl is mentally ill.' I, who am a chatterbox, not doing anything for entire days! Not reading a line!" ("Interview"). The physical and psychological pain obliged Miriam to bottle-up her feelings and wall herself off as a defense against dehumanization.

The anxiety resulted from boredom because of "stupid discussions that make you forget everything you ever knew" (*Journal*, 79), constant fear and endangerment, but also isolation in "filthy Djurin, with the scorching sun and the blistering wind" (*Journal*, 81), determined Miriam to chronicle her life[23] in the diary she got from Bondy:

> I had it [the diary], a pencil, and had no girl friend. And Bondy – we used to get along well back then – who had to find food for his folks. I didn't get along with my father. Mother was the one who got the food. She would go with a shirt and barter with the peasants. I had to do something. My sister [who was born in 1927] was four years younger than I and she did not grasp the gravity [of the situation].

Miriam confessed that the journal only recorded of some of the experiences lived in exile, disclosing some of her impressions, perceptions, and emotions in the Transnistrian ghettos. She avoided unveiling the cruel reality of the distressing experiences of the Jews in Transnistria, lest the discovery of her journal by the authorities have repercussions for her and her family:

> I didn't write everything. I wrote a thousand times less. [...] When I started this journal I promised myself I would not write anything political, that anything could happen, I would only write banal things, so as to not endanger anyone. For that reason, the journal is just a thousandth part of

---

23  She started from November 4, 1941, onward.

what I thought and what I have been through. I only wrote what went through my mind momentarily. ("Interview")

At the same time, part of her sentimental life was also deliberately overlooked. Miriam did not write too much in her journal about her first romances, "my loves from those three years," probably because the feelings triggered by the misery, the unrest that more often than not turned into anger, accentuated by the uncertainty of tomorrow, these feelings were more pressing than the other preoccupations that were common for her age. This does not mean that they did not exist at all, but they faded away because of the overpowering reality of the ghetto where "rich or poor, it's still the same," because everyone had left what they owned to be "prey for the wolfish hands that feast on them" (*Journal*, 61). Miriam declared several times how much she wanted to live "for just a minute" (*Journal*, 61) without the need to make money in order to ensure her future, yearning for "some sympathy – or rather some trouble" (*Journal*, 73). Several times she experienced an intense feeling of longing for a compatible partner with whom she could establish a connection and a strong bond. Compared to the necessity to offset her distressed emotional state, Miriam expressed her need for a loving relationship which would provide her with a deep fulfillment.

On the one hand, realizing that no other boy showed any interest in her in Transnistria, Miriam was convinced she had lost her feminine beauty: "As a matter of fact, nobody thought or showed interest in me, so it seems I lost my sex appeal once I crossed the Nistru River" (*Journal*, 73). Her personal charm did not even work when she tried to barter her body for the free-dom of her 52-year-old father who had been taken for labor: "And when they took Father, I went to the soldier. I offered myself to him, but I was so skinny and scrawny that no soldier would lay their hands on me" ("Interview"). The lack of interest of a man for her body caused great anguish, Miriam developing at times a sense of numbness and indifference regarding the filthy moral and physical surrounding world.

On the other hand, the impossibility of fulfilling a relationship of love is caused by the fact that the partner is perceived as part of a coping strategy: "Since I left home, I can't even think this way about a boy, other than as a comrade who carries the luggage" (*Journal*, 73). In a world where "cold, fear, insomnia, dark thoughts, regrets, wishes" (*Journal*, 28) were all part of the daily reality of the Jews, a world where "death lost its mystery" (*Journal*, 23), as Miriam saw deaths that did not "leave any special impression" (*Journal*, 28) on her, in this world, adolescent romances brought her back to life to a certain extent and resuscitated her hope of being rescued from that distressing world. First she was in love with Bondy, but her friendship with him faded as soon as the shortages overwhelmed them all: "We sat so close to one another and we were almost not acknowledging each other. I could not have imagined it. But he was protecting his family and I, somewhat, was protecting mine" ("Interview"). The poignant need to share her feelings with someone close to her soul always sends her to Bondy, especially because in the ghetto "you've got nobody to talk to" (*Journal*, 89). She writes several times with sadness about this unraveled friendship:

> [Bondy and I] were very good friends up until we got to know each other too well, and then everything went to hell. I am sorry for our beautiful friendship – it would have been very useful now. I would have had somebody to tell what I feel, what I think. Now he doesn't have anybody and neither do I, and although we live in adjoining rooms, we are hundreds of kilometers away from each other. All is over. (*Journal*, 89)

These moments of feeling alone and not having anyone to communicate with made Miriam close up inside. However, there were also people who managed to restore her wish to live:

> I feel there has been a big change in me. Judith transformed me completely. Just two years ago, I wanted to live, I wanted to dance; I wanted to feel I am young. There is an

unknown torrent in me, a new spring that I feel gushing hot. What would I give to be free, to be able to go where I want, to swim, to skip. But it's in vain. We are all sinners and all is endless. (*Journal*, 105)

Actually, Miriam "shamefully" confessed in the journal that there were moments when she danced "at Moghilev," that "she dared to forget for a moment the catastrophe" (*Journal*, 24):

Go figure! I also danced! [...] I tried to forget everything and I danced. I say I tried because I did not manage for one moment to forget where I was and all the time I was very sad. The beautiful view: in a sorry room, a few youngsters dance and in the other room Father stays with the neighbors (two months have passed since the loss of his parents), he hears the music and cuts firewood. (*Journal*, 65)

Thinking about other young people, she declared that "if you got a moment when you could dance, you wanted to dance. You were young. I don't know what the women did. They probably made love there, too, with their men or with others" ("Interview"). From a masculine perspective, "there was a boy, Burşi Braun, who later went to medical school in Iași with me. He woke me up a bit from my lethargy, from my being mute" ("Interview"). At some point, she fell in love with

a Ukrainian Jew who was older. Later on I heard that he was part of the resistance. I fell in love with him. [...] He was a 37-year-old gentleman who felt pity for me. I was in over my head for him and when they took Father for labor, we managed thanks to him. I was very sick. He would bring us milk, bread, firewood. Days in a row. Without asking for any reward. ("Interview")

The feelings of love and pity become confused as the beloved man protected her and her family from starvation, and therefore from death, at a difficult time when she was ill, her father was taken for labor, and her mother could not cope anymore with their deprivation.

The beautiful experiences from a past spent close to dear people whom she could talk to were still flickering in her memory, exposing her inability to make new friends: "For the moment, I need to live here. Maybe I should look for friends here. How nice that would be" (*Journal*, 97). Miriam is alienated and cannot adapt to the new social and physical environment: "I know it's above my strength to say to somebody more than ten words and these are words that are strange to me, not what I feel. What is in my soul I cannot express with simple words" (*Journal*, 97).

Impoverished both materially and spiritually, Miriam experienced profound moral suffering: "I feel a great pain in my soul, a great wound that bleeds every time my thoughts lead me to the past" (*Journal*, 97). Being away from home, she deeply regrets her lovely childhood days, at that time vanished: "When I look at the road to Moghilev, it appears to me that I am closer to home. There are days when I'm so painfully homesick that I would do anything only to be able to see our house from afar" (*Journal*, 97). The difficulty of enjoying activities typical of young people leaves her with a sense of apathy about her life: "I am young and I need to remind myself that there are hundreds of young people in my situation who are somehow cheerful" (*Journal*, 97–98). Miriam objectifies her pain, but she cannot explain her malaise: "Why can't I be like them [the cheerful youngsters]? Why? It is a question that I alone cannot answer" (*Journal*, 97–98). Miriam's asocial behavior is translated into a personal psychological disorder: "Maybe it's my nature that makes me be solitary or I lack the will" (*Journal*, 97–98).

Knowledge – as well as the cognitive processes linked to it – is a dynamic process embedded in a social environment. As the relational capital resulting from connections with other people living in the ghetto does not bring about knowledge sharing and the development of intellectual capital, the lack of qualitative intellectual debates exacerbates her pain. Because of the growing moral degradation triggered by "stupid discussions" which imposed severe anguish on her, Miriam preferred solitary confinement and social deprivation: "I find it impossible to laugh, to be cheerful. I feel better when I sit and watch the road to Moghilev, just like so, for no reason, than to talk about stupid things" (*Journal*, 97–98).

Uncertainty, insecurity, and the incapacity of getting over her tragic situation deepened her anxiety and self-isolation even more. Her emotions were worn out and words become useless in expressing the pain: "I have nothing else to write. I have no more words to express what I feel, that's how full my heart is with longing, pain and spite! What do words express compared to what I feel?" (*Journal*, 82). Miriam highlights the inadequacy of language and the emptiness of words to render her horrific and incomprehensible Transnistrian experience – "Words are empty, stone drops!" (*Journal*, 82) – as well as the grief associated with it.[24] Deep sadness led to an apathetic outlook on her life: "Everything is nothing and all my thoughts revolve around this nothing. I find it hard to specify what I think about and everything revolves so crazily fast around my memories that are all nothing today" (*Journal*, 82).

Her emotional fatigue is accompanied by severe anxiety leading to apathy. Her psychological sickness is reflected in the monotony of the landscape, the physical reality around her, of the Ukrainian steppe, contrasting with the landscape at home:

> Days and nights fly past quickly. A fourteen-hour night, that's how long we stay in bed. I wish the cold would go away, too! It's terribly cold. It's so cold your bone marrow freezes and the steppe wind bites with a violence unknown to us Muntenians. And always the same worry: What do we eat today?! What will we eat tomorrow? (*Journal*, 46)

The monotony of the days passing by, as the trapped Jews waited for their situation to change, was the opposite of the busy daily life they had lead back home:

---

24  A similar problem, of putting words on the unspeakable, encountered other Holocaust survivors, such as Elie Wiesel, whose words were "obstacles rather than vehicles" (Catrina, "The Production," 212).

But we are here on the steppe, far from my dear mountains that I was used to, which evoked so many pleasant memories. Here everything is too smooth, too wide, too uniform. As far as you can see there is only a plain, not a hill to break the flat monotony. The river bank is not as beautiful as the one at home. We have willows and some poplars, but the rest is only high and dry plain. The water is so tranquil, not like our Moldova, alive and whimsical, full of life. Everything here flows so slowly, without nerve, without vigor. (*Journal*, 76)

Besides the material shortages, lethargy is also generated by an overwhelming sadness: "I don't know why, but I feel so weak and drowsy. I don't have enough power to lift my hand. I feel a general weakness, a kind of laziness about talking or moving, an overwhelming sadness" (*Journal*, 76). Miriam cannot escape from her childhood memories and, compared to them, the present is miserable and the future is a desert, this being the reason why her heart is breaking: "I am not allowed to think about home anymore. I have to imagine that I have never had my home, that we are nomads. This will be easier, maybe" (*Journal*, 66).

But the memories are stronger than her will to repress them "and they unspool one after another and they revolve into a vicious circle: my home, my childhood, the past, the sad present, the empty future" (*Journal*, 66). The passing of time marks the loss of childhood and Miriam's coming of age: "I cut my hair. Yes, I don't have ponytails anymore. I comb my hair in all kinds of ways. I broke with childhood!" (*Journal*, 101). Her lost adolescence is outlined, and concomitantly all the vanished caring, loving, and affectionate moments of her loved ones: "It doesn't make any difference that I look more mature. But with the ponytails went so many beautiful memories!" (*Journal*, 101). The tight bond with her loved ones vanished and her soul lost its vitality: "I felt that when I cut my ponytails I had also cut off a part of my soul, of the child that I once was" (*Journal*, 101). In a country which, for Miriam, signified "the cold, the cruel wind, the hunger, and all that mess in which we live and sink" (*Journal*, 49), it was impossible to find "peace and tranquility" (*Journal*, 85), especially for her childlike soul, as she saw it. Because of the dehumanization that eroded her sense of self and her will to live, death seemed an acceptable alternative:

> There are days when I would rather die, when I wish for death eagerly, just like once I wished to learn medicine. There are days when I wish I will live to see the end of this war, to live beautiful days like before. But death is better; it's quiet, it's peaceful, without tears. (*Journal*, 85)

Despite all this, sometimes the longing to live is inexplicable: "Why is there such a wish to live in us? Why don't we put an end to our misery?" (*Journal*, 49). This is stimulated by the memory of the childhood lands, the places and the people she met: "Our mountains, our dear mountains, where are you? Why do you follow me even in my sleep? Firs, dark forests, clean houses, beautiful people, homeland, I miss you" (*Journal*, 51–52). The obsessive recollection of her birthplace shows her the importance of belonging to a homeland: "I did not think of Romania, or better yet Câmpulung, as my homeland. The reason was that we were always insulted and discriminated against by the Romanians" (*Journal*, 51–52). Racial segregation and denial of a homeland reify the deliberate separation between "them" and "us": "But today, when we are far away, when hundreds of kilometers set us apart from our small Câmpulung, I feel how much I miss my homeland and how close it is. *Heimat*, how much this word can say?" (*Journal*, 51–52).

Being stripped of their homeland, the metaphor of wandering turns out to be a frame through which Jewishness is perceived: "Why are we such sinners so as to not have a homeland to love us? We have been banished by our homeland into the emptiness, among the strangers, and among the oppressive words I am being followed by the eternal 'wandering kike'" (*Journal*, 53).

In Miriam's interpretation, all of it – the hardships of everyday dehumanization that Jews were subjected to – was a trial at the end of which "maybe all of this will make humans out of us and in other times we will know how to cherish the good" (*Journal*, 49).

"Cold, fear, insomnia, dark thoughts, regrets, wishes" (*Journal*, 28), all these feelings are mixed up while waiting to go home. In such a context, spreading false information around the ghetto about going back home resulted from every deported Jew's wish to leave Transnistria: "We did not know anything, but we knew too much. So many things were said! News was circulating from one person to another and many of them voiced their wishes rather than the reality." Jews called this kind of rumor circulation "IPA – Plotkesagentur" (The Jewish Agency of Lies). And everyone "said what they wished," "some to calm down, others to become nervous." At times, hope of going back home would give the deported the power to overcome their despair:

> Today there was another rumor, just like so many other times, that we are leaving, going back home. And although I am sure it is just another rumor in these bleak times, which it is a lie wished by everybody, although I know that in one hour somebody will come with sad news about the concentration camp, or new about the front, a ray of hope is flickering in my soul and I smile, I smile with tears. Humanity, don't let yourself tricked by the delusion; for one and a half years we have been living in misery, kept alive only by our hope to go back home at some point, but until now all of it was lies made up of our wishes. (*Journal*, 100)

On the other hand, fake news regarding the return home also generated anger and disorientation:

> [I]n the afternoon it is rumored that we would surely leave, but it is not known where to. [...] People are angry. Immediately the illusion is shattered. We're not leaving for anywhere for now. We are all disoriented. The majority claims

that a denial is in fact a confirmation. So, who knows? (*Journal*, 104)

The impossible wish turned into panic: "People are desperate, there are fights everywhere. What is that sound? What are we going to do? Nobody knows anything positive" (*Journal*, 89). Waiting for the news telling them that they can go home, mistrust grows in the truthfulness of the news and so does the impatience of "getting away from the ordeal – because, really, it is an ordeal" (*Journal*, 29). This pushed Miriam to explain what drove her to write about her experiences:

> Today, after so many months of silence, I feel the need to write, to ask for a justification from Providence, from the cruel fate that banished us to the edge of the earth (because that's what Djurin is like). It condemned us, without hope, to ordeals, torments of the soul, worse than those of the body. (*Journal*, 99)

Thus, in such a context where "the powers and means from home are long gone" (*Journal*, 90), where "people are tired, empty, sapless" (*Journal*, 90), Miriam tries to understand the reason why they were cast away to become "colonists without land, without home. We are colonized in the air, prey to diseases and hunger" (*Journal*, 73). Moreover, Miriam searches for explanations regarding the hatred that settled the cruel fate of the Jews: "And even as weak as we are, we are thorns in their eyes, they're looking to destroy us. What an unfair fight! The German colossus and a handful of sapless Jews" (*Journal*, 90). More to the point, she considers that Jews are "people between two borders whom nobody wants and whom everybody casts away" (*Journal*, 74). While waiting for a change, Miriam reconfirmed an essential aspect of the absurd situation in which she found herself: the fact that the Jewish origin was a stigma upon which racist hatred was built. The meaningless "journey" of the Jews is explained by the metaphor of wandering, repeated frequently throughout the journal:

"Further, wandering kike" – these words keep ringing in my ears. But where to go? Why don't we have the courage to die? Are we cowards? How many have died, how many more will die, how many talents will we lose? And this is the civilization of the twentieth century! (*Journal*, 90–91)

Yet again, the perpetual migration to which the Jews were condemned equals stigma:

What was I expecting, what can save us still? We only lie to ourselves that maybe spring will bring the much expected change. But who knows what it will bring? Oh, wandering kike, continue your travels! You are not a human, you are a kike. This stigma is more powerful than that of Cain. Just like him, you cannot find your rest in the world. Everybody knows your fate and they cast you away, further on. (*Journal*, 64)

Jews are thus portrayed as subhuman, separated from their human nature. Because of the stigma they have to carry, Jews were forced to live at the margins of society. Moreover, being judged as inferior beings, Jews were condemned to eternal martyrdom in the name of which they had to go through torments of the soul and physical ordeals, as a form of penitence for the sins they had committed:

[T]oday I realize that it would have been better if we had all been killed then, in our home, rather than being sent into the desert, to die of cold and hunger, because this is the aim followed by those who sent us here. It would have been more humane. But it is obvious that we are fated to writhe in spasms, and not for one minute, like facing the wall, but for years. God knows for how long! (*Journal*, 46)

Miriam referred to the myth of the Jewish race which had existed for centuries, and, according to which, the faith of the Jews in being errant people is a punishment for their biblical sin. This frame of reference, which eternalizes anti-Semitism, eroded her sense of self.

Yet, even if her Transnistrian trauma disrupted the foundations of her personal and social self, "leaving her marked by the lived experiences" (Afterword, 124), Miriam would not accept her fatalism. On the contrary, coming back to the country on May 2, 1944, "after traveling on foot for two weeks" (Afterword, 124), she finally found the ambition to adapt to a "normal life." Furthermore, after the war, Miriam did not give up school, but instead became a doctor. She earned a PhD in medicine and became the head of the Pediatric Oncology Department at the Fundeni Hospital in Bucharest, Romania. In addition to publishing her *Ghetto Journal*, Miriam talked about her life in oral history interviews. She also transmitted her Holocaust memories to later generations during her visits to various schools and universities.

*Recrafting a Fractured Self in the Aftermath of World War II and Overcoming Dehumanization*

Researchers showed that dehumanization impacts on identity building in diverse and complex ways, as traumatic events "crosscut all dimensions of self-structure and result in self-fragmentation."[25] In Miriam's case, dehumanization aroused anxiety, shaping her emotional and cognitive reactions to other people living in the harsh, hostile, and depressing Transnistrian milieu. The deplorable moral and physical conditions, in which she had lived for three years, in the absence of highly qualitative interpersonal relations, deeply affected the "architectural framework of the self-structure,"[26] her ego being warped by extreme anxiety and grief experiences. Aware of her vulnerability to being inscribed to a category discriminated against in varied manners, after the war she found herself in "a vacuum state" "in which the vitality of the self was emptied."[27] Trauma affected her self-structure, leading to symptoms of psychological distress and agony.

---

25  Wilson and Keane, *Assessing Psychological Trauma*, 34.
26  Wilson, *The Posttraumatic Self*, 34.
27  Wilson, *The Posttraumatic Self*, 34.

Exposed to the extreme strain of being the target of hostility, stigmatization, persecution, and state discrimination until 1945, when coming back from Transnistria, Miriam was challenged by the task of coping with stigma-related distress, restoring her lost humanity, and recrafting her fractured self. Therefore, in spite of "the catastrophic devastation of every aspect" of her life and even her "culture and existence,"28 her altered identity and emotionally fragmented self needed to be reconfigured in accordance with the new living conditions Miriam found when she returned home. When she was deported, every time she felt hungry, cold, dirty, disoriented, disempowered, and alone, Miriam used to close her eyes and project herself into her joyful childhood home. Displaced, dispossessed, and deprived of any rights, Miriam felt alienated. Facing terrible hardship and humiliation, Miriam, like any other deported Jewish child or adolescent, was obliged to grow up in a hostile world, which violently fractured her identity. This was, in her view, a crucial step in her transformation from a person into a subhuman creature. Miriam stated in the afterword of her Ghetto Journal that she managed to survive "only because of unusual strength in fighting 'evil' and unjustified hope" (Afterword, 123). In spite of her traumatized and fractured war existence, Miriam dreamed of a homecoming. Being aware that she could not recover her happy and comfortable prewar life, Miriam did not give up on being optimistic. This explains why, in spite of the empty world she found in her native country, she embraced the homeland that had cast her away. The joy of returning was immense, being followed by "a new battle for readjustment to a normal life" (Afterword, 124). Since her response to dehumanization was disengagement, silence, isolation, and, finally, apathy, Miriam also had to cope with the rift in her social and psychological existence. Because of the physical abolition and loss of self-respect, her social reintegration was difficult. So was the recovery of her human dignity. This explains why no

---

28  Wilson, *The Posttraumatic Self*, 34.

one recognized "the smart and chic student" that she used to be before deportation and who returned in the country on May 2, 1944, under the appearance of "a ragged, barefoot beggar, hungry, burned by the sun and the windy road" after two weeks of travel (Afterword, 124). In 2019, she stated in an interview for the newspaper Libertatea that, first of all, she felt persecuted by her own poverty and the deplorable state she was in: "I came back barefoot [and] skinny as hell." On top of that, contrary to expectations, nobody helped her in any way. Instead, "[e]verybody felt profoundly sorry for me: 'Look at how elegant and beautiful Miriam ended up!'" Moreover, several Jewish colleagues saw her as "a curiosity" ("Interview"). The major problem she had to deal with was to repress and recover from her traumatic memories, as she returned from Transnistria "sick in the head":

> I am a human being who has been sleeping for decades with the help of sleeping pills. Even now, I sleep with two sleeping pills, one for falling asleep and one for staying asleep. [...] Sometimes I sleep, sometimes I don't. Why did I have to resort to sleeping pills? I would dream about my grandparents. I would dream of them calling, "Mimi, we need you!" I would wake up with terrifying nightmares. ("Lecția de viață a lui Mirjam Bercovici," hereafter "Bercovici's Life Lesson")

Coming back to life meant she had to find a new meaning to her existence. To recover the "broken connection,"[29] Miriam had to restart school, although she had to start all over with reading and writing as she had lost some of these abilities in the Transnistrian ghetto. Consequently, this contributed to her psychical degradation: "In the first three years it was very hard to learn. I could not adapt to the learning rhythm. [...] I could not organize my mind. But step by step, I rose back up" ("Interview"). The wish to go on to medical school helped her regain her appetite for learning and thus to overcome the psychological and social barriers inflicted on her by trauma.

---

29  Lifton, *The Broken Connection.*

In spite of finding a motivation to readjust to a normal way of living, Miriam could not overcome the psychological pain of losing her grandparents in an absurd situation, and, with them, all the beautiful moments she lost while being deported. Thus, for Miriam, to visit her hometown was unbearable, even though during the deportation, the memory of her town was a way of repressing the traumatizing reality of the ghetto and the unthinkable atrocities done to the Jews. Seeing her birthplace after more than half a century, in 2007, was insufferable as she was come over with "a state of unrest" and everything seemed black ("Interview"). To defend herself against unbearable memories, Miriam preferred not to spend time in her childhood city, declaring that she wanted to "keep it in her memory as she remembered it" ("Interview"). Her self-defense was activated by the interplay of the overwhelming childhood and adolescent memories and distress caused by intolerable trauma, which caused her severe agony.

Moreover, after 1945 she did not tell anyone about her adolescent experiences, considering that "people do not want to hear horror stories" ("Interview"). She tried to detach herself from those memories, looking for meaning in her life. In 1967 she found her journal, which her mother had cared for after bringing it along when leaving Transnistria. This threw her back into the harsh reality of deportation, declaring that "in that night I cried, I think, more than I had ever cried in my life" ("Interview"). Although she knew that the journal "was nothing compared to the rest" ("Interview"), to the actual experience of the deportation that could not be put into words, the suffering produced by those memories was still profound. The journal was published in 1992, in Germany, and then in 1995, in Romania, even though "nobody was interested in it" ("Interview"), as if the author talking about her Holocaust experience was a voiceless figure. When there was a possibility of emigrating to Israel, Miriam confessed that she could not start all over again, as the clash between the stability gained in Romania and another change would have destabilized her again:

71

Sometimes I think I should have made myself go. [...] But I had a workplace where I was cherished, where I advanced. I did not feel up to starting all over again. [...] In Israel, I would have been the same as the other workers. Maybe I would not have been a head of department, I would not have had so many jobs, and maybe I would not have done a doctorate. But I would have had enough to live on and a house at least as good as this one. ("Bercovici's Life Lesson")

Adopting such a stance on emigration, Miriam rejected the biblical guilt and marking of Cain, "guilty of the crime of fratricide for murdering Abel [and] condemned by God to wander the earth as a fugitive (Genesis 4:8–16)."[30] Refusing the errant life, as well as the restraint of having to build a new life from scratch, Miriam dissociated herself from a mark she thought as an epistemic framework turning the destiny of the Jews into a mythological fatality. This attitude was reinforced by her refusal to be perceived through her Jewishness, which is an objectified and dehumanized representation of a person:

I am allergic when they say that the Romanian people are tolerant. I do not want to be tolerated. I want to have the same rights as any Romanian citizen. I do not need tolerance. One tolerates what is difficult to bear. Why should I be tolerated? Am I wrong? Am I different from others? I am not different. I do not "tolerate" others. I take the Romanian people as they are and they should take me as I am, not tolerate me. ("Interview")

More to the point, Miriam felt profoundly offended, pointing out the reification of anti-Semitic stereotypes in contemporary Romanian society, as far as the Jew is still depersonalized by stereotypical caricatures. Using the word "kike" and its symbolic burden is a social situation which involves psychological dehumanization. Miriam felt it again when, going into a school to

30  McGlothlin, *Second-Generation*, 26.

talk about her war experience as an adolescent, a student in the audience remarked that "kike" means "a man who steals just by looking" ("Interview"). Refusing to be perceived differently from other human beings, in other words, to be subjected to objectification and categorization, Miriam rejected the internalization of stigma and prejudice, as well as the humiliating feelings associated with these social mechanisms. Her rejection of tolerance eventually means not accepting psychological degradation.

## Concluding Remarks

In her *Ghetto Journal*, Miriam Korber-Bercovici has mainly disclosed personal feelings and attitudes about suffering and dehumanization, combined with examples of psychological rupture. Given the prevalence of the personal aspects encompassed by the reality Miriam illustrates in her *Ghetto Journal*, in this chapter we particularly wanted to expose their significance. The goal was to explain Miriam's silences in relation to her physical and emotional changes and her maturity, as well. By giving voice to this young Jewish girl's suffering and hopes in a time of rampant violence against Jews from the Romanian territories, the major objective was to highlight the extent to which familiarity with suffering and death redefined her identity, relationships, and perceptions of the world around her and the values she endorsed.

Compared to the warm times of her childhood, in the Transnistrian social setting imposed by the Romanian authorities Miriam felt overwhelmed by uncertainty and insecurity. The feelings of deep distress triggered severe anguish. Her chronic fatigue led to depression, and, finally, to social anxiety. The lack of social capital which enables her to cope with extreme insecurity and to feed emotional comfort turned Miriam inward. Yet, her silences did not equal the absence of a message, but the incomprehensibility of the situation of the Jews. Whereas for the canonical author Elie Wiesel, silence, a sort of cognitive dissonance, denoted his failure to speak about the unspeakable,[31] for Miriam Korber-Bercovici it designated her inability to see a way to escape her destiny, which was similar to that of other Jews, men or women, part of the same violent and traumatic experience. Not only was language insufficient to fully capture the meaning of the "traumatic experiences" of the Jews, but the words were not able to explain their horrific and incomprehensible Transnistrian experience.

While acknowledging that there is a wide variety of Jewish religious responses to the Holocaust, in Miriam's personal interpretation, her destiny, and that of other displaced Jews, was explained by comparison to that of Jesus Christ. In trying to interpret their grief, Miriam referred to it as the Jews' "road to Golgotha" (Afterword, 116). Relying on "Golgotha," the site of the crucifixion of Jesus, the author has used the idea of eternal suffering that has been the hallmark of the Jewish people throughout their long history. This view has turned "Golgotha" into a symbol for collective suffering. From this perspective, Korber-Bercovici's *Ghetto Journal* could be integrated in the category of autobiographical documents that present the theological implications of the Holocaust. Among the prominent modern Jewish writers on the Holocaust that represent this approach are Eliezer Berkovits, Arthur Cohen, Emil Fackenheim, Irving Greenberg, Hans Jonas, Ignaz Maybaum, Richard Rubenstein, and Elie Wiesel. Unlike the novelist Elie Wiesel, for whom "the Holocaust is inexplicable with God, but also it cannot be understood without Him,"[32] Miriam introduces the idea of "sin," which is a frequent term used in her memoirs. Her insistence on this aspect explains her disengagement with action. In this regard, her attitude resembles Melissa Raphael's acts of nonviolent resistance explained

---

31 The inappropriateness of language, invoked by Elie Wiesel and other Holocaust survivors who decided to talk or write about their Holocaust experiences, means that "their personal narratives and testimonies cannot entirely capture a traumatic experience that remains to a great extent unspeakable" (Catrina, "The Production," 226).

32 Cohn-Sherbok, "Jewish Faith and the Holocaust," 1.

by the image of God. Yet, while Raphael constructs a "theology of the presence of God"[33] under the appearance of Shekhinah, "a medieval, mystical, female image of the divine who goes into exile and suffers with the Jewish people,"[34] Miriam asserts that Jews have to suffer like Jesus, on behalf of their sin.

The image of sin within Miriam's feminist theological approach is a personal view among the wide variety of Jewish religious responses to the Holocaust that is meant to explain the tremendous suffering of the Jews. While Miriam has internalized this biblical frame of reference in deportation, her survival proves that she would not accept its fatal consequences. Although trauma eroded her personal and social self, in the aftermath of World War II Miriam has tried to restore her lost humanity and overcome her deeply damaged mental, behavioral, and physical health. In addition, she committed to speak out and spread the legacy of the Holocaust throughout the generations. While transmitting her trauma, concomitantly she refused to be perceived as different and rejected tolerance. Practically, Miriam refused categorization which once had institutionalized discrimination along ethnic and religious lines, leading to social disorder, identity fragmentation, prejudice, violence, and, finally, genocide.

---

33  Umansky, "The Presence of God at Auschwitz," 5.
34  Umansky, "The Presence of God at Auschwitz," 5.

# Bibliography

Primary Sources

BHEC. "Elsa Binder – Stanislawow, Poland." Birmingham Holocaust Education Center. https://bhecinfo.org/wp-content/uploads/Elsa-Binder.pdf, accessed August 20, 2020.

"Elsa Binder – Stanisławów, Poland." In *Salvaged Pages: Young Writers' Diaries of the Holocaust*, edited by Alexandra Zapruder, 301–328. New Haven: Yale University Press, 2002.

Facing History and Ourselves. "Elsa Binder." https://www.facinghistory.org/resource-library/text/elsa-binder, accessed August 20, 2020.

Facing History and Ourselves. *"Teaching Salvaged Pages: Young Writers' Diaries of the Holocaust."* https://www.facinghistory.org/teaching-salvaged-pages, accessed August 20, 2020.

Holocaust Memorial Resource & Education Center of Florida. "The Diary of Elsa Binder." https://www.holocaustedu.org/education/research/this-week-in-history/december-27-1941-elsa-binder/, accessed August 20, 2020.

"Interviu Miriam Korber-Bercovici. Data şi locul interviului: 31 octombrie 2009, Bucureşti. Interviu realizat de Cosmina Guşu" [Interview with Miriam Korber-Bercovici. Date and place of the interview: October 31, 2009, Bucharest. Interview conducted by Cosmina Guşu]. Institutul Naţional pentru Studierea Holocaustului din România "Elie Wiesel" [Elie Wiesel National Institute for the Study of the Holocaust in Romania], 2009. http://www.inshr-ew.ro/ro/marturii/162-interview-miriam-korber-bercovici.html, accessed April 20, 2020.

Korber-Bercovici, Miriam. *Jurnal de ghetou* [Ghetto journal]. Bucharest: Curtea Veche Publishing, 2017.

"Lecţia de viaţă a lui Mirjam Bercovici, supravieţuitoare a Holocaustului: 'Colegii mă înmormântaseră deja, renunţaseră la mine'" [The life lesson of Miriam Bercovici, Holocaust survivor: "Colleagues had already buried me, given up on me"].

Carried out by Maria Andrieş, Bogdan Sorocan (video), and Marius Tatu (montage). *Libertatea*, July 19, 2019. https://www.libertatea.ro/stiri/video-interviu-lectia-de-via-ta-a-lui-mirjam-bercovici-supravietuitoare-a-holocaus-tului-colegii-ma-inmormantasera-deja-renuntasera-la-mi-ne-2699873, accessed April 20, 2020.

"Miriam Bercovici, Bucharest, Romania." Oral history interview carried out by Ana-Maria Hincu, August 2003. *Centropa: Preserving Jewish Memory – Bringing History to Life*. https://www.centropa.org/biography/miriam-bercovici#During%20the%20War, accessed April 20, 2020.

"Miriam Korber – Transnistria." In *Salvaged Pages: Young Writers' Diaries of the Holocaust*, edited by Alexandra Zapruder, 243–270. New Haven: Yale University Press, 2002.

## Scholarly References

Adelman, Tzvi Howard. "Self, Other, and Community: Jewish Women's Autobiography." Nashim: A Journal of Jewish Women's Studies & Gender Issues 7 (2004): 116–127. doi:10.1353/nsh.2004.0037.

Catrina, Sonia. "The Production, Usages and Circulation of Holocaust Testimonies within Mainstream Societies: Identity Stakes." In Holocaust Memoryscapes: Contemporary Memorialisation of the Holocaust in Central and Eastern Countries, edited by Sonia Catrina, 190–237. Editura Universitară: Bucharest, 2020.

Cohn-Sherbok, Dan. "Jewish Faith and the Holocaust." In Issues in Contemporary Judaism, 1–18. London: Palgrave Macmillan, 1991. https://doi.org/10.1007/978-1-349-21328-3_1, accessed August 18, 2020.

Crocker, Jennifer, Brenda Major, and Claude Steele. "Social Stigma." In Handbook of Social Psychology, edited by Susan T. Fiske, Daniel T. Gilbert, and Gardner Lindzey, 2 vols., vol. 2, 504–553. Boston: McGraw-Hill, 1998.

Eidheim, Harald. "When Ethnic Identity Is a Social Stigma." In Ethnic Groups and Boundaries: The Social Organization of Culture Difference, edited by Fredrik Barth, 39–57. Long Grove: Waveland Press, 1998.

Florian, Alexandru. Foreword. In Miriam Korber-Bercovici, Jurnal de ghetou [Ghetto journal], 5–8. Bucharest: Curtea Veche Publishing, 2017.

Goffman, Erving. Stigma: Notes on the Management of Spoiled Identity. New York: Simon and Schuster, 2009.

Korber-Bercovici, Miriam. Afterword. In Miriam Korber-Bercovici, Jurnal de ghetou [Ghetto journal], 115–126. Bucharest: Curtea Veche Publishing, 2017.

Lifton, Robert Jay. The Broken Connection: On Death and the Continuity of Life. New York: Simon and Schuster, 1979.

McGlothlin, Erin. Second-Generation Holocaust Literature: Legacies of Survival and Perpetration. New York: Camden House, 2006.

Stets, Jan E., and Peter J. Burke. "Identity Theory and Social Identity Theory." Social Psychology Quarterly 63 (2000): 224–237.

Umansky, Ellen M. "The Presence of God at Auschwitz: Theological Reflections on the Work of Melissa Raphael." Holocaust Studies 15.3 (2009): 5–12. DOI: 10.1080/17504902.2009.11087243, accessed August 17, 2020.

Wilson, John Preston. The Posttraumatic Self: Restoring Meaning and Wholeness to Personality. New York: Routledge, 2006.

Wilson, John Preston, and Terence Martin Keane. Assessing Psychological Trauma and PTSD. New York, Guilford Press, 2004.

## 2. "When the Shabbat Became Sunday": Religious and Social Life of Polish Jews in the USSR during World War II

*Katharina Friedla*

© United States Holocaust Memorial Museum, Washington, DC.

The above photograph shows Polish Jews, the Szczukowski and Bankir families, baking matzah for the Passover holiday. This picture was taken in the spring of 1945, in the Uzbek town of Zaamin, located between Tashkent and Samarkand. The young man sliding a peel with matzah into the stove is Mojżesz Szczukowski. He was born in 1920 in Łódź, where he worked as a cobbler and shohet. After the war had broken out he went to Białystok and married Hela Krakower (sitting in the front row in the picture, holding the child). The Szczukowskis were deported to Siberia by the NKVD. When Polish citizens were granted "amnesty" in the summer of 1941, they went to Zaamin. It was this photograph, among many other similar pictures deposited in the United States Holocaust Memorial Museum in Washington, DC, as well as hundreds of testimonies and reports depicting religious life of Polish Jews in exile in the USSR, that prompted me to write this chapter.[1]

Holocaust research has never really focused on the life and world of the religious Jews, nor has it been the center of interest in the historiography of Polish Jews in exile in the Soviet Union during World War II.[2] Until now, the issue of religious Jews from Poland in the USSR has only been briefly discussed in chapters in Yosef Litvak's book on Polish-Jewish refugees in the USSR, 1939–1946,[3] as well as in the monograph by Dov Levin, which describes the fate of religious Jews under Soviet occupation in the years from 1939 to 1941 in some short passages.[4] Eliyana

---

1   This chapter is based on the research on the project *Topography, Experience, and Memory of Life in Transition: Polish Jews in the Soviet Union (1939–1959)*, funded by the research grant from the Gerda Henkel Foundation, and Fondation pour la Mémoire de la Shoah Paris. Editorial work on this article was carried out during the research stay at the Polish Institute of Advanced Studies of the Polish Academy of Sciences in Warsaw. I would like to thank Dr. Arkadi Zeltser, the director of the Moshe Mirilashvili Center for Research on the Holocaust in the Soviet Union, Yad Vashem, for his valuable and critical comments on this text during the workshop (Jewish Experiences and the Holocaust in the Soviet Union) at the United States Holocaust Memorial Museum in Washington, DC, which took place in the summer of 2019. I would like to express my gratitude to Lidia Zessin-Jurek for her invaluable suggestions.
2   See Huberband, *Kiddush Hashem;* Dreifuss, "The Work of My Hands"; Michman, *Jewish Religious Life,* 147–165; Farbstein, *Hidden in Thunder.* Havi Dreifuss writes about historiography and research on Jewish religious life during the Shoah in "Badania nad życiem religijnym Żydów," whereas the problem of Jewish religiousness in the USSR is analyzed in Altshuler, *Religion and Jewish Identity;* Shternshis, *Soviet and Kosher* and "Passover in the Soviet Union"; Levin, *Toldot Chabad;* Litvak, *Plitim Jehudim mi-Polin be-Brit ha-Moatzot;* Bemporad, *Becoming Soviet Jews* and "Behavior Unbecoming a Communist."
3   Litvak, *Plitim Jehudim mi-Polin be-Brit ha-Moatzot,* 155f., 198–200.
4   Levin, *The Lesser of Two Evils,* especially chapter 7 ("Religious Life"), 151–178.

Adler's article should also be mentioned here. In it she analyzes the attitudes of Orthodox Jews from Poland in the Soviet exile during World War II, simultaneously giving some methodical inputs regarding the analysis of testimonies of religious Jews.[5] Despite these few attempts to explore the fate of religious Jews from Poland in the Soviet exile, there are still many unanswered questions that require a more detailed analysis.[6] It must also be stressed that in recent years, a growing number of papers and lectures are oriented toward the subject of Polish-Jewish refugees, the paradox of their survival, and the memory of that survival, in a more in-depth, detailed approach. One of the newest publications is a collection of seven texts, published in 2017, devoted entirely and exclusively to this subject: Edele et al., eds., *Shelter from the Holocaust: Rethinking Jewish Survival in the Soviet Union*.[7] Natalie Belsky's contribution in this anthology is devoted to the subject of the meetings and encounters of Polish and Soviet Jews. The author also mentioned religious practices during which Polish and Soviet Jews participated together.[8] Also noteworthy is Markus Nesselrodt, *Dem Holocaust entkommen. Polnische Juden in der Sowjetunion, 1939–1946* (the first monograph in German on this topic).[9] The newest results of the present-day historians' research on history and memory of the Polish Jews has come out in the form of two new anthologies: one directed at the Polish reader (Zessin-Jurek and Friedla, eds., *Syberiada Żydów polskich. Losy uchodźców z Zagłady*) and one at the international reader (Nesselrodt and Friedla, eds., *Polish Jews in the Soviet Union (1939–1959): History and Memory of Deportation, Exile and Survival*).[10] Beside

---

5    Adler, "The Miracle of Hanukkah."
6    The problem of Catholic religiousness of Poles in exile was investigated by some Polish historians, e.g. Pakuza, "Przyczynek" and *Życie religijne;* Srebrakowski, "Życie religijne"; Siemiaszko, "Życie religijne."
7    Edele et al., *Shelter from the Holocaust.*
8    Belsky, "Fraught Friendships," 167–171.
9    Nesselrodt, *Dem Holocaust entkommen.*
10   Zessin-Jurek and Friedla, *Syberiada Żydów polskich;* Nesselrodt and Friedla, *Polish Jews in the Soviet Union.*

these two volumes, Eliyana R. Adler's monograph *Survival on the Margins: Polish Jewish Refugees in the Wartime Soviet Union* is expected to be published by the end of 2020.[11] All of these new publications notwithstanding, the subject of the Polish-Jewish experience in the USSR still leaves many issues to be explored by researchers. One of these subjects is their religious life in the Soviet exile, which call for a more structured analysis.

In this chapter I wish to present the trajectories of the lives of Polish Jews who remained faithful to their religion in the face of persecution and mass violence in the Soviet Union during World War II.[12] What specific experiences did religious Jews undergo? How did they respond to persecution, violence, and restrictions on their religious rituals? What form did the religious life take – if there was one – in the atheistic Soviet reality? How did religious Jews try to endure their ordeal in the "inhuman land"[13]? I will attempt to find answers to these and many other questions, based on the analysis of the early testimonies recorded either during World War II or in the immediate postwar period, as well as memoirs and interviews published later. The corpus of sources concerning this subject matter is remarkably extensive. In my analysis I will refer to early accounts from the Hoover Institution Archives at Stanford University (including the Władysław Anders Collection and Ministerstwo Informacji i Dokumentacji Records), the Yad Vashem Archives in Jerusalem, the Polish Institute and Sikorski Museum Archive in London (especially the Wincenty Bąkiewicz Collection). Until now historians very often overlooked these early testimonies, which were created as part of

---

11  Adler, *Survival on the Margins*.

12  It must be stressed that not all Polish Jews who found themselves in the interior of the Soviet Union were victims of the NKVD deportations. Some of them managed to live through those hard times, experiencing the hardship of war like any ordinary member of Soviet society. They would cross the Soviet Union in search of employment, or as volunteers seeking work, while others found themselves in the Soviet hinterland as part of the general evacuation following the outbreak of the German-Soviet war.

13  In pursuit of the book title by Czapski, *Inhuman Land*.

the records of the fates of Poles in the Soviet Union, prepared by the Polish Information Centre for the East at the Ministry of Information and Documentation of the Polish government-in-exile. The only exceptions are the so called Palestinian Protocols, which were published in fragments in some source editions.[14] The following presentation of only a small part of these testimonies highlights the enormous potential for further research on this valuable corpus of sources. Nevertheless, it should be noted that working with these early testimonies as well as with later oral history interviews recorded many years after the events described also brings many difficulties in interpreting certain processes.

It is important to be aware of the context in which the testimonies and reports were recorded, and interpret carefully and accurately facts such as names, dates, and locations. For example, in almost all accounts information about the complete extinction of Jewish religious life in the USSR can be found. This fact cannot be confirmed in the accounts of Soviet Jews, in which the description of religious practices and cultivating Jewish tradition in hiding are often cited.[15] Beside this, especially in the early testimonies, there is a tendency visible to a self-representation meant not only to prove Polish-Jewish religious and cultural superiority over the Soviet Jews, but in general a sense of arrogance toward the Soviet way of life and culture as well.

In order to meet the methodological requirements I have analyzed a critical mass of testimonies and personal reports from various proveniences, early and later testimonies and interviews,

---

14  Tych and Siekierski, *Widziałem anioła śmierci;* Grudzińska-Gross and Gross, *War through Children's Eyes*. Regarding the early testimonies of non-Jewish Poles, see Jolluck, *Exile and Identity*.

15  Fortunoff Video Archive for Holocaust Testimonies at Yale, Victor E., 24.XI.1982, New Haven, hvt 0200; Id., Mikhael K., 16.XII.1991, New York, hvt 1924; Interview no. 9, T. Lib. and I. Lib., in Erlich, Summary Report; Interview no. 11, a woman doctor from Kharkov, in Erlich, op. cit.; Interview no. 13, Rotstein, in Erlich, op. cit.; Interview no. 16, Mr. Weinbrand, in Erlich, op. cit.; Interview no. 18, Mrs. W., in Erlich, op. cit. I would like to thank Markus Nesselrodt for sharing these interviews with me.

checking them against other sources and comparing them with each other, including testimonies authored by Soviet Jews. Despite the cognitive and psychological limitations, these sources proved to be best window into the war trajectories of religious Jews of Poland investigated below.

Periodization is a prerequisite for the analysis of religious life in the Soviet Union. From the very beginning the Soviet regime tended toward antireligious and antichurch policies. Over the course of time instructions were issued that provided a legal basis to the open war with religion. Although the constitution guaranteed freedom of conscience, norms of criminal law were framed in order to prevent churches, synagogues, and Orthodox churches from providing their normal service and to practically ban religious observance from the public sphere.[16] As Aleksander Srebrakowski points out: "Decisions that seemingly defended freedom of faith were in fact aimed at preventing any religious rituals under the pretext of protecting public order and civil rights."[17] Disobedience to these rules was subject to very severe punishment.[18] Mordechai Altshuler, the author of a monograph on the religious identity of Jews in the USSR, proves that after a wave of repression and terror against religious institutions in the 1920s and early 1930s, Soviet antireligious propaganda was relatively mitigated and slackened by the mid-1930s.[19] Along with the surge of terror from 1936 to 1938 the management of all religious issues was assumed by the security forces. At that time many rabbis and Catholic and Orthodox Church officials were

---

16  Srebrakowski, op. cit., 264. Srebrakowski mentions the following offences cited in the Soviet penal code (Arts. 119–125): teaching religion to minors in state or private companies and schools, performing religious rituals in state institutions and companies.

17  Srebrakowski, op. cit., 265.

18  Beizer, "The Destruction of Jewish Religious Life"; Weinberg, "Demonizing Judaism."

19  Altshuler, op. cit., 1. Similar conclusions are presented by Shternshis, *Soviet and Kosher;* Bemporad, *Becoming Soviet Jews.*

arrested by the NKVD on charges of anti-Soviet activity.[20] Just before the outbreak of World War II there were over three million Jews living in the Soviet Union. The few synagogues and prayer houses which operated legally, including the Great Synagogue in Moscow or the synagogue in Kharkov, were kept under permanent supervision of the NKVD.[21] A resident of Kharkov, an Orthodox Jew, comments on the religious Jews in the city:

> For the 200,000 Jews in Kharkov there was one synagogue. It was guarded by the NKVD. This synagogue had an official rabbi registered with the NKVD; all other rabbis had been exiled and no one knows how many of them perished. This official rabbi had to report to the NKVD everything that was talked about in the synagogue. He was simply an informer. Perhaps he was compelled to do so, but what Jew would have anything to do with such a rabbi?[22]

Many reports of Russian Jews shows that religious people chose different strategies to observe religious laws and practiced religious rituals, despite restrictions and persecution by the authorities. Ritual slaughter as well as circumcisions were practiced in the underground.[23] Religious Jews usually met in private houses for prayers, and most of them bypassed synagogues, which were officially approved for use, in order to avoid surveillance by the NKVD. In the underground there were also Orthodox schools

---

20  Altshuler, op. cit., 2; Interview no. 18, Mrs. W., in Erlich, op. cit., 2; Interview no. 16, Wainbrand, in Erlich, op. cit., 1.

21  The Polish Institute and Sikorski Museum Archive in London (afterward: PISM), the Wincenty Bąkiewicz Collection (afterward: Col. 138), testimony of Izaak Szachter, no. 10576; The Hoover Institution Archives (afterward: HIA), the Władysław Anders Collection (afterward: WAC), Box 43, folder 3, testimony of Józef Edelsberg, no. 12333.

22  Interview no. 16, Wainbrand, in Erlich, op. cit., 1f.; see also: Interview no. 18, Mrs. W., in Erlich, op. cit., 2.

23  Ibidem; Interview no. 14, Mr. H., in Erlich, op. cit., 6; Yad Vashem Archives (afterward: AYV), O.3/1644, Testimony Gustaw Austzaler, 2.

in which children and youth were taught Hebrew.[24] The biggest difficulty for religious Jews was practicing the Sabbath. In connection with this celebration, there was the problem of working on Saturdays, which were working days in the Soviet Union. In Judaism, however, Saturday is strictly a day off from work. Therefore, many Orthodox Jews decided to set up joint cooperatives, or devoted themselves to outwork to avoid working Saturdays.[25]

After the USSR had annexed eastern parts of Poland (present-day western Ukraine and Belarus), as well as Lithuania, Latvia, Estonia, Bessarabia, and North Bukovina in 1939 and 1940, the number of Jewish inhabitants of the lands controlled by the Soviets increased to five million.[26] Most of them were attached to their tradition and religion. The occupied territories had hundreds of synagogues, prayer houses, Jewish political, cultural, and social service organizations, and schools. The security apparatus immediately targeted religion as well as other spheres of social life. The new authorities began closing Talmud Torah schools and rabbinical academies (yeshivas) and most of the leaders of these institutions were arrested.[27] Witold Lewin, born in Radom in 1916, a dentist by education, witnessed the invasion of the Red Army in Lwów (today the Ukrainian city of Lviv) in September 1939. In his testimony he describes the Soviet repression of the

---

24 In the Soviet Union, Yiddish schools operated until 1951, but it was prohibited to teach Hebrew. See Halevy, *Jewish Schools;* Altshuler, *Ha-Yevsektsyah be-Brit Ha-Moatzot;* Zeltser and Selemenev, "The Jewish Intelligentsia."

25 Interview no. 16, Wainbrand, in Erlich, op. cit., 2; Interview no. 18, Mrs. W., in Erlich, op. cit., 2; Interview no. 14, Mr. H., in Erlich, op. cit., 6; Interview no. 11, A woman doctor from Kharkov, in Erlich, op. cit., 3, 5; Interview no. 10, E. G., in Erlich, op. cit., 7; Interview no. 9, T. L. and I. L., in Erlich, op. cit., 7; Interview no. 4, Traitman, in Erlich, op. cit., 2; Interview no. 5, L. L., in Erlich, op. cit., 2.

26 See Poliakov and Žiromskaya, *Nasielenie Rosii,* 10.

27 Levin, *Tkufa be-Sograyim.*

Polish citizens, but also shows and analyzes the situation of Jewish religious life in the Soviet Union:

> It is impossible for someone living in Europe to grasp with their mind the immensity of the tragedy brought about by the Soviets: the Jewish religion, which over the centuries had been repeatedly repressed, became the object of ruthless persecution at that time. [...] I saw those savages, who changed the living conditions in the USSR beyond recognition in a little more than 20 years! There are no synagogues in the Soviet towns, no prayer houses; it is strictly forbidden to have prayer books. Jewish people are persecuted, and younger generations of Jews from their earliest days wallow in godlessness and deceit. Religious observance is punishable by exile or imprisonment. Rabbis, except for a handful of opportunists, were deported to the north or other places of isolation, where many of them died and others were doomed to extinction.[28]

After Germany invaded the USSR in June 1941, the Soviet regime was forced to seek support from the Allies. As a result of this, and owing to the intercession of many Jewish organizations in the USA and the United Kingdom, the authorities became more liberal toward religious matters.[29] Simultaneously, the Soviet regime was desperately looking for support to wage

---

28 HIA, WAC, Box 41, folder 4, testimony of Witold Lewin, no. 10583, 4.

29 Ivan Maiski, the USSR ambassador to the United Kingdom, met representatives of Agudat Yisrael, a Jewish religious political party, who appealed to him to release rabbis kept in Soviet prisons and to restore religious freedom for the Jews in the USSR (Davar, August 8, 1941). The Polish government-in-exile and Ignacy Schwarzbart, a member of the National Council at the Polish government in London, also pursued diplomatic efforts to release Polish rabbis and students of rabbinic academies from Soviet prisons. See HIA, Poland, Ministerstwo Informacji i Dokumentacji Records [Ministry of Information and Documentation] (afterward: MID), Box 546, folder 8; PISM, Ministerstwo Spraw Zagranicznych [Ministry of Foreign Affairs] (afterward: MSZ), A.11.49/Sow/24, Situation of Polish civilian population in Russia, 58; id., A.11.49/Sow/681.

war against Germany among the disappointed and embittered Soviet population. This appeal to the population also contained elements that supported the liberalization of the religious policy. The Orthodox Church and Jews supported the fight in the Great Patriotic War (as World War II was called in the Soviet Union). As early as the end of 1941 prayers were offered for the victory of the Red Army in the Great Synagogue in Moscow.[30] Soon after the signing of the Sikorski-Mayski agreement (a Polish-Soviet treaty) in July 1941, the Polish Embassy in Moscow made demands on the Soviet government in regard to Poles living in the USSR. Apart from "amnesty" for Polish citizens detained by the Soviets, aid plans, and humanitarian transport missions from the USA and UK, or the possible evacuation of the Polish people, the embassy raised some religious issues. All priests and Polish citizens irrespective of their religion were expected to be released, Soviet authorities were also asked to return an appropriate number of Catholic and Orthodox churches and synagogues in the centers of the Polish population, to provide Polish adherents of non-Catholic religions, especially members of the Orthodox Church, Greek Catholics, and Jews, with the same religious care as Catholics. As the Polish Army was being formed in the USSR, a claim was made that the choice of chaplaincy services should belong solely to internal competence of the army.[31] In August 1943 a pro-Soviet Palestinian daily newspaper, *Mishmar*, wrote: "The attitude of the Soviet state toward religion has not changed whatsoever. Public fighting against religion was ceased, but only

---

30 *Jewish Chronicle*, January 2, 1942, 2. When the Jewish New Year was celebrated in September 1942 the Moscow synagogue was full to the brim and many congregants wore Red Army uniforms (*Jewish Chronicle*, September 25, 1942).

31 31 PISM, MSZ, A.11.49/Sow/24, op. cit., 54–60.

because of a more immediate war with the enemy and because of some tactical reasons."[32]

This shift, however slight, in the Soviet policy on religious issues provides a context which sheds new light on the circumstances of taking the above photograph, which shows Polish Jews baking matzah for the Passover holiday. In many interviews and reports of Jewish refugees from Poland in the USSR, witnesses emphasize a kind of liberalization in matters of performing religious practices after the Sikorski-Mayski agreement was signed in the summer of 1941.[33]

As I have already mentioned, the photograph was taken in the spring of 1945. Soon afterward, Mojżesz and Hela Szczukowski joined a group of repatriated Polish citizens. They went to their home in Łódź and then decided to defect from Poland to a DP (displaced person) camp in Hofgeismar near Kassel. In 1948 the family immigrated to Canada. The Szczukowskis, like thousands of Polish Jews, had gone through the harrowing escape route from German-occupied Poland, Soviet deportation to Siberia,

---

32 PISM, Col. 138/254, Menachem Buchwajc: Położenie Żydów w Rosji Sowieckiej [Situation of Jews in the Soviet Russia], "Mishmar," August 17, 1943, 67. Tactical reasons included the Lend-Lease Act. In March 1944 "Aleph-Bet" (formerly "Eshnav") reported on: "an increase in religious tendencies in the USSR and expansion of church institutions. [...] In view of a renewal of the Orthodox Church and strengthening of the position of Muslims [the USSR Supreme Muslim Council had recently been appointed], it is vital to officially recognize the Jewish religion. The Jewish Community in Moscow was acknowledged to be a representative of Jewish religion in numerous cases, and presently opening an academy for rabbis in Moscow is being negotiated," PISM, Col. 138/237, Aleph-Bet, March 5, 1944.

33 University of Southern California, Shoah Foundation, Institute for Visual History and Education (afterward: USC VHA), Roman Litman, Interview 28343, Lublin, February 22, 1997, tape 1.

facing hard living conditions in an Uzbek town, repatriation to Poland and another escape, and emigration.

## And There the Red Messiah Came...[34]

The Szczukowskis, like thousands of Jews who would later become expatriates, faced their ordeal in the early days of September 1939. The attacking German Army was so ruthless that roads leading to the eastern border of Poland filled up with refugees. On September 17, 1939, Soviet troops entered the eastern part of Poland. Many Jewish fugitives saw this as hope for salvation. Tens of thousands of desperate and horrified people fled toward the German-Russian demarcation line, including thousands of Orthodox and religious Jewish families. Many of them had undergone traumatic experiences witnessing extreme German brutality and cruelty toward Jewish people. These events prompted them to seek refuge in the Soviet occupation zone, which at first seemed a temporary asylum.[35] This was how most Polish-Jewish refugees saved their own lives.

Considering all the events accompanying this miserable wandering around the Soviet Union, memories of religious life are no less emotional than other dramatic experiences. Usually religious oppression is recalled. General efforts to eradicate religious practice in the Soviet Union were determinedly pursued in the newly occupied territories. By gradual elimination of religion the invaders intended to remodel and break social structures in the occupied territories and thus make sure they could take complete control over the local people. To persecute rabbis and other Jewish religious figures the Soviet authorities employed the same methods as against Catholic and Orthodox priests. Their main objective was atheization. Jewish institutions may have not been officially disbanded, but religious communities and social and cultural institutions affiliated with them were beginning to col-

---

34  HIA, MID, Box 123, folder 6, testimony of Meir Szpalter, Report no. 120, 3.
35  Adler and Aleksiun, "Seeking Relatively Safety"; Gurjanow, "Żydzi jako specpierieselency," 111; Żbikowski, *Archiwum Ringelbluma*, 13.

lapse at a fast pace. This was due to the high taxes imposed on the communities and the rapid impoverishment of their members.[36] The new administration started to take over the infrastructure and functions of the communities, closing Talmudic academies (yeshivas), Jewish schools (cheders, Talmud Torah, or Tarbut schools).[37] Teaching religion in private homes was also forbidden; therefore, Soviet officials not only took action in synagogues and prayer houses, but also confiscated ritual objects: Torah scrolls, books of Talmud, prayer books, tallits,[38] and phylacteries.[39] Most severe antireligious acts of repression were aimed at the "cult functionaries," including Catholic and Orthodox priests, but rabbis, yeshiva students, executives and personnel of Jewish communities, teachers, and Jewish political activists were persecuted with equal ruthlessness.[40] Rabbi Mojżesz Stupiczewski explains the situation in Brześć (present-day Brest-Litovsk, Belarus) after the invasion of Soviet troops:

> In September 1939 Bolsheviks entered Brześć. They turned out to be ruthless as regards religious matters. From the very beginning of their rule they took massive action against the Jewish religion. It was done through closing Jewish schools and prayer houses. I was arrested on November 3, 1939, as a religious person who with others fiercely opposed this

---

36 HIA, WAC, Box 41, folder 4, testimony of Morduch Migdałowicz, no. 10587, 17; id., Box 43, folder 3, testimony of Maks Orenstein, no. 12299, 78; PISM, Col. 138, testimony of Wiktor Fiszler, no. 12338, 26; Levin, *Tkufa be-Sograyim*, 177–190.

37 PISM, Col. 138, testimony of Chaim Piekarczyk, no. 14520; id., testimony of Jakob Rochman, no. 12300; HIA, WAC, Box 41, folder 4, testimony of Ludwik Wegner, no. 10579.

38 *Tallit* (in Hebrew), a rectangular shawl covering the head during prayers.

39 *Tefilin* (in Hebrew), leather boxes with verses from Torah worn during daily prayers.

40 HIA, testimony of Ludwik Wegner, op. cit., 8; id., WAC, Box 45, folder 1, testimony of Leopold Spira, no. 14527, 1; PISM, Col. 138, testimony of Samuel Kahan, no. 12301, 23; id., testimony of Józef Kestenbaum, no. 10581; id., testimony of Morduch Migdałowicz, no. 10587.

antireligious campaign. In prison, I spent six weeks alone, in a single cell, for religious observance. [...] After fourteen months in prison in Brześć I was sent to the labor camp in the north, 1,000 kilometers beyond Pechora.[41]

In dozens of accounts and testimonies of rabbis and their relatives who describe the first months of the Soviet occupation the same theme can be found – increased repression by new authorities against religious people. Most rabbis and Orthodox Jews, however, did not stop following religious observances, as religious Soviet Jews did, going underground and keeping their worship private, praying and teaching at home.[42] Roman Ferszt reports that he witnessed prayer services which were held in Jewish cemeteries.[43] Cemeteries remained the only places administered by Jewish communities.[44]

The "underground tactics," which were adopted, for instance, by Rabbi Alter Perlow from Baranowicze, was not always an effective shield against persecution. The NKVD accused him of espionage and threatened to send him to Siberia unless he stopped rabbinic activity. But Rabbi Perlow never ceased teaching children and yeshiva students. As a result of continuing threats and harassment by the NKVD, the rabbi and a group of yeshiva students decided to defect to Wilno (present-day Vilnius, Lithuania), at that time controlled by Lithuania.[45] According to estimates by historians, about 18,000 Polish Jews had attempted to save their lives by fleeing to Lithuania since the end of October

41  PISM, Col. 138, testimony of Rabbi Mojżesz Stupiczewski, no. 10578, 219f.
42  HIA, MID, Box 123, folder 6, testimony of Zeew Frenkel, rep. no. 121, 2; id., testimony of Jechoszua Frydman, rep. no. 107.
43  PISM, Col. 138, testimony of Roman Ferszt, no. 10572, 14.
44  PISM, Col. 138, testimony of Emil Adler, no. 14525, 13; id., testimony of Szymon Kimmel, no. 10571, 144.
45  HIA, MID, Box 123, folder 6, testimony of Jakub Rabinowicz, rep. no. 131, 1f.; see also: id., Box 123, folder 5, testimony of Gitla Rabinowicz, rep. no. 77.

1939.[46] Among thousands of exiles seeking refuge in Lithuania there were many Polish Orthodox Jews, rabbis, and students of Talmudic academies.[47] One of these schools was the famous Mirer Yeshiva, which managed to relocate to Lithuania, and later to Japan and Shanghai, being the only school that survived the war as a whole.[48]

*On the Way to "the East" – "Orthodox Jews Say Prayers in the Carriage"*[49]

Many Jewish fugitives from German occupation tried to come back to their homes in the first months of living under the Soviet rule, specifically as at the beginning of 1940 the Soviet authorities announced that people could register to return. In March 1940 the so-called "passportization" was introduced, which forced refugees to accept Soviet citizenship. Many of them did not agree to it and declared their intention to return to German-occupied territory, including many religious Jews, who hoped to follow their religious observance more freely under German occupation, but most important of all, to have access to kosher food.[50] The so-called *bezentsy* (refugees) as a result of registering to return home became the majority of the deportees sent to Siberia and, consequently, the majority of authors of the accounts and memories presented here.[51] Repressive measures were also targeted at activists of Jewish political parties, rabbis, members of the establishment, or those who refused to accept Soviet citizenship.[52] Between February 1940 and June 1941 the NKVD organized four

---

46  Strelcovas, "Refugees," 46; Arad, "Concentration of Refugees"; Bauer, "Rescue Operations through Vilna"; Zuroff, "Rescue via the Far East."

47  See Levin, "Lithuanian Jewish Refugees"; Liekis, "Jewish-Polish Relations"; Adler, "Exile and Survival."

48  AYV, M.2/358, 3, 47, 53, 67; Eber, *Wartime Shanghai;* Leitner, Operation: *Torah Rescue;* Warhaftig, *Refugee and Survivor.*

49  HIA, MID, Box 123, folder 5, testimony of Adela Weindling, rep. no. 43, 3.

50  Idem, testimony of Józef Rosenberg, rep. no. 65.

51  See Boćkowski, "Losy żydowskich uchodźców."

52  See PISM, Col. 138, testimony of Lieber Gottlob, no. 12128; id., testimony of Chemia Grejnec, no. 12279; id., testimony of Maurycy Grüss, no. 14498.

mass deportations of Polish citizens to the Soviet interior. The largest group of Polish Jews, more then 70,000 people, was deported in June 1940.[53] It should be mentioned that the deported refugees had gone through the hardship of the escape to the east from the Germans in 1939, and so some of them had experienced German ruthlessness and violence firsthand. These Jews had already been robbed of their possessions, knew the ordeal of traumatic flight, and spent months in exile, uncertain of their own future.

They were deported in disastrous conditions: crowded stock cars, no sanitary facilities, inadequate food supplies. Many of the deportees fell ill and died on the way to their destination. Importantly, in almost every Jewish account we can find passages about religious Jews praying in cars and refusing to eat nonkosher foods.[54] Simcha Shafran, a yeshiva student, wrote in his memoir that even traveling by train for weeks he and other students had found a space for prayer in the corner of a car which had been bursting at the seams. They had always managed to assemble a minyan.[55] Shafran recalls that yeshiva students continued their study and Talmudic deliberations under Rabbi Nekritz's tutelage during deportation.[56] As proved by tens of accounts by Polish Jews, who were driven to the trains headed into the heart of Russia, many of them sought support and comfort in prayers, which invigorated them. Some of them, which need to be emphasized

53  Kaganovitch, "Jewish Refugees," 99; Hryciuk, "Victims 1939–1941"; Gurjanow, "Cztery deportacje"; Edele and Warlik, "Saved by Stalin?," 105.

54  HIA, WAC, Box 45, folder 1, testimony of Sima Siebcesser, rep. no. 112, 1; HIA, testimony of Jakub Rabinowicz, op. cit., 2; HIA, MID, Box 123, folder 6, testimony of Eliezer Kretner, rep. no. 114, 2f.; id., testimony of Zeew Frenkel, rep. no. 121, 2; id., testimony of Jechoszua Frydman, rep. no. 107, 2; USC VHA, Henry Galler, Interview 6574, Toronto/Canada, September 8, 1995, tape 4.

55  *Minyan* (in Hebrew), the quorum of ten adult men above the age of thirteen required for Jewish communal worship.

56  Shafran, *Fire, Ice, Air*, 43; USC VHA, Simcha Shafran, interview 47557, Baltimore, MD, USA, August 10, 1998, tape 5.

again, still respected laws of kashrut and, despite hunger and exhaustion, refused to eat the minimal food rations allotted to them.[57]

*Kiddush HaShem*[58] – *Religion, Dignity and Resistance in Exile, Prison, and Special Settlements*

Polish Jews deported in June 1940 were placed in the NKVD-supervised special settlements, the so-called *spetsposeloks*,[59] in the Autonomous Soviet Republics of Yakut and Mari, in Altai and Krasnoyarsk Krai and in the Oblasts of Archangelsk, Chelyabinsk, Irkutsk, Molotov, Omsk, and Sverdlovsk.[60] They were quartered in a total of 250 settlements supervised by 158 local units of the NKVD.[61] The deportees were forced to labor at clearing forests, in lead, coal, gold, and platinum mines, at building roads and railroads. There was a large group of Orthodox Jews among them. As proved in hundreds of accounts, memoirs, and diaries, despite the inhuman conditions many religious Jews still followed religious rituals, celebrated Shabbat and Jewish holidays, held circumcision ceremonies and bar mitzvahs,[62] religious weddings and funerals.[63]

---

57  USC VHA, Regina Mansdorf (born Leidner), interview 16412, Jerusalem, June 11, 1996, tape 3; HIA, testimony of Sima Siebcesser, op. cit.; id., testimony of Eliezer Kretner, op. cit.; id., testimony of Zeew Frenkel, op. cit.

58  *Kiddush HaShem* (in Hebrew), sanctification of God's Name (in Yiddish, Kidesh-Hashem); in Judaism this rule means being ready to sacrifice one's life rather than transgressing laws of the religion (Torah, Book of Leviticus, 22:32). It is synonymous to martyrdom for the faith.

59  Special settlement, a camp in the USSR where civilians were forcibly kept.

60  HIA, Poland, Ambasada (United States) Records, Box 30, folder 8, Deportations of Polish Citizens from Soviet-Occupied Poland to the Interior of the USSR, 1–8; id., Poland, Ministerstwo Spraw Zagranicznych Records, Box 525, folder 6, Rejony, w których są umieszczeni zesłańcy [Areas where exiles are placed], October 24, 1941.

61  Boćkowski, "Żydzi polscy w ZSRR," 116.

62  At this ceremony boys become legal adults at age thirteen and are able to obey commandments of the Law of Moses.

63  USC VHA, Doris Urman (born Arbesfeld), interview 44699, Cliffside Park, NJ, USA, September 1, 1998, tape 4; id., Meyer Rosenberg, interview

According to the accounts, before every Jewish holiday the authorities became increasingly vigilant.[64] Leaving one's workplace on Shabbat or a holiday or baking matzah for the Passover holiday were considered acts of counter-revolutionary sabotage.[65] The traditional circumcision ceremony, a religious imperative of Judaism, was seen by the Soviet authorities as a "counter-revolutionary superstition." These rituals were severely punished, at least until the summer of 1941. Sometimes the exaggerated eagerness of the NKVD officers in following antireligious instructions led to comical situations. Dawid Klajman, a doctor born in 1899 in Lublin, tells a story from a special settlement:

> We, Jews, were forbidden to pray and were forced to work, especially on our holidays. [...] I recall when one of the Jewish bookkeepers was arrested, because on a holiday he sang an aria from an opera in his room, and an exceptionally smart NKVD officer thought it was a Jewish religious song.[66]

Collective services on Shabbat and holidays were specially watched and often violently dispersed. When caught participating in collective prayers, Jews were mostly punished by solitary confinement, deprived of already minimal food rations, often beaten; prayer books revealed during a search were torn or burned.[67] On

16124, Toronto, Canada, June 6, 1996, tape 4; id., Minnie Premsky (born Kleparda), interview 44124, Toronto, Canada, August 12, 1998, tapes 3, 4; id., Solomon Scharf, interview 2866, New York, NY, May 28, 1995, tapes 2, 3; id., Murray Zoltak, interview 16182, Toronto, Canada, June 9, 1996, tape 3; id., Asher Scharf, interview 28003, Brooklyn, NY, February 5, 1997, tapes 4, 5, 6.

64 PISM, testimony of Chaim Piekarczyk, op. cit.
65 HIA, WAC, Box 46, folder 1, testimony of Aron Glikman, rep. no. 201, 2f.; PISM, testimony of Emil Adler, op. cit., 14; id., testimony of Morduch Migdałowicz, op. cit., 118; id., testimony of Samuel Muszkat, no. 14502, 185.
66 HIA, WAC, Box 41, folder 4, testimony of Dawid Klajman, no. 10574, 2; see PISM, Col. 138, testimony of Edmund Lusthaus, no. 10573.
67 PISM, testimony of Emil Adler, op. cit.; id., testimony of Marceli Ardel, no. 14523 (he testifies: "In Asino, in Siberia, a few older Jews were beaten

the other hand, the rebel spirit was rising, even taking the form of strikes. Such a response from the Jewish deportees, even if frequent, must have been surprising to the Soviet authorities.[68] It bears testimony to the strong determination of religious people, who heedless of repression, threats of imprisonment and starvation, followed religious rules and celebrated holidays.[69] Judyta Patasz, who was thirteen at that time, in her testimony describes religious observances in one of the special settlements near Archan-

---

by the NKVD officers during their prayer on the Day of Atonement only because they gathered for the service"); id., testimony of Dawid Cynberg, no. 10588 (he testifies: "In the settlement I saw the stark reality of religious persecution of Jews. In the early days of our imprisonment an old Jew was beaten by a policeman for praying during working hours"); id., testimony of Abram Czarnocha, no. 10568 (he testifies: "In my camp a group of Jews gathered secretly on the Day of Atonement, the holiest Jewish day, and prayed in hiding with a few tallits. We were assaulted, the tallits were confiscated and used as curtains in the office just to annoy us"); id., testimony of Fiszel Krygier, no. 10700 (he testifies: "On the Day of Atonement, when Jews did not turn up for work and met for prayers, investigation was conducted, but as the name of person leading the prayer was not revealed, three Jews were arrested as instigators and sent to a labor camp"); id., testimony of Dawid Halpern, no. 10584 (he testifies: "I remember one of the wardens seeing a Jew who prayed on the upper bunk. He caught him by the tefillin, dragged him down and kicked violently, screaming: 'We don't need God here!'").

68 PISM, Col. 138, testimony of Dawid Klajman, no. 10574, 153; id., testimony of Fiszel Krygier, op. cit.; id., testimony of Michał Zarnower, no. 10566; id., testimony of Wilhelm Kluger, no. 14528; HIA, testimony of Jakub Rabinowicz, op. cit.; id., testimony of Jechoszua Frydman, op. cit.; HIA, MID, Box 123, folder 6, testimony of Eliezer Hochmeister, rep. no. 113; id., testimony of Estera Barasz, rep. no. 119; id., testimony of Zeew Frenkel, op. cit.; id., Box 123, folder 5, testimony of Józef Wajdenfeld, rep. no. 123; id., testimony of Eliezer Helfman, rep. no. 31; id., testimony of Dawid Cwibel, rep. no. 40; id., testimony of Gitla Rabinowicz, op. cit.; Katz, From the Gestapo to the Gulags, 57f.

69 USC VHA, Dora Tenenbaum (born Fuks), interview 22845, Bielawa, Poland, November 8, 1996, tape 1; AYV, O.3/1553, testimony of Rena Szklaniewicz, 5; Interview no. 8, K. Red, in Erlich, op. cit., 6.

gelsk. On Yom Kippur[70] her family and other Jews decided to refrain from work and gather for prayers. The NKVD reacted immediately, threatening to punish them and bring them to court: "Unmindful of punishment, we did not stop praying. The next day I was taken to court with the adults, but as a minor I was not convicted," Judyta recalls.[71]

Seventeen-year-old Jakub Kalman from Bochnia was involved in a similar situation:

> Our settlement was in the Mari Republic, not far from the Volga River. [...] During Rosh Hashanah[72] 30 Jews did not turn up for work. The Russian commissar made a strict search and caught all those participating in an illegal service. People were dispersed and threatened with severe punishment. Nevertheless, they conducted the service to the end. My father was sentenced to six weeks in jail, others had their wages cut. But nobody got scared of the punishment and people were getting ready for the Yom Kippur service. None of the Jews in the settlement went to work and were not afraid of the punishment.[73]

In the broad Polish historiography and memoirs on exile we can find numerous passages about riots of the imprisoned, which were typically generated by living conditions in the special settlements, hunger, and slave labor. But religiously motivated revolts and strikes have a different dimension as they refer not only to a struggle for human dignity in its physical side, but also and above all to the spiritual aspect.

Religious restrictions were not imposed with equal strictness in all special settlements. It largely depended on the decision of

---

70 The Day of Atonement, one of the most important Jewish religious holidays devoted to repentance. The observance consists in refraining from work and absolute fasting.

71 HIA, MID, Box 123, folder 5, testimony of Judyta Patasz, rep. no. 37, 5.

72 The New Year, the first day in the Jewish calendar. It marks the beginning of the period of repentance (Yamim Noraim), which ends with Yom Kippur.

73 HIA, MID, Box 124, folder 1, testimony of Jakub Kalman, rep. no. 214, 2.

a commandant. Sometimes a commandant turned a blind eye to religious ceremonies, or worshipers negotiated with him for absence from work during holidays.[74] Gitla Rabinowicz, a rabbi's daughter, testifies that her father held Shabbat prayers in the hut for crowds of religious Jews living in the settlement. He was repeatedly arrested by the NKVD commandant. But his perseverance proved effective and on Yom Kippur the warden excused all Jews from work and allowed them to pray together on Shabbat.[75]

Religious Jews were in a similar situation in Soviet prisons and penal colonies. Tallits, prayer books, and other liturgical objects raised laughs among prison and camp guards, provoked blasphemous sneers and curses, and a worshiper faced charges of counter-revolutionary activity and a new sentence, when using them in secret. Religious paraphernalia were confiscated and sometimes even desecrated. Chrel Zylber, a 47-year-old shohet from Tarnów, recalls: "During the search everything was taken away, not only tallits and prayer books, but tablecloths were made out of tallits and phylacteries were turned into reins for horses."[76] Chaim Lubelski, an industrialist from Warsaw, born in Baranowicze (present-day Baranavichy, Belarus) in 1909, gives an account of his stay in the labor camp near Kotlas, where he met a rabbi from Minsk. Lubelski remembers that the rabbi was: "persecuted and most savagely abused at any time for his godliness."[77] He also admits that: "We had some fervent communists among our boys, who gradually began to pray. Some of them became almost fanatically pious. It was clear they wanted to rectify their youthful mistakes."[78]

---

74  HIA, WAC, Box 41, folder 4, testimony of Dawid Cynberg, no. 10588; id., testimony of Jakob Federgrum, no. 10590; HIA, MID, Box 123, folder 7, testimony of Motel Gejer, rep. no. 135; id., testimony of Józef Geller, rep. no. 181; id., testimony of Jakub Kalman, op. cit.; Ettinger, Erinnerungen, 105.
75  HIA, testimony of Gitla Rabinowicz, op. cit., 4.
76  PISM, Col. 138, testimony of Chrel Zylber, no. 10565, 146.
77  PISM, Col. 138, testimony of Chaim Lubelski, no. 14015, 144.
78  Ibidem.

A similar phenomenon of the "return to religion" is mentioned by Rabbi Pinkas Rosengarten, who became the Chief Rabbi in the Polish Armed Forces in the East after the "amnesty" had been announced. In his memoirs he describes a situation during transportation of prisoners from the Odessa prison to Vorkutgulag, a forced-labor camp in Vorkuta:

> Against the ethnic mosaic a group of religious Jews stood out, who refused to eat nonkosher foods. [...] Strong believers supported and consoled many our brothers from the House of Israel who had broken down, despaired of life itself, and were on the verge of suicide. It should also be added that those good Jews managed to organize evening prayers on Yom Kippur on board the ship, and they were joined by many Jews who had previously considered themselves atheists or communists.[79]

Often rabbis and Orthodox Jews gave moral support, encouragement, and hope to their fellow believers in Soviet prisons. The accounts of witnesses describing the activities of the chief rabbi of the Polish Army, Baruch Steinberg, who was imprisoned in the POW camps in Starobilks and Kozelsk, are truly moving; he provided immense support to prisoners imprisoned in these camps, and organized religious services. In the spring of 1940, Rabbi Baruch Steinberg was murdered in the Katyn Forest.[80] The same pattern – priests bolstering up their fellow believers – can be found in numerous accounts of Catholic Poles.[81] Both Christians and Jews saw people who had previously been religiously indifferent turn to religion, which is mentioned by Rabbi Rosengarten, Chaim Lubelski, and many Catholic deportees.[82] Many Jews with ambivalent attitudes toward religion sympathized with the

---

79  Rosengarten, *Zapiski rabina wojska polskiego*, 37.
80  Slowes, *The Road to Katyn;* Meirtchak, *Żydzi.*
81  See Kobryń, *Wspomnienia sybiraków;* Przewłocki, *Wspomnienia sybiraków.*
82  Begin, *Czas białych nocy*, 64; Katz, op. cit., 55; USC VHA, Melta Huppert (born Zilz), interview 44102, New York, NY, June 9, 1998, tape 2.

believers and often participated in their prayers.[83] This helped the exiles and prisoners cherish their hopes and remain strong enough to survive. Moreover, religious observance reinforced their Jewish identity. Zev Katz gives an account of the Yom Kippur celebrations in his memoirs:

> Not that I myself was religious, nor were many of us, especially among the young, but Yom Kippur was deeply embedded in our tradition. We found a way to mark it even during our brief time under the Germans. Besides, in the barrack conditions, this was a matter of "national-ethnic" self-assertion, of being Jews.[84]

Joint religious observance in prisons, labor camps, and special settlements were also of considerable psychological importance, giving the deportees the sense of a close and supporting community, which helped them survive. This mechanism was aptly described by Aleksander Wat, who as the only Jew in a prison cell did not belong to the group of confessors of Christ. Therefore, he not only felt rejected, but also could not see any sense in struggle for life. This experience induced him to consider converting to Christianity. Aleksander Wat confides his very intimate reflections on religion to Czesław Miłosz:

> In the stink, in that horrible misery and hardship – every day Marian songs. All around me only believers. And me, lying alone in the corner, excluded from the community. [...] I was excluded from the community of believers. [...] Later in Saratov [Prison] I experienced a conversion, which had probably been ripening when I had that sense of being rejected, and particularly of being excluded from the social community.[85]

---

83  PISM, Col. 138, testimony of Alfred Süsser, no. 14501.
84  Katz, op. cit., 56.
85  Wat, *Mój wiek*, 331.

Apart from alienation and solitude, which affected Aleksander Wat, however, quite different situations arose. Testimonies often mention instances of solidarity and mutual help among prisoners of different faiths and beliefs.[86] Anatol Krakowiecki, a Polish Catholic imprisoned in Stanisławów (present-day Ivano-Frankivsk, Ukraine), tells a heartbreaking story. In his memoirs he reports that together with other inmates he spared no efforts to ensure that the Orthodox president of the Jewish community in Łuck (present-day Lutsk, Ukraine), who shared the cell with them, observed the laws of kashrut. They prepared a meal for him with two kosher pots received in a parcel: "After three months Werman could at last drink some hot tea and eat some bread. We enjoyed watching it."[87] Rabbi Samuel Cywiak, a former yeshiva student in Baranowicze (present-day Baranavichy, Belarus), who fled to Wilno (present-day Vilnius, Lithuania) after the war had broken out, and in the summer of 1941 was deported to a forced-labor camp in the Uzbek city of Nukus, asserts that his fellow prisoners helped him enormously to observe Shabbat. According to his account, the inmates usually hid him in the hut on Shabbat, which is Saturday, a working day, and protected him from the Soviet guards so that he could devote himself to prayers.[88]

Sometimes Catholics and Jews celebrated holidays together. Jerzy Gliksman, one of the prominent representatives of the Bund Party in Poland before the war, Wiktor Alter's brother, transferred from a Soviet prison to a special camp in Kotlas, where he was on a December 24, Christmas Eve. He was invited to the Christmas celebration by the Poles from his hut.[89] Aron

---

86  HIA, WAC, Box 41, folder 4, testimony of Maurycy Klotz, no. 10593.

87  Krakowiecki, *Książka o Kołymie*, 42.

88  Cywiak, *Flight from Fear*, 125; see PISM, testimony of Alfred Süsser, op. cit. On the solidarity of prisoners with religious Jews, see USC VHA, Izydor Einziger, interview 44445, Union, NJ, USA, August 4, 1998, tape 4.

89  Gliksman, *Tell the West*, 218; YIVO Archive New York, Jerzy Gliksman, "Jewish Exiles in Soviet Russia (1939–1943)," Part I–III (1947), Papers, Record Group 1464, Box 4, folder 41.

Glikman in his account of his stay in the Soviet prison in Oszmiana (present-day Ashmyany, Belarus) describes the celebration of Passover with his Polish inmates, who were invited to the rituals by a group of Jews:

> We celebrated the Passover Seder. We did not have Haggadah[90] but our shohet knew it by heart. That evening we cried. In our group we had some assimilated Jews, who also cried. Our Polish inmates were deeply moved, when we translated the prayer for them.[91]

Some Polish fellow prisoners, on the other hand, displayed hostility to religious Jews.[92] Particularly heartrending are the stories of Jewish children who describe persecution in Polish orphanages.[93] Jakub Piwko, placed in a Polish orphanage in Samarkand by his mother, recalls his relationship with other children: "I spent a year in the orphanage. We were severely bullied by Polish children. They forced us to say Christian prayers, and those who refused, were beaten."[94] Nevertheless, thanks to being in the orphanage Jakub was able to evacuate from the USSR. In August 1943 he arrived at Palestine via Tehran; he had to leave his mother and brother in Russia.[95]

---

90  The Passover Haggadah, the story commemorating the liberation of the Israelites from slavery in Egypt; it consists of passages from Torah, commentaries and prayers; read during a Seder dinner, which marks the beginning of the Passover holiday.

91  HIA, testimony of Aron Glikman, op. cit., 5; the joint celebrations of holidays held by Poles and Jews is also mentioned by Komito, *Between Two Crazy Dictators*, 48; Ettinger, op. cit., 105.

92  PISM, Col. 138, testimony of Miriam Krambajn, rep. no. 144 (15562).

93  HIA, testimony of Jechoszua Frydman, op. cit.; id., testimony of Eliezer Hochmeister, op. cit.; id., testimony of Zeew Frenkel, op. cit.; USC VHA, Pinchas Doron, interview 46850, Brooklyn, NY, November 11, 1998, tape 3; id., Zvi Potash, interview 44731, Melbourne, Australia, May 24, 1998, tape 2.

94  HIA, MID, Box 123, folder 7, testimony of Jakub Piwko, rep. no. 140, 4.

95  Ibidem, 5.

Jewish refugees from Poland celebrate a wedding together with their Uzbek friends, Bukhara, May 1942 (© USHMM).

*Meetings and Confrontations: Bukharan Jews and Soviet Marranos*[96]
Signing the Sikorski-Mayski agreement and the announcement of the "amnesty" for Polish citizens in August 1941 mark the turning point in biographies of most of the deportees and prisoners. Polish Jews represented a large percentage of former exiles who made a disorderly rush southward, to the Central Asian Soviet republics, in hopes of finding better living conditions and food. The biggest centers of Jewish population were formed near Samarkand, Bukhara, Tashkent, Dzhambul (present-day Taraz,

---

96 This term dates back to the late fourteenth century, when Jews were persecuted during the Inquisition. Marranos were Jewish converts in Spain and Portugal, suspected of practicing Judaism in secret. Gennady Estraikh also cites examples of the use of the term "Marranos" by Yiddish writers from Poland in relation to Soviet poets and writers of this language (Estraikh, "The Missing Years"). For the newest publication on this topic, see Schulz, "The Deepest Self."

Kazakhstan) and Jalal-Abad.[97] A number of Jewish organizations, such as the Jewish Agency for Palestine or the American Jewish Joint Distribution Committee, supported refugees by sending gifts, food, and funds.[98] It was possible to allow Jewish organizations to begin charitable work in the USSR, although under the umbrella of several embassies, including the Polish one, because at that stage Stalin was compelled to cooperate with the Allies.

At that time the Ministry of Foreign Affairs of the Polish government in London, in response to the constantly arriving requests and interventions of Jewish religious organizations from the USA, compiled lists of rabbis and students of rabbinical academies who were in the USSR.[99] According to the documents, large groups of rabbis and their students reached, for example, the town of Merke (present-day Merki) in Dzhambul Oblast in Kazakhstan. Over a hundred students attended the yeshiva in Merke, on Sadowa Street.[100] Furthermore, larger groups of yeshiva students with rabbis were located in the Uzbek city of Jizzakh (Samarkand Oblast) or in Chimkent (present-day Shym-

97  HIA, Poland, Ambasada (Soviet Union) Records, Box 16, folder 3, Udzielona pomoc i opieka nad ludnością żydowską w ZSRR [Aid granted to the Jewish population in the USSR] (by Zygmunt Sroczyński), Teheran w sierpniu 1943 roku, 35, 54; id., Box 7, folder 3, Pismo Ambasadora Kota do Ministra Spraw Zagranicznych w Londynie [Letter from ambassador Kot to the Foreign Minister in London], November 8, 1941, 1f.; Report on the Relief Accorded to Polish Citizens by the Polish Embassy in the USSR, with Special Reference to Polish Citizens of Jewish Nationality, Tehran, Iran, September 1941–April 1943.

98  HIA, Poland, Ambasada (United States) Records, Box 34, 64, 109; id., Ministerstwo Spraw Zagranicznych Records, Box 148, folder 19, Brief outline of relief work among Jewish refugees in the USSR, through the Parcels Service, Charles Passman, Jerusalem, February 25, 1944, 1–4; On the aid actions by Joint to the USSR during WWII, see Grossmann, "Joint Fund Teheran."

99  HIA, MID, Box 123, folder 3, folder 4; id., Box 45, folder 6; id., Poland, Ambasada (United States) Records, Box 67.

100 PISM, MSZ, A.11.E/681, Lista studentów szkół rabinackich i rabinów, uchodźców w ZSRR [List of students of rabbinical academies and rabbis in exile in the USSR].

kent) in Kazakhstan.[101] Rabbi Leib Nekritz with his family and a group of his students from the yeshiva Beit Yosef were in the special settlement of Nekrasovka in Novosibirsk Oblast. As proved by the accounts and memoirs, rabbis and their students continued their study and prayers in exile in the USSR.[102] Additionally, many Polish rabbis met in Dzhambul in Kazakhstan, where they established a yeshiva for 20 young men, a Talmud Torah school for 70 children, a mikvah,[103] and a rabbinic court[104]; Samarkand, thanks to the massive influx of Polish-Jewish refugees, also became a vibrant center of Jewish religious life.[105]

The period following the announcement of the "amnesty" for the polish citizens in the USSR marks one of the most interesting chapters in the odyssey of religious Polish Jews in the Soviet exile. Accounts of the refugees who encountered the local Jewish population when wandering across the Soviet Union are truly fascinating.[106] In the Central Asian republics such as Uzbekistan, Kyrgyzstan, and Kazakhstan, they encountered Bukharan Jews.[107] Polish Jews were particularly impressed by the admirable religious determination of their Bukharan brothers in faith.[108]

---

101 Ibidem.

102 Shafran, op. cit.; USC VHA, Simcha Shafran, op. cit.; Cywiak, op. cit.; Goldberg, *The Unexpected Road;* Pomerantz, Itzik, *Be Strong!*

103 A ritual bath house.

104 Interview no. 4, Traitman, in Erlich, op. cit., 3.

105 Litvak, "Jewish Refugees," 144; USC VHA, Shyfra Scharf (born Leser), interview 28004, Brooklyn, NY, February 5, 1997, tapes 3, 4.

106 PISM, testimony of Szymon Kimmel, op. cit.; PISM, Col. 138, testimony of Rafał Sunilowicz, no. 14519; id., testimony of Szymon Wittman, no. 10563; id., testimony of Aron Wajer, no. 10559; id., testimony of Natan Zylberstein, no. 14017; HIA, testimony of Maurycy Klotz, op. cit.; USC VHA, Zenon Goldberg, interview 15959, Łódź, Poland, May 31, 1996, tape 2. On the relation between Polish and Soviet Jews in the USSR during World War II, see Belsky, "Fraught Friendships."

107 On Bukharan Jews, see Levin, "How It All Began"; Loy, *Bukharan Jews;* Kaganovitch, *Druzya po nevolye.*

108 Interview no. 1, Dr. R., in Erlich, op. cit., 5; Interview no. 4, Traitman, in: op. cit., 1; Interview no. 10, E. G., op. cit., 6; Interview, Mrs. H., op. cit., 10; Interview no. 15, Mr. Ent, op. cit., 3.

David Azrieli fondly recalls: "I arrived in Bukhara. Its oriental architecture made an impression on me. [...] I was fascinated by Bukharan Jews, their utterly different customs and exotic rituals, but I felt remarkably connected to them."[109] Chaim Lubelski in his testimony describes his meeting with Bukharan Jews in the following words:

> I left Tashkent for Bukhara. There I met the famous Bukharan Jews, who maintain Jewish religion and tradition even today. It is a very tough task as they are persecuted by the authorities. They have no temples, which were confiscated for clubs or other needs of the government. Hence, they pray in private apartments. Most of them do outwork, so they can celebrate Shabbat and holidays. They speak Uzbek and Hebrew.[110]

Polish Jews were often invited by Bukharan Jews to their homes to observe Shabbat and holidays with them. Nachum Teper writes that a group of Bukharan Jews warmly received his family in their home, even though they had nothing to eat themselves. The hosts took good care of them and they prayed together.[111] It was not the only form of support from Bukharan Jews, who often helped refugees find a job, a place to live, or food.[112]

Meetings with Soviet Jews offered many Polish Jews new opportunities for understanding the reality of Soviet life. They often established closer contacts, which provided a basis for mutual trust. The confidence and dialogue resulted in initiating Polish Jews into the underground religious life of their Soviet fellow believers. Some Polish Jews referred to Russian and Bukharan Jews as "Marranos" and called their secret religious observance

---

109 Azrieli (Azyrelewicz), *One Step Ahead*, 85.
110 PISM, testimony of Chaim Lubelski, op. cit., 144.
111 HIA, MID, Box 123, folder 5, testimony of Nachum Teper, rep. no. 74, 4.
112 HIA, testimony of Zeew Frenkel, op. cit., 5; HIA, MID, Box 123, folder 6, testimony of Nachman Elbojm, rep. no 55; Begin, op. cit., 302; USC VHA, Henry Galler, op. cit., tape 5.

"a Spanish system." Morduch Migdałowicz says: "I was present at the Rosh Hashanah service held in a small house, where I met those people and saw someone like medieval 'Spanish Marranos' [...] – people who prayed eagerly and with enthusiasm."[113] Rabbi Mojżesz Stupiczewski met a Soviet Jew who was a member of the Communist Party. When he learned that his Polish fellow believer was a rabbi "he told me the whole truth that although he and his father were members of the party, they still practiced the old Jewish religious rituals in the Spanish system. But they did it in closely guarded secret from their neighbors and even their family and friends."[114]

Chaim Lubelski, the soldier of Anders' Army, describes his impressions on the Passover holiday in Guzar in Kyrgyzstan:

> At Easter we, Polish soldiers of Jewish faith, held a traditional service in the military theater building in Guzar. The ceremony was attended by a great number of Russian Jews, refugees from central Russia. Each of them had his tallit, which proved they often prayed, since those who do not pray, do not tend to carry their tallits with them. It broke our hearts to see those people crying. When talking to them, we were certain that they had never lost their hope in God![115]

The sudden and massive influx of Polish Jews into the Soviet Union during the war also offered Soviet Jews who lived in isolation an opportunity to renew their contact with Judaism and Jewishness. Some Jews in the USSR preserved their tradition and practiced religion in secret. Many of them showed solidarity to the newcomers from Poland. As a result of over 20 years of Soviet indoctrination, repressions, and persecution, most of the Soviet

---

113 PISM, testimony of Morduch Migdałowicz, op. cit., 118.
114 HIA, WAC, Box 41, folder 4, testimony of Mojżesz Stupiczewski, no. 10578, 1; see PISM, Col. 138, testimony of Mejer Parnes, no. 10570; id., testimony of Perec Rachman, no. 10567.
115 PISM, testimony of Chaim Lubelski, op. cit., 144.

Jews were forced to cultivate Jewish tradition, culture, and religion in secret. Therefore, the encounter with Polish Jews was a significant experience to them as they met a lot of religious, well-educated people who spoke Yiddish and had graduated from Jewish or Hebrew schools. For some Soviet Jews, it was a chance to "come out of the closet," if only for a moment, and celebrate holidays or Shabbat with their fellow believers.

## Conclusions

The above testimonies and accounts of Polish Jews who remained faithful to their religion illustrate various paths in the Soviet exile and experiences with persecution, but also strategies and opportunities which helped them follow religious practice. Religiousness was a significant factor determining attitudes and behavior of many Jews in exile. It is aptly observed by Yitzchok Pomerantz, a yeshiva student:

> I knew full well that, as a yeshivah student, my chances of survival were very slim. However, I was ready to sacrifice my life for the sake of my beliefs. I was given the task to preserve my *tzelem Elokim*,[116] my divine image, and I would resist with all my power the tendency to assimilate with the savages around me.[117]

This attitude was also characteristic of the majority of Catholic deportees from Poland. Both Polish Jews and Catholics found themselves in a completely new situation, especially in terms of the limited possibilities of satisfying their religious needs. Jews connected with Judaism by their *kehila* (community), centuries-old tradition, morality, and emotions were suddenly deprived of their rabbis and all religious infrastructure, and, most importantly, of the opportunity to observe religious practices. Nevertheless, from the very beginning of their lives under the Soviet rule many Polish Jews did not abandon their rituals. With

116 The image of God.
117 Pomerantz, op. cit., 161.

great determination they tried to organize their religious lives by pursuing different strategies, which were often similar to those chosen by Soviet Jews. One form of resistance was a religious internal emigration, or individual performance of rituals in secret to avoid repression, but respecting the laws of their religion, even if reduced to a bare possible minimum. Many deportees met in the camp barracks for prayers or sneaked onto the taiga to pray out of sight of the NKVD officers.[118] Others fought for their religious rights through collective rebellion, especially on the holiest days in the Jewish calendar.

Religion definitely helped deportees maintain spiritual strength and an awareness of their national and social identity. Faith and religious practices were also elements of keeping their dignity, motivating them to help other exiles and prisoners. Religious rituals allowed them to symbolically separate themselves from the overwhelming reality and were part of their survival strategy, necessary in extremely difficult conditions, to overcome alienation and external pressure. It is worth drawing attention to the accounts and reflections which describe nonreligious people who find a sense of community in collective prayer, a cure for homesickness in exile, and, most importantly, a source of hope and solace.

Most religious Jews who had the opportunity to participate in joint prayers or the celebration of Shabbat and holidays felt and remembered it as something which strongly affected their attitudes, giving them enormous strength to survive in the "inhuman land." These feelings are illustrated by a passage in the memoir of Rabbi Simcha Shafran:

> In Siberia, we learned what prayer really means. We had no idea how long our exile would last, or indeed if it would ever end. We never knew if we would survive the week, the month, the year. [...] When we allowed our Jewish souls full expression, we felt that Siberia, somehow, would not

---

118 USC VHA, Henry Galler, op. cit., tape 7.

prove to be our end, that there would be a future for us. Rabbi Nekritz would often tell us – looking back now, prophetically – that one day, with G-d's help, we would be in a better place, and that, in fact, we would look upon our Siberia sojourn as a precious time of spiritual growth.[119]

Apart from a very small group of Jewish refugees from Poland, evacuated to Iran and then to Palestine with the Anders' Army, most of the deportees and refugees from Poland were forced to stay in the USSR until the end of the war.[120] The final decision regarding "repatriation" was made on July 6, 1945. According to the agreement signed by the Soviet Union and the Provisional Polish Government of National Unity, the right of return was granted to all individuals who on September 17, 1939, had Polish citizenship and were of Polish or Jewish nationality. Until the end of 1946, more than 200,000 Jews returned from the USSR to Poland.[121] Most of the transports went to the former German territories that had been ceded to Poland, mostly to Lower Silesia and West Pomerania.[122] Among thousands of repatriated Jews to Poland, there were many religious people, rabbis, and yeshiva students. As it was reveled in a recent article by Serafima Velkovich, the repatriation of Polish citizens from the Soviet Union offered an opportunity for a group of Soviet Jews, mostly represented

---

119 Shafran, op. cit., 43; USC VHA, Simcha Shafran, op. cit., tape 5.

120 During the evacuation of the Polish Army under the command of General Anders from the USSR in 1942, approximately 4,000 Jewish soldiers and around 1,500 civilians reached Palestine, HIA, MID, Box 136, folder 6, Dowódca Armii Polskiej na Wschodzie, Memoriał w sprawie żydowskiej podczas ewakuacji W.P. z Sowietów na teren Iranu [The head of the Polish Army in the East, Memorial in the Jewish case during the evacuation from the USSR to Iran], Teheran, Iran, September 19, 1942.

121 Hornowa, "Powrót Żydów polskich"; Kaganovitch, "Stalin's Great Power Politics"; Litvak, "Polish-Jewish Refugees"; Novik, Eyrope, 130f.

122 The Potsdam Conference in August 1945 redrew the borders in Europe. Accordingly, large parts of eastern Germany fell under Polish administration, including two-thirds of Pomerania and the bulk of Silesia.

by religious Orthodox Jews and Zionists, to escape the Stalinist regime.[123]

The majority of the Jewish repatriates from the Soviet Union had been strongly affected by the turmoil of the war. Their exile in Siberia and Central Asia had been characterized by hunger, illness, and poverty. Returning from the Soviet Union, they were exhausted and in poor health. Besides, they returned home with great curiosity but also unsettled by their uncertainty and fears regarding the relatives and friends they had left behind when they went to the USSR. As soon as they arrived, they found out that their relatives who had stayed behind had been murdered and their former homeland had become a Jewish cemetery. Given the unimaginable scale of the tragedy, they could barely grasp the reality after the Shoah. The world they had left behind in 1939 no longer existed. There was nowhere they could return to. They were not welcome in their former houses. The situation in war-ravaged Poland alarmed many. When the returnees reached the Polish border, they were often confronted with virulent anti-Semitism. Many faced similar questions and statements: "What are you coming back for? Couldn't you stay in Russia?", "A pity that Hitler didn't finish you all off to the last one", "Look, unslaughtered chickens are returning."[124]

Obviously, the experience of the war had done nothing to ameliorate the stereotypes and prejudices that had long been wide-

123 Velkovich, "Polski paszport."
124 USC VHA, interview 34313, Rita Berger (born Adler), September 21, 1997, Lido Beach, NY, USA, tape 3; id., interview 11719, Norbert Fluss, February 4, 1996, New York, NY, USA, tapes 2, 3; id., interview 3498, Max Wozniak, 25 June, 1995, Los Angeles, CA, USA, tape 4; id., interview 30264, Sara Brokholc, April 10, 1997, Szczecin/Poland, tape 2; id., interview 30068, Sara Bergman, April 6, 1997, Melbourne, Australia, tape 3; id., interview 44445, Izydor Einziger, August 4, 1998, Union, NJ, USA, tape 6; id., interview 14395, Morris Gruda, April 22, 1996, Thornhill, Ontario, Canada; Gruda, *Tricks of Fate*, 236; Tytelman-Wygodzki, *The End and the Beginning*, 36; Lipiner, *Long Journey Home*, 142.

spread in Polish society.[125] Most Poles showed neither empathy for nor solidarity with the returnees. In the summer of 1945, anti-Jewish unrest and pogroms erupted in some Polish cities, such as Rzeszów, Lublin, Radom, Częstochowa, and Kraków.[126] This atmosphere culminated in the July 1946 pogrom in Kielce, which killed an estimated 42 Polish Jews.[127] After arriving in Poland, all those refugees were confronted with the unimaginable destruction of their prewar community. The first postwar months, however, were replete with new traumatic experiences. Without a homeland and their culture and language robbed from them years before, they were forced to look for new destinations and a new homeland. Their flight and emigration were motivated not least by their experience of the communist regime in the Soviet Union during the years of their exile there.

Many religious Jews and rabbis left Poland shortly after arriving from the USSR and headed primarily to the American occupation zone of Germany, where many DP (displaced person) camps were established. Thanks to this influx of religious refugees, rabbinical schools were founded in the DP camps, among others, in Bergen-Belsen and Föhrenwald. Religious life was rapidly reviving in many other DP camps as well. Soon, many leading rabbis and Orthodox Jews left the DP camps in Germany and Austria, mainly for Israel and the USA. For most of them, this emigration brought an end to the protracted, painful, and distressing trajectory of exile, flight, deportation, "repatriation," and renewed exile, which had led them across several constantly shifting borders.

---

125 The complex and dramatic Polish-Jewish "coexistence" in Poland immediately after the war has been studied extensively. See Gross, Fear; Gross and Grudzińska Gross, Golden Harvest; Zaremba, *Wielka Trwoga;* Tych and Adamczyk-Garbowska, *Jewish Presence in Absence;* Krzyżanowski, *Dom którego nie było;* Engelking and Grabowski, *Dalej jest noc;* Tokarska-Bakir, *Pod klątwą.*

126 Tych and Adamczyk-Garbowska, *Jewish Presence in Absence.*

127 Tokarska-Bakir's two-volume monograph, *Pod klątwą,* is the most recent study on the pogrom in Kielce.

# Bibliography

## Archives

The Hoover Institution Archive (AIH), Ministerstwo Informacji i Dokumentacji Records (Ministry of Information and Documentation).

AIH, the Władysław Anders Collection.

AIH, Ambasada (Soviet Union) Records (Embassy Soviet Union).

AIH, Ambasada (United States) Records (Embassy United States).

AIH, Ministerstwo Spraw Zagranicznych Records (Ministry of Foreign Affairs).

The Polish Institute and Sikorski Museum Archive in London (AIPiM), the Wincenty Bąkiewicz Collection.

AIPiM, Ministerstwo Spraw Zagranicznych (Ministry of Foreign Affairs).

University of Southern California, Shoah Foundation, Institute for Visual History and Education (USC VHA).

Yad Vashem Archives (AYV).

YIVO Archive New York.

United States Holocaust Memorial Museum Archive

# General Bibliography

Adler, Eliyana R. "Exile and Survival: Lithuanian Jewish Deportees in the Soviet Union." In *That Terrible Summer: Seventy Years since the Destruction of the Jewish Communities of Lithuania*, edited by Michal Ben Yaakov, Gershon Greenberg, and Sigalit Rosmarin. Jerusalem: Efrata College, 2013 (in Hebrew).

———. "The Miracle of Hanukkah and Other Orthodox Tales of Survival in Soviet Exile during World War II." *Dapim: Studies on the Holocaust* 32 (2018), no. 3: 155–171.

———. *Survival on the Margins: Polish Jewish Refugees in the Wartime Soviet Union*. Cambridge, MA: Harvard University Press, 2020.

Adler, Eliyana R., and Aleksiun, Natalia. "Seeking Relatively Safety: The Flight of Polish Jews to the East in the Autumn of 1939." *Yad Vashem Studies* 46.1 (2018): 41–71.

Altshuler, Mordechai. *Ha-Yevsektsyah be-Brit Ha-Moatzot, 1918–1930: Ben Lemiyut le-Komunizm* [Yevsektsya in the Soviet Union, 1918–1930: Between nationality and communism]. Jerusalem: Hebrew University Press, 1980.

———. *Religion and Jewish Identity in the Soviet Union, 1941–1964*, Waltham: Brandeis University Press, 2012.

Arad, Yitzhak. "Concentration of Refugees in Vilna on the Eve of the Holocaust." *Yad Vashem Studies* 9 (1973): 201–206.

Azrieli (Azyrelewicz), David J. *One Step Ahead: Memoirs: 1939–1950*. Jerusalem: Yad Vashem, 2001.

Bauer, Yehuda. "Rescue Operations through Vilna." *Yad Vashem Studies* 9 (1973): 215–223.

Begin, Menachem. *Czas białych nocy. Opowieść o aresztowaniu i przesłuchaniach Menachema Begina* [Time of white nights: A story of the arrest and interrogation of Menachem Begin]. Cracow: Austeria, 2010.

Beizer, Michael. "The Destruction of Jewish Religious Life in Leningrad, 1929–1939." *Shvut* 24.8 (1999): 58–86.

Belsky, Natalie. "Fraught Friendships: Soviet Jews and Polish Jews on the Soviet Home Front." In *Shelter from the Holocaust: Rethinking Jewish Survival in the Soviet Union*, edited by Mark Edele, Sheila Fitzpatrick, and Atina Grossmann, 161–176. Detroit: Wayne State University Press, 2017.

Bemporad, Elissa. *Becoming Soviet Jews: The Bolshevik Experiment in Minsk*. Bloomington: Indiana University Press, 2013.

———. "Behavior Unbecoming a Communist: Jewish Religious Practice in Soviet Minsk." *Jewish Social Studies* 14.2 (2008): 1–31.

Boćkowski, Daniel. "Losy żydowskich uchodźców z centralnej i zachodniej Polski przebywających na Kresach Północno-Wschodnich w latach 1939–1941" [Experiences of Jewish refugees from central and western Poland in the North-Eastern Borderlands in 1939–1941]. In *Swiat NIEpożegnany: Zydzi na dawnych ziemiach wschodnich Rzeczpospolitej w XVIII–XX wieku* [A world we bade no farewell: Jews in the eastern territories of the Polish republic from the eighteenth to the twentieth century], edited by Krzysztof Jasiewicz, 91–108. Warszawa: Oficyna Wydawnicza RYTM, 2004.

———. "Żydzi polscy w ZSRR w czasie II wojny światowej" [Polish Jews in the USSR during World War II]. In *Żydzi i komunizm* [Jews and communism], edited by Michał Bilewicz and Bogna Pawlisz, 104–128. Warszawa: Stowarzyszenie Jidele, 2000.

Cywiak, Samuel. *Flight from Fear: A Rabbi's Holocaust Memoir*. New York: Dreamer Publications, 2010.

Czapski, Jozef. *Inhuman Land: Searching for the Truth in Soviet Russia, 1941–1942*. London: Chatto & Windus, 1951.

Dreifuss, Havi. "Badania nad życiem religijnym Żydów w Polsce podczas Zagłady – główne źródła i podstawowe zagadnienia" [Research on Jewish religious life in Poland during the Holocaust – Major sources and fundamental issues]. *Zagłada Żydów. Studia i Materiały* [Holocaust studies and materials] 9 (2013): 48–85.

———. "The Work of My Hands Is Drowning in the Sea, and You Would Offer Me Song?!: Orthodox Behaviour and Leadership in Warsaw during the Holocaust." In *Warsaw. The Jewish Metropolis:*

*Essays in Honor of the 75th Birthday of Professor Antony Polonsky*, edited by Glenn Dynner and François Guesnet, 467–495. Leiden: Brill, 2015.

Eber, Irene. *Wartime Shanghai and the Jewish Refugees from Central Europe: Survival, Coexistence, and Identity in a Multi-Ethnic City*. Berlin: De Gruyter, 2012.

Edele, Mark, and Wanda Warlik. "Saved by Stalin? Trajectories and Numbers of Polish Jews in the Soviet Second World War." In *Shelter from the Holocaust: Rethinking Jewish Survival in the Soviet Union*, edited by Mark Edele, Sheila Fitzpatrick, and Atina Grossmann, 95–160. Detroit: Wayne State University Press, 2017.

Edele, Mark, Sheila Fitzpatrick, and Atina Grossmann, eds., *Shelter from the Holocaust: Rethinking Jewish Survival in the Soviet Union*. Detroit: Wayne State University Press, 2017.

Engelking, Barbara, and Jan Grabowski, eds. *Dalej jest noc. Losy Żydów w wybranych powiatach okupowanej Polski* [Night without an end: The fate of Jews in selected counties of occupied Poland]. Warsaw: Centrum Badań nad Zagładą Żydów, 2018.

Erlich, Rachel, ed. *Summary Report of Eighteen Intensive Interviews with Jewish DP's from Poland and the Soviet Union*. New York: American Jewish Committee Library of Jewish Information, 1949.

Estraikh, Gennady. "The Missing Years: Yiddish Writers in Soviet Bialystok, 1939–41." *East European Jewish Affairs* 46.2 (2016): 176–191.

Ettinger, Mark. *Erinnerungen. Von Warschau durch die Sowjetrepublik Komi nach Astrahan, 1922–1999*. Konstanz: Hartung-Gorre, 2005.

Farbstein, Esther. *Hidden in Thunder: Perspectives on Faith, Halachah and Leadership during the Holocaust*, 2 vols. Jerusalem: Feldheim Publishers, 2007.

Gliksman, Jerzy. *Tell the West, by Jerzy Gliksman: An Account of His Experiences as a Slave Laborer in the Union of Soviet Socialist Republics*. New York: Gresham Press, 1948.

Goldberg, Hilel. *The Unexpected Road: Storied Jewish Lives around the World*. New York: Philipp Feldheim, 2013.

Gross, Jan T. *Fear: Anti-Semitism in Poland after Auschwitz.* Princeton: Princeton University Press, 2006.

Gross, Jan T., with Irena Grudzińska Gross. *Golden Harvest: Events at the Periphery of the Holocaust.* Oxford: Oxford University Press, 2011.

Grossmann, Atina. "Joint Fund Teheran: JDC and the Jewish Lifeline to Central Asia." In *The JDC at 100: A Century of Humanitarianism*, edited by Avinoam Patt et al., 205–244. Detroit: Wayne State University Press, 2019.

Gruda, Morris. *Tricks of Fate: Escape, Survival, and Rescue, 1939–1945.* Toronto: Holocaust Centre of Toronto UJA Federation, 2006.

Grudzińska-Gross, Irena, and Jan T. Gross, eds. *War through Children's Eyes: The Soviet Occupation of Poland and the Deportations, 1939–1941.* Stanford: Hoover Institution Press, 1981.

Gurjanow, Aleksandr. "Cztery deportacje, 1940–1941" [Four deportations, 1940–1941]. *Karta* 12 (1994): 114–136.

———. "Zydzi jako specpierieselency – bieżeńcy w Obwodzie Archangielskim (1940–1941)" [Jews as special deportees – refugees in the Arkhangelsk region]. In *Swiat NIEpożegnany: Zydzi na dawnych ziemiach wschodnich Rzeczpospolitej w XVIII–XX wieku* [A world we bade no farewell: Jews in the eastern territories of the Polish republic from the eighteenth to the twentieth century], edited by Krzysztof Jasiewicz, 109–121. Warszawa: Oficyna Wydawnicza RYTM, 2004.

Halevy, Zvi. *Jewish Schools under Czarism and Communism: A Struggle for Cultural Identity.* New York: Springer, 1976.

Hornowa, Elżbieta. "Powrót Żydów polskich z ZSRR oraz działalność opiekuńcza Centralnego Komitetu Żydów w Polsce" [The return of Polish Jews from the USSR to Poland and the aid actions of the Central Jewish Committee in Poland]. *Biuletyn Żydowskiego Instytutu Historycznego* 133/134 (1985): 105–122.

Hryciuk, Grzegorz. "Victims 1939–1941: The Soviet Repression in Eastern Poland." In *Shared History – Divided Memory: Jews and Others in Soviet-Occupied Poland, 1939–1941*, edited by Elazar Barkan, Elizabeth A. Cole, and Kai Struve, 173–200. Leipzig: Leipziger Universitätsverlag, 2007.

Huberband, Shimon. *Kiddush Hashem: Jewish Religious and Cultural Life in Poland during the Holocaust*. Hoboken, NJ: Ktav Publishing House/New York: Yeshiva University Press, 1987.

Jolluck, Katherine. *Exile and Identity: Polish Women in the Soviet Union during World War II*. Pittsburgh: University of Pittsburgh Press, 2002.

Kaganovitch, Albert. *Druzya po newolye. Rosiya i Bukharskiye Evrejie 1800–1917*. Moscow: Novye literaturnye obozrene, 2016.

———. "Jewish Refugees and Soviet Authorities during World War II." *Yad Vashem Studies* 38.2 (2010): 85–121.

———. "Stalin's Great Power Politics, the Return of Jewish Refugees to Poland, and Continued Migration to Palestine, 1944–1946." *Holocaust and Genocide Studies* 26.1 (2012): 59–94.

Katz, Zev. *From the Gestapo to the Gulags: One Jewish Life*. London: Vallentine Mitchell, 2004.

Kobryń, Jerzy, ed. *Wspomnienia sybiraków. Zbiór tekstów źródłowych*. [Memoirs of Siberian deportees: Collection of source texts], vol. 2. Bystrzyca Kłodzka: Koło Związku Sybiraków, 2010.

Komito, Max. *Between Two Crazy Dictators*. New York: M. Komito, 1991.

Krakowiecki, Anatol. *Książka o Kołymie* [The book on Kolyma]. London: Veritas, 1987.

Krzyżanowski, Łukasz. *Dom którego nie było. Powroty ocalałych do powojennego miasta* [A house that was not there: Survivors returning to the postwar city]. Wołowiec: Czarne, 2016.

Leitner, Yecheskel. *Operation: Torah Rescue: The Escape of the Mirer Yeshiva from War-torn Poland to Shanghai, China*. Jerusalem: Feldheim Publishers, 1987.

Levin, Dov. *The Lesser of Two Evils: Eastern European Jewry under Soviet Rule, 1939–1941*. Philadelphia: Jewish Publication Society, 1995.

———. "Lithuanian Jewish Refugees in the Soviet Union during World War II, 1941–1945." *Studies in Contemporary Jewry* 4 (1988): 185–209.

119

―――――. *Tkufa be-Sograyim: 1939–1941, Tmurot ba-Hayey ha-Jehudim ba-Etzorim shesufchu le-Brit ha-Moatzot be-tchila Milchemet ha-Olam ha-Shniya* [Closure times: 1939–1941, changes in Jewish life in areas annexed to the Soviet Union at the beginning of World War II]. Jerusalem: Hebrew University, 1989.

―――――. *Toldot Chabad be-Russia Ha-Sovietit be-Shanim 1917–1950* [History of Chabad in the USSR, 1917–1950]. Brooklyn: Otzar Hasidim, 1989.

Levin, Zeev. "How It All Began: Bukharan Jews and the Soviets in Central Asia, 1917–1932." In *Bukharan Jews in the 20th Century: History, Experience and Narration*, edited by Ingeborg Baldauf et al., 23–36. Wiesbaden: Dr Ludwig Reichert, 2008.

Liekis, Sarunas. "Jewish-Polish Relations and the Lithuanian Authorities in Vilna, 1939–1940." *Polin* 19 (2007): 521–536.

Lipiner, Lucy. *Long Journey Home: A Young Girl's Memoir of Surviving the Holocaust*. New York: Usher Publishing, 2013.

Litvak, Yosef. "Jewish Refugees from Poland in the USSR, 1939–1946." In *Bitter Legacy: Confronting the Holocaust in the USSR*, edited by Zvi Gitelman, 123–150. Bloomington: Indiana University Press, 1997.

―――――. *Plitim Jehudim mi-Polin be-Brit ha-Moatzot, 1939–1946* [Polish-Jewish refugees in the USSR, 1939–1946]. Jerusalem: Hebrew University, 1988.

―――――. "Polish-Jewish Refugees Repatriated from the Soviet Union at the End of the Second World War and Afterwards." In *Jews in Eastern Poland*, edited by Antony Polonsky and Norman Davies, 227–239. London: Palgrave Macmillan, 1991.

Loy, Thomas. *Bukharan Jews in the Soviet Union: Autobiographical Narrations of Mobility, Continuity and Change*, Wiesbaden: Dr Ludwig Reichert, 2016.

Meirtchak, Benjamin. *Żydzi – żołnierze Wojsk Polskich polegli na frontach II wojny światowej* [Jews – Soldiers of the Polish Army who died on the fronts of World War II]. Warsaw: Bellona, 2001.

Michman, Dan. "Jewish Religious Life under Nazi Domination: Nazi Attitudes and Jewish Problem." *Studies in Religion* 22 (1993): 147–165.

Nesselrodt, Markus. *Dem Holocaust entkommen. Polnische Juden in der Sowjetunion, 1939–1946*. Berlin: De Gruyter, 2019.

Nesselrodt, Markus, and Katharina Friedla, eds. *Polish Jews in the Soviet Union (1939–1959): History and Memory of Deportation, Exile and Survival*. Boston: Academic Studies Press, 2021 (forthcoming).

Novik, Peysakh. *Eyrope – Tsvishn Milhome un Sholem*. New York: Ikuf, 1948.

Pakuza, Joanna. "Przyczynek do rozważań nad życiem religijnym polskich kobiet zesłanych do Związku Radzieckiego w latach 1939–1945" [Contribution to a discussion on the religious life of Polish women exiled in the Soviet Union, 1939–1945]. *Studia Teologiczne* [Theological studies] 32 (2014): 389–403.

―――. *Życie religijne wygnańców polskich w Związku Sowieckim w latach 1939–1945 na podstawie wspomnień* [Religious life of Polish exiles in the USSR, 1939–1945, based on memories]. Katowice: Wydawnictwo WueM, 2018.

Poliakov, Yuri, and Valentina Žiromskaya, eds. *Nasielenie Rosii v XX. vekie: Istoricheske Ocherki, vol. 2, 1940–1959* [Russian population in the 20th century: historical overview], Moscow: ROSSPeN, 2001.

Pomerantz, Yitzchok. *Itzik, Be Strong!* New York: CIS Publishers, 1993.

Przewłocki, Janusz, ed. *Wspomnienia sybiraków: "Polsza budiet kakda woron zbieliejet,"* vol. 1 [Memories of Siberian Deportees]. Warszawa: Wyd. Pomost, 1990.

Rosengarten, Pinkas. *Zapiski rabina wojska polskiego* [Diary of a rabbi in the Polish Army]. Warsaw: Stowarzyszenie Dokumentacji i Upowszechniania Dorobku Kulturalnego Żydów Europy Środkowej i Wschodniej "Pamięć Diaspory," 2001.

Schulz, Miriam. "The Deepest Self Denies the Face: Polish-Jewish Intellectuals and the Birth of 'Soviet Marrano." In *Polish Jews in the Soviet Union (1939–1959): History and Memory of Deportation, Exile and Survival*, edited by Markus Nesselrodt and Katharina Friedla. Boston: Academic Studies Press, 2021 (forthcoming).

Shafran, Simcha. *Fire, Ice, Air: A Polish Jew's Memoir of Yeshiva, Siberia, America*. New York: Hashgacha Press, 2012.

Shternshis, Anna. "Passover in the Soviet Union, 1917–1941." *East European Jewish Affairs* 31.1 (2001): 61–76.

—————. *Soviet and Kosher: Jewish Popular Culture in the Soviet Union, 1923–1939*. Bloomington: Indiana University Press, 2006.

Siemiaszko, Zbigniew S. "Życie religijne obywateli polskich w głębi ZSRR w latach 1939–1957" [Religious life of Polish citizens in the heart of the USSR, 1939–1957]. In *Polacy w Kościele katolickim w ZSRR* [Poles in the Catholic Church in the USSR], edited by Edward Walewander, 129–139. Lublin: Redakcja Wydawn. Katolickiego Uniwersytetu Lubelskiego, 1991.

Slowes, Salomon W. *The Road to Katyn: A Soldier's Story*. Oxford: Blackwell, 1992.

Srebrakowski, Aleksander. "Życie religijne i obrzędowość" [Religious life and rituals]. In *Życie codzienne polskich zesłańców w ZSRR w latach 1940–1946. Studia* [Everyday life of Polish exiles in the USSR, 1940–1946], edited by Stanisław Ciesielski, 263–286. Wrocław: Wydawnictwo Uniwersytetu Wrocławskiego, 1997.

Strelcovas, Simonas. "Refugees: Between Myth and Reality." In *Casablanca of the North: Refugees and Rescuers in Kaunas, 1939–1940*, edited by Linas Venclauskas, 43–53. Vilnius: Versus aureus; Kaunas: Sugihara Diplomats for Life Foundation, 2017.

Tokarska-Bakir, Joanna. *Pod klątwą. Społeczny portret pogromu kieleckiego* [Under the curse: Social portrait of the Kielce pogrom]. Krakow: Czarna Owca, 2018.

Tych, Feliks, and Maciej Siekierski. *Widziałem anioła śmierci: losy deportowanych Żydów polskich w ZSRR w latach II wojny światowej: świadectwa zebrine przez Ministerstwo Informacji I Dokumentacji Rządu Polskiego na Uchodźstwie w latach 1942–1943*. Warsaw: Rosner I Wspólnicy, 2006 [I saw the Angel of Death: Experiences of Polish Jews deported to the USSR during World War II. Testimonies collected in 1943–1944 by the Ministry of Information and Documentation of the Polish Government in Exile].

Tych, Feliks, and Monika Adamczyk-Garbowska, eds. *Jewish Presence in Absence: The Aftermath of the Holocaust in Poland, 1944–2010*. Jerusalem: Yad Vashem, 2014.

Tytelman-Wygodzki, Rachel. *The End and the Beginning: August 1939– July 1948*. Author's edition, 1998.

Velkovich, Serafima. "Polski passport jako droga do wolności. Żydowscy uchodźcy z ZRSS po II wojnie światowej" [The Polish passport as a way to freedom: Jewish refugees from World War II]. In *Syberiada Żydów polskich. Losy uchodźców z Zagłady* [The Siberian odyssey of the Polish Jews], edited by Lidia Zessin-Jurek and Katharina Friedla, 619–626. Warsaw: Jewish Historical Institute, 2020.

Warhaftig, Zorach. *Refugee and Survivor: Rescue Attempts during the Holocaust*. Jerusalem: Feldheim Pub., 1988.

Wat, Aleksander. *Mój wiek. Pamiętnik mówiony* [My century: Spoken diary], vol. 1. Warsaw: Czytelnik, 1990.

Weinberg, Robert. "Demonizing Judaism in the Soviet Union during the 1920s." *Slavic Review* 67.1 (2008): 120–153.

Zaremba, Marcin. *Wielka Trwoga. Polska 1944–1947. Ludowa reakcja na kryzys* [The great fear: Poland, 1944–1947: People's responses to the crisis]. Krakow: Znak, 2012.

Żbikowski. Andrzej, ed. *Archiwum Ringelbluma. Konspiracyjne Archiwum Getta Warszawy, vol. 3: Relacje z Kresów* [Ringelblum's Archive: The underground archives of the Warsaw Ghetto, vol. 3: Reports from the Eastern Borderlands]. Warszawa: Żydowski Instytut Historyczny, 2000.

Zeltser, Arkadi, and Viacheslav Selemenev, "The Jewish Intelligentsia and the Liquidation of Yiddish Schools in Bielorussia, 1938." *Jews in Russia and Eastern Europe* 43 (2001), 78–97.

Zessin-Jurek, Lidia, and Katharina Friedla, eds. *Syberiada Żydów polskich. Losy uchodźców z Zagłady* [The Siberian odyssey of the Polish Jews]. Warsaw: Jewish Historical Institute, 2020.

Zuroff, Efraim. "Rescue via the Far East: The Attempt to Save Polish Rabbis and Yeshiva Students, 1939–1940." *Simon Wiesenthal Center*

*Annual* 1 (1988). http://motlc.wiesenthal.com/site/pp.asp?c=gvKVL-cMVIuG&b=394985, accessed March 30, 2018.

## 3. The Roots of the Rashomon–like Story of Eliezer Gruenbaum/Leon Berger[1]

*Tuvia Friling[2]*

There would be no reason to bother reader with the story of Eliezer Gruenbaum if it was not a story of many Jews who were nominated by the Nazis to be *kapos* in the concentration camps, or members of *Judenrats* (Jewish local leadership) at many ghettoes. And, as such, part of a genius yet wicked and vicious system where the victim took an initial part in a "self – annihilation" process.

It is a story that can illustrate the deep presences of the Shoah in Israeli life[3] and has the potential to be a fruitful test case for dealing with the complicated, entangled, and fragile "relations" between history, memory, and politics that radiates and plays on them both. It would not be worth readers' precious time if it was not a story that offers a fruitful infrastructure for a methodological query of the problems, odds, and challenges of judicial documentation.

This is a journey into the intriguing life of Eliezer Gruenbaum – a Jewish *kapo*, a communist, an anti-Zionist, a secularist, and the son of Yitzhak Gruenbaum, the most prominent secular leader of interwar Polish Jewry and Israel's first Minister of the Interior. The story of Eliezer Gruenbaum became a symbol exploited by opponents of the movements to which both the father and the son alike were linked. A *Rashomon*-like journey within the cultural and political contexts, it illuminates key debates that rented the Jewish community in Europe and Israel from the 1930s to today and centers on the question of what constitutes – and how to evaluate – moral behavior in Auschwitz. This is a

---

1   The chapter is based on Tuvia Friling, *Who Are You, Leon Berger?* and *A Story of a Jewish Kapo.*
2   For a previous version of this article, see Friling, "Contested Memory."
3   Friling, "Introduction."

125

journey which attempts to unravel the historical, political, and psychological issues that underlay the tragedy of Eliezer Gruenbaum, a young Polish Jew, who was denounced after the war as a *kapo* at Auschwitz-Birkenau.

Eliezer Gruenbaum/Leon Berger

Eliezer Gruenbaum was the second son of Yitzhak and Miriam Gruenbaum, the younger brother of Binyamin-Benio and older than Yonatan. The three of them were sons of the leading Zionist politician in interwar Poland, which had the largest, most culturally vibrant, and most politically fragmented Jewish community in the world. He was also the initiator and the chair of the "Minorities block" in the Sejm, the lower house of the Polish parliament. A champion of a secular, nationalist conception of Jewishness, whose major opponents included the communists – who sought to overcome Jewish particularity through universalist revolution – and the ultra-Orthodox, who condemned the Zionists as heretics for their attempt to establish a Jewish state.[4]

4    On Zionist politics in Poland, see Bartal and Gutman, *Kiyyum ve-Shever;* Guterman, *Warsaw Jewish Community.* On Gruenbaum's role in the "Minorities block," see Frister, *Without Compromise;* Gruenbaum, *Speeches in the Polish Sejm.*

Orthodox Jews struggled to understand how, while so many of the Polish Jewry observed the religious commandments, they were being dragged under the leadership of supposedly radical and belligerent Zionists who refused to appease the feudal lord and thus, they argued, provoked the gentile world to no good end. The tensions caused by this political and cultural diversity ran within families, including the Gruenbaums. Eliezer, like his elder brother Binyamin, initially joined the socialist-Zionist pioneer youth movement HaShomer HaTzair cell in Warsaw.[5] But he left soon afterward for the communist movement, and in 1929, at age 20, Eliezer was arrested by the Polish secret police owing to his clandestine activity in the Polish Communist Party.[6]

After Eliezer's quick trial, conviction, and incarceration in Łęczyca Prison, Eliezer's mother, who refused to wait for her son's prison term to end, used the family's status and connections to work for his release. After he had served about two and a half years of his sentence, he was freed.[7]

Loyal to its revolutionary principals, France continued to open its doors to migrant workers and political fugitives looking for asylum. Paris had been a "little Poland" since the first wave of Eastern European immigrants settled there in the late nineteenth century, and it remained a safe haven for Jewish runaways in the 1920s. Young Gruenbaum was one of the asylum seekers who

---

5  Founded in 1913 in Galicia, in Austria-Hungary. For more details, see Tsur, *Before Darkness Fell;* Zertal, *Den of Youth;* Zait, *Shomer Dreams of Utopia.*

6  The Communist Party in Poland was banned after the May 1926 coup by Józef Piłsudski. The legal issue is discussed in J. Gutner et al., 1929, No. 105/1454, Duracz Archives, situated in the Archive of the Institute of Party History of the United Polish Workers' Party, at the Archiwum Akt Nowych (Central Archives of Modern Records, Warsaw) [hereafter AAN-PPR].

7  Frister, *Without Compromise,* 267–277; Gruenbaum, unpublished manuscript, chapter on Eliezer Gruenbaum. Yonatan Gruenbaum's unpublished manuscript has no title. A portion is in the possession of the author. Other portions are quoted by other writers, as noted. The section "HaTragedia shel Eliezer Gruenbaum" was kindly shown to me by Matti Regev.

arrived in Paris in 1931. He became an activist in the Polish cell of the French Communist Party and a journalist for its press. Like many romantic communist freedom fighters in the late 1930s, Eliezer left France illegally to go to Spain. With a group of comrades from his Parisian club he enlisted in the all-Jewish Naftali Botwin Company, one of units among the International Brigades, for service the Spanish Civil War.[8] He fought side by side with members of the noncommunist left, veterans of strikes, demonstrations, and "hunger marches" in many countries, who viewed the civil war in Spain as a continuation of their own campaigns against exploiters of the working class, fascism, and Nazism. Standing along with "La Pasionaria," Dolores Ibárruri, the legendary secretary general of the Communist Party in Spain, and others to fight under the antifascist slogan "¡No pasarán!" (They shall not pass!).

In the company he met, among others, Emanuel Mink, its famous commander, and David Szmulewski, who were later to be two of his fellow prisoners in Birkenau.[9] While fighting in the Spanish Civil War Eliezer Gruenbaum adopted a nom de guerre, "Leon Berger," cutting the last tie connecting him with his father and the rest of his family.

After the International Brigades were disbanded (in September 1938), Eliezer wanted to return to France. Along with other foreigners, he was confined in the detention camp at Saint-Cyprien as a stateless refugee and an immigrant who had left France illegally. Once again, his mother used her connections to legalize his status in France, now standing at the precipice of war with

---

8   The establishment of a Jewish company was first proposed by Albert Nahumi (whose original name was Aryeh Weitz), a communist activist in Paris who arrived in Spain at the beginning of the war. He gained the support of André Marty, commander of the International Brigades' basic training camp and chief of the communist delegation in the Brigades. See also the account of a discussion between supporters and opponents in Zaagsma, *Jewish Volunteers in the Spanish Civil War*, 12–13.

9   The number of Jews in the International Brigades was disproportionately high. See Stein, *Der birger-krig in Shpanye Zikhroynes fun a militsioner*.

Germany. With the defeat of French armies in the summer of 1940, Eliezer and his communists friends had new problems, namely, the German occupation of Paris and the advent of the right-wing Vichy regime.

Eliezer's continued involvement in the French underground Communist Party led to his arrest in Paris by French authorities in April 1941. He was subsequently interned in the Beaune-la-Rolande internment camp, where he became one of the inmate leaders.[10] In the second half of June 1942, as the Germans began mass deportations to Auschwitz with the help of the Vichy authorities, most of Beaune-la-Rolande's detainees were also deported. Eliezer, along with the rest of the foreign Jewish prisoners, was deported to Auschwitz-Birkenau.[11] As in other cases, the "organized" groups within the camp tried to place their own members in privileged positions in the inmate hierarchy. Gruenbaum became *Blockaelteste* (block elder) in Birkenau, earning him the epithet of *kapo*.[12]

Eliezer Gruenbaum's role in Birkenau subsequently became a matter of bitter contention. Sometimes he acted with brutality toward the inmates, but whether his deeds were born of cruelty or, as he later argued, a strategic necessity under the morally intolerable conditions of the camp, remained a matter of dispute. During the post-1942 period, as far as we can learn from the

---

10  Gruenbaum testimony, Gruenbaum file no. 15087, AAN-PPR; Gruenbaum testimony in front of Kowalski and Eisner, August 13, 1945, November 29,1945, André Ballot, Private Collection (Paris); Jerome, *Les Clandestins*, 50–52.

11  It was part of a larger deportation from the unoccupied zone of 11,000 to 13,000 foreign Jews agreed between Vichy premier Pierre Laval and Theodore Dannecker, Eichmann's representative in France.

12  André Ballot argument, November 29, 1945, André Ballot, Private Collection (Paris); Gruenbaum Diary, August 13, 1945 (located in the possession of his heirs). A portion of Gruenbaum's Diary was published in Avinoam, *Gevilei Esh*. See also Mark, *Megilat Oshvits*, 54–55; "The Truth about Gruenbaum," Charles Pepernik, Massuah Archives, Kibbutz Tel Yitzhak, no date.

documentation that we have, he was a central figure in the communist underground cell in Birkenau.[13]

In February 1944, as a part of the Nazis decision to remove Jews from *kapo* positions, Gruenbaum ended his *kapo* role at Birkenau. He was transferred to the Auschwitz III camp at Buna-Monowitz, where he stayed for a few days until he was sent to the coal-mining camp of Jawischowitz, another subcamp of Auschwitz. There, feeling the cold shoulder of the members of the underground, rumors reached Eliezer about an investigation of his actions in the camp, conducted in absentia by his communist comrades from Auschwitz-Birkenau. One of Eliezer's associates told him that the investigation evolved based on the way Eliezer functioned as a *Blockaelteste*, particularly with regard to the depth of his connections with the Nazis. Aggressive defenses were made on his behalf, all actually ex officio. He later found out that he had been exonerated.[14]

As Soviet forces approached in January 1945, Gruenbaum and his fellow inmates were part of a forced marched to Buchenwald, one of the infamous death marches. Immediately after the liberation, Gruenbaum was put on trial twice at Buchenwald by a tribunal of inmates for his role in the Auschwitz camps. The first investigation was conducted by three members of the Communist Party underground cell in Buchenwald. The charges included beating inmates for no reason, giving preferential treatment to Polish inmates while abusing Czech inmates, stealing food portions, and participating in the extortion of money from Czechs. The second investigation was conducted by a group of "reactionary" Poles, based on political and ideological differences. In both

---

13 Issac Ochshorn affidavit, documents of the legal proceeding, André Ballot, Private Collection (Paris); Gruenbaum, unpublished manuscript, chapter on Eliezer Gruenbaum, 18–19; testimonies from the hearing, Paris, 1945–1946, Ochshorn testimony, February 17, 1946, Levana Frenk private collection in Israel. Another testimony of Ochshorn can be found in the Yad Vashem Archives in Jerusalem. See also Mark, *The Scrolls of Auschwitz*.

14 Gruenbaum testimony, August 13, 1945, ANN-PPR, Gruenbaum file no. 15087; see also Victor Majzlik testimony, July 18, 1945, in the same file.

cases, Eliezer was acquitted on the ground of inconclusive evidence.[15]

Under the orders of the Polish Communist Party, he returned to postwar Paris as its representative. While he was there, a judicial inquiry by the Polish Communist Party – held at the same time in Warsaw and in Paris – found him guilty of having been a brutal *kapo* at Birkenau and a communist apostate. This time he was expelled from the party.

Subsequently, he was arrested in August 1945 in Paris and investigated by a French investigating judge (*Un juge d'instruction*) for the same charges, based on a French criminal statute concerning collaboration with the enemy. His friends and his father (by now the deputy chair of the Jewish Agency Executive in Palestine) hired a talented local advocate to ensure that investigators would hear Eliezer's side of the story. The charges – during this fourth or fifth investigation – were dismissed for insufficient evidence.[16]

An impartial eye notes significant differences between the testimonies of the communist cell members in Birkenau during the communist-led investigation and at the French state investigation.[17] Comparing part of the testimonies with Nazi registrations

---

15  Gruenbaum's testimony, August 13, 1945, Gruenbaum file no. 15087, 1–20, AAN-PPR. It is not clear from Gruenbaum's words whether two proceedings were held in Buchenwald or only one. However, we can determine from his testimony that the accusations were unfounded, and that he did not act differently from the camp custom. See also André Ballot summation, 110–134 in the file, André Ballot, Private Collection (Paris).

16  Document from Ministry of Justice, Directorate for War Crime Investigations Service, Paris, March 20, 1946, in André Ballot, Private Collection (Paris). Letter from the director to the Legal Assistant of Commissaire de Governement, 11 rue Boissy d'Anglas, Paris, reference no. 2805-ac-jm-52-334, office of Mr. Marchessaux, André Ballot, Private Collection (Paris).

17  See Daniel Finkelkraut testimony, October 1945, André Ballot, Private Collection, Paris, and compare with his testimony, file no. 15087, August 9, 1945, AAN-PPR.

from Arollsen and the Yad Vashem Archives shows even more inconsistencies in them.

Still, Eliezer Gruenbaum, now a man without a party, was soon also a man with no country. The French government ordered his expulsion as an undesirable alien. The ruling communist-dominated government of Poland, embarrassed by its association with a man increasingly stigmatized as a Nazi collaborator, refused Eliezer's request to return there. Thus Gruenbaum, who had rejected Zionism throughout his adult life, changed his name to Leon Berger and was forced to seek refuge in the only place that would accommodate him. Accompanied by his father, Eliezer arrived in Palestine on May 1, 1946, which was (ironically) International Workers' Day.[18]

In the Yishuv (the Jewish community in Palestine) Eliezer and his father made repeated attempts to explain his role at Auschwitz-Birkenau to the skeptical officials of the Jewish Agency Executive and anyone else who was ready to hear what it meant to be a *kapo* in Auschwitz-Birkenau.

Still, as a devoted communist, Eliezer sought once more to return to Poland, but in November 1947 he was again denied entry by senior Communist Party members now holding key positions within the new Polish government – so by both the Communist Party and the state. While in Jerusalem, isolated and lonely, he met Stefa (Stefania) Rosenzweig, a childhood friend and fellow survivor of the Holocaust, a widow of Jozef Rosenzweig. She was also the daughter of the renowned Shmuel Abraham Poznanski, a historian and one of the world's leading figures in the study of the Karaite sect, who has also served as the senior rabbi of Warsaw's Great Synagogue.[19]

---

18  Gruenbaum, unpublished manuscript, chapter on Eliezer Gruenbaum, 19; Frister, *Without Compromise*, 299.

19  Ben-Hanan, "A Grandson from the War"; Galia Glasner-Heled interview with Rivka Gruenbaum, Eliezer's sister-in-law, private collections in Israel held by Glasner-Heled and Eran Turbiner; Frister, *Without Compromise*, 300–301.

When the fledgling state of Israel came under attack in May 1948, Eliezer, perhaps under paternal or family pressure, volunteered to join the Haganah – the Jewish army soon known as the Israeli Defense Forces. But rumors of his role as a *kapo* in Auschwitz-Birkenau led the Haganah – in a very unusual decision in those days – to reject him. Once again, his father, now a member of the Provisional Government of Israel – intervened. Eliezer was permitted to enlist and join in the defense of Jerusalem, which was under attack by the Arab Legion of Transjordan's King Abdullah, a battalion from Egypt and local Arab-Palestinian militias. On May 22, 1948, eight days after Israel's declaration of independence, Eliezer fell in the battle on the outskirts of the city during the defense of Kibbutz Ramat Rachel.[20]

By that very evening, rumors circulated that Eliezer was not killed in action as a combat soldier, but that he was executed by his comrades in revenge for his role in Auschwitz. The source of these rumors was ultra-Orthodox extremists in Jerusalem. On learning of his death, that same evening, Stefa committed suicide.

The Gruenbaum family thereafter grappled with the rumors about Eliezer's execution and struggled to rehabilitate his reputation. Eliezer's "aftermath life," his "life" after his death in Israeli discourse, continued for decades. Eliezer Gruenbaum's public memory became a recurrent point of tension in Israeli political culture. His father, Yitzhak, expended much of his political capital to have Eliezer included in *Scrolls of Fire*, the prestigious memorial volumes devoted to the fallen heroes of the War of Independence.[21] The perceived pressure exerted by Yitzhak Gruenbaum on the volume's editors ultimately damaged his own rep-

---

20  Ben-Hanan, "A Grandson from the War"; Frister, *Without Compromise*, 302; Glasner-Heled and Bar-On, "Eliezer Gruenbaum."

21  Barnea, "King of the Jews and His Sons"; Yitzhak Gruenbaum, the former Minister of Interior (as appears on the letterhead), 8 Dizengoff Street, Tel Aviv to IDF Immortalization Department at the Ministry of Defense, August 6, 1952, courtesy of Doron Avi-Ad, IDF and Defense Establishment Archives, Tel Aviv.

utation, but Eliezer was officially recorded as an independence fighter in 1952.

Nine years later, Eliezer's memory resurfaced in entirely different context. He served as the model for the fictional character Früchtenbaum in one of the most famous early Israeli Holocaust memoirs, *Piepel* (1961, translated into English as *Atrocity*) by the author Ka-Tzetnik (Yehiel De-Nur), who himself had survived Auschwitz-Birkenau.[22] Früchtenbaum was represented as a loathsome aide of a *kapo* and as a persecutor of Orthodox Jews. Yet the name Früchtenbaum (meaning "fruit tree") is also a play on words, and a clear reference to Gruenbaum ("green tree"). In this case the fruit – the son – the secular communist *kapo* who persecuted religious Orthodox Jews in Auschwitz, came from the tree – the father – the ultra-secular Zionist and the chairman of the Rescue Committee of the Jewish Agency in Palestine, a committee which allegedly did not try to rescue Orthodox Jews. The fruit, Ka-Tzetnik suggests, did not fall far from the tree. Like father, like son.

Right-wing groups in Israel joined the chorus in attacking the son and father together. Isaac Rembah was the chief editor of *Herut*, the leading newspaper of the Zionist right. In the early 1960s, not long after Ka-Tzetnik's book appeared, Rembah published two articles. The first listed many leaders, authors, and intellectuals – Jewish and non-Jewish – who were ashamed of their adult children. The article included Theodor Herzl, Winston Churchill, Franklin D. Roosevelt, Mendele Mocher Sfarim, and others. This unfortunate phenomenon, said Rembah, was not limited to the fate of Yitzhak Gruenbaum – the dedicated and important Zionist leader. "If that were the case, I would not have

---

22 Ka-Tzetnik is the pen name of Yehiel De-Nur (1909–2001), an Orthodox Jewish writer and Holocaust survivor. De-Nur, one of few who met Eichmann at Auschwitz and survived, testified at Eichmann's trial in June 1961, fainted, and was subsequently unable to resume his testimony. Among his books: *Salamandra* (1946); *House of Dolls* (1953); *Atrocity* (1961); and *Stars of Ashes* (1966), all deal with his Auschwitz experience.

written this article at all," wrote Rembah, "and I would have not mentioned poor Gruenbaum's story."[23] However, in the next article, Rembah promised, he would tell readers why he had an "open and a bitter account" with Yitzhak Gruenbaum.

And so, he did. He urged the readers to read Ka-Tzetnik's book. "This book," he said, "is an illustration of what *really* happened during the Holocaust. In the book you will find the despicable character of Früchtenbaum." Nevertheless, Rembah wrote:

> I would not have written my article, just to remind you that there were Jews like Früchtenbaum, who was a communist, but also that [they] murdered Jews during the Holocaust. [...] I wrote this article because the father of this despicable murderer dared to exploit his political power to insert this filth into the *Scrolls of Fire* – our holy of holies, of our hero children. What to an idol in our Temple?

Moreover, he continued:

> [A]t the same time the father exploited his status to convince the corrupted Mapai [David Ben-Gurion's Labor Party] leaders to include his *kapo* son in Israel's Bravery Hall of Fame, they rejected our sons, the Lehi [Lohemai Herut Israel] and IZL [Irgun Zvai Leumi] heroes, who sacrificed their lives to resurrect our homeland, and refused to include them in this pantheon for political reasons. Our brave sons were left out – but Gruenbaum the *kapo* was included.[24]

The Polish, French, Zionist, communist, ultra-Orthodox, and other documentation reveal a wide range of Eliezer Gruenbaum's activities and different aspects of his character. They

---

23  Rembah, "When Not Fathers but Sons Eat Sour."
24  Rembah, "What of Früchtenbaum and the *Scrolls of Fire?*" Lehi and IZL forces were irregular paramilitary groups connected with the right-wing movements in the prestate Israel. Menachem Begin was the commander of IZL and Yitzhak Shamir was the commander of Lehi.

covered his youthful underground period in Poland, his jail days in Łęczyca Prison, his political activity among the communist groups in Paris, and his days in the cities and hills in Spain. Documents covering his time in the leadership of Beaune-la-Rolande, Auschwitz-Birkenau, Jawischowitz, and Buchenwald highlighted his participation in the underground resistance in the death camps, offering a rather more complex personality than his alleged ill-treatment of Orthodox Jews while serving as a *kapo*. The documentation records his sometimes courageous actions to save his communist comrades and other inmates in the camps.

It allows us, at least, to present a *Rashomon*-like account of four main narratives: a communist, an ultra-Orthodox, a Zionist (left and right wings), and a familial – and their battle among all four for hegemony. A tale that was sequestered from Leon Berger and from his family, and was transformed into a symbol, ultimately served the all four narratives, all of which had axes to grind.

*An Ultra-Orthodox Narrative*

The first was an ultra-Orthodox narrative, ensuing from the need to create a connection between the father and his son. It was an argumentative smoke screen that enabled an "easy" escape from weighty theological questions about God's presence or absence in the Holocaust. Within the ultra-Orthodox group were those who saw the Zionist state as the mother of all sins. They did not recognize the state or its army, soldiers, and commanders, but who oddly enough were alarmed by the very notion that the *"Früchte,"* the "rotten fruit," would be included in the state's secular pantheon. They and the vast majority of their sons devoted themselves almost exclusively to studying Torah. Still, they not only thought it inappropriate that Eliezer had fought for the country – which they neither wanted nor recognized – they did everything in their power to deprive him of the honor reserved for those who fell in battle in the state's defense. The cultural swings of the Gruenbaum family came full circle when a younger Eliezer Gruenbaum, Yitzhak's grandson and the son of Eliezer's brother

136

(named in memory of his uncle), came under the influence of the ultra-Orthodox and rabidly anti-Zionist rabbi and publicist Menachem Gerlik, one of Yitzhak's most implacable foes.[25] The "defection" of the scion of the Gruenbaum family to its ideological adversaries was trumpeted in the ultra-Orthodox press.

Other "sins" of the father were his role as the chair of the Jewish Agency Rescue Committee[26] during the Holocaust which allegedly did not try to help and rescue Orthodox Jews. Another "sin" was his part on shaping the "Status Quo agreement" (1947) which defined the relations between the state and religion in the forthcoming modern and secular Jewish state.

## A Zionist Narrative

The second narrative, a Zionist one, was of an embryonic, nascent society that underwent complex processes of nation and society building as well as a bloody war for independence. In order to build its hall of role models its selected from ancient Jewish history heroes like Judas Maccabeus or Bar Kokhba and from Yishuv (modern) times it embodied figures such as Joseph Trumpeldor, fighters from Hashomer, and Hannah Szenes and Enzo Sirenni; from the Warsaw Ghetto it adopted Antek [Yitzhak Zuckerman], Zivia Lubetkin, Mordechai Anielewicz, and so; it also included "Alik who came from the sea," Uri and Ayala, "the young and handsome," who had helped immigrants disembark in the dark night and "carried their people on their shoulders." A society building its foundations needed its own heroes and symbols that were utterly different from those embodied by a bald, communist Polish lawyer who had never wanted to be a part of the Zionist state, and who, on top of everything else, had been

---

25  Glasner-Heled and Bar-On, "Eliezer Gruenbaum."; Galia Glasner-Heled interview with Rivka Gruenbaum, Eliezer's sister-in-law, Glasner-Heled collection; H. Copper "Who Will Laugh Last" cited Eliezer from an interview he gave to the journalist Bezalel Kahan; Menachem Gerlik comment to Eran Turbiner, Turbiner collection.

26  Friling, *Arrows in the Dark*, chap. 3, "Lightening Rod: Establishing the Rescue Committee."

137

a controversial block commander in Birkenau, and then in death became a part of the state of Israel's pantheon by accident of his father's position.

## A Communist Narrative

The third was a communist narrative stemming from the fear within the French and Polish Communist Parties, including Polish communist exiles in Paris. They worried that the personality of Eliezer and his like would threaten their increasing political power and thus their chance of coming to power in the immediate postwar world. Eliezer's story threatened to pull them into the depths of collaborationist narratives that had thoroughly discredited the political right. This threat was of such intensity that the communist leadership in Poland and France simply erased Eliezer Gruenbaum, not only from the account of the recent past of communists in concentration camps but also from his role as a courageous resistance fighter in France and even from their shared history in the International Brigades during the Spanish Civil War. In this realm played the independent stands he took when he resisted orders from communist headquarters in Paris to flee from Beaune-la-Rolande. If we, the leaders, will escape who will lead our comrades here? Who will be punished for helping others to escape? He asked. Or when he told his comrades, at one of the evening meetings, that the Red Army was being attacked by the Nazis in Operation Barbarossa[27] and, unfortunately, had to withdraw. To withdraw? The Red Army? The Red Army never withdraws!

---

27 Operation Barbarossa, the code name for the Axis invasion of the Soviet Union, started on Sunday, June 22, 1941. It was the largest invasion force in the history of warfare and opened the Eastern Front with more forces than in any other theater of war in history. It was one of the war's largest battles and experienced the highest casualties of the Soviet and Axis forces alike. The German armies captured some 5,000,000 Soviet Red Army troops, a majority of whom never returned alive. This was the first move in the last stage of the Final Solution, Nazis mass shootings of Soviet Jews, as part of the Holocaust.

His partners in the leadership "corrected" him. A real communist would never demoralize his group with accurate historical facts...! Other comrades did not like to hear his criticism of the Molotov-Ribbentrop Pact.[28] How could this pact coexist with fighting for freedom on the Aragon front, the Ebro River or the hills of Malaga and Granada? How could Mother Russia and Father Stalin negotiate at the same time with Nazi Germany on dividing Poland between them...? Nor did they liked his clear voice about his devotion to communism, while at the same time being a Polish nationalist, who wanted to see an independent communist Poland and not Poland as a new seventeenth Soviet republic in the USSR. Others from within his circle, all enthusiastic communists, did not approve of his connections with the right-wing Armia Krayova[29] members in the underground in Auschwitz. For his part, he advocated for any kind of coalition against the real enemy: the Nazis. The result was that the only group, the only side, that could point out his brave and devoted acts, his glory, "evaporated" him, abandoned him, left him alone with the alleged stain of blood on his hands.

*A Personal and a Family Narrative*
There was also a personal and a family narrative. Despite his role as his family's black sheep, his father, others in his nuclear family, and a few relatives believed – and still believe – in his innocence. Based on their talks with him and with his parents and brothers, on his testimonies at the Polish communist quasi-judicial processes, on the French investigation and verdict, on reading a kind

---

28  The Molotov-Ribbentrop Pact, a nonaggression pact between the Soviet Union and Nazi Germany that enabled them to divide Poland between them, was signed in Moscow on August 23, 1939, by Soviet Foreign Minister Vyacheslav Molotov and German Foreign Minister Joachim von Ribbentrop.
29  The Armia Krayova (Home Army), the dominant Polish resistance movement in occupied Poland during World War II, was formed in February 1942 by absorbing and uniting most of the Polish underground forces. Its allegiance was to the Polish government-in-exile.

of a diary he left, they presented to the Israeli public the dilemmas that a person in his position faced while being a *kapos* and a member of a *Judenrat*.

They tried to force on the Israelis this narrative at a time when Israel was being torn apart by the raucous, heated public debates over the issue of accepting reparations from Germany,[30] in Knesset sessions on the "Nazis and Nazi Collaborators Punishment Law,"[31] the "Yad Vashem Law,"[32] in discussions on the shaping of Holocaust Remembrance Day and its symbolic proximity to

---

30 The Reparations Agreement between Israel and the Federal Republic of Germany was signed on September 10, 1952. According to the agreement, West Germany was to pay Israel for the costs of "resettling so great a number of uprooted and destitute Jewish refugees" after the war and to compensate individual Jews, via the Conference on Jewish Material Claims against Germany, for losses in Jewish livelihoods and property resulting from Nazi actions. Negotiations were held between Israeli Foreign Minister Moshe Sharett and his team and West German Chancellor Konrad Adenauer and his aides. The discussions with Germany just a few years after the Holocaust led to a bitter controversy in Israel, as the coalition government, headed by David Ben-Gurion, claimed that reparations were necessary to meet the basic needs of the young state in absorbing the huge wave of immigrants. Public debate was among the fiercest in Israeli history. Opposition to the agreement came from both the right (Herut and the General Zionists) and the left (Mapam) of the political spectrum; both sides argued that accepting reparation payments was the equivalent of forgiving the Nazis for their crimes. It was a dramatic challenge for Ben-Gurion and the young and vulnerable democracy of Israel.

31 Israel's Nazis and Nazi Collaborators Punishment Law was enacted on August 1, 1950. Between 1950 and 1961, this law was used to prosecute about 40 Jewish kapos. Based on the same law, on December 15, 1961, Adolf Eichmann was sentenced to death and then executed. For more, see Yablonka, "The Development of Holocaust Consciousness in Israel."

32 Yad Vashem Law was enacted on August 19, 1953, by the Knesset, Israel's parliament, close to the tenth anniversary of the Warsaw Ghetto uprising. It established the Martyrs' and Heroes' Remembrance Authority for "the commemoration in the Homeland of all those members of the Jewish people who gave their lives, or rose up and fought the Nazi enemy and its collaborators." The idea was to set "a memorial to them, and to the communities, organizations and institutions that were destroyed," for education, research and documentation, and commemoration.

"Memorial Day for the Fallen Soldiers."[33] This proximity was not accidental. It testifies to the Israeli wish to highlight what constituted important ideological links between what would eventually become the symbols of the Holocaust and the destruction of European Jewry, on the one hand, and the symbols of redemption and national rebirth, on the other.

The Holocaust as a central component in the discussions on the meaning of "valor" and resistance, on what was defined, so horribly, as "going like sheep to the slaughter," in the "*kapo*" trials of the 1950s, in research and in the public furor over the actions of the *Judenrats*, and in the creation of memorial institutes[34] and sites

---

33 "Holocaust Remembrance Day" and "Memorial Day for the Fallen Soldiers" – The "General Memorial Day for the Heroes of the War of Independence" – is commemorated every year at the 4th of Aiyar, the day preceding Independence Day. It was established upon the recommendation of the Public Council for Soldiers' Commemoration that was set up in January 1951 and won government approval that same year. The first Holocaust Remembrance Day in Israel took place on December 28, 1949, following a decision of the Chief Rabbinate of Israel that an annual memorial should take place on the 10th of Tevet, a traditional day of mourning and fasting in the Hebrew calendar. In 1951, the Knesset began deliberations to choose a date for Holocaust Remembrance Day. On April 12, 1951, after also considering as possibilities the 10th of Tevet, the 14th of Nisan, which is the day before Passover and the day on which the Warsaw Ghetto uprising (April 19, 1943) began, and September 1, the date on which World War II began, the Knesset passed a resolution establishing the 27th of Nisan in the Hebrew calendar, a week after Passover, and eight days before Israel Independence Day, as the annual "Holocaust and Ghetto Uprising Remembrance Day." For more, see Brog, "Victims and Victors"; Azaryah, "Mount Herzl."

34 Regarding memorial institutes: despite the state decision to establish Yad Vashem as a central memorial of the Holocaust and although the left wing in young Israel tried to present a unified front, its different groups and factions jockeyed over who "owned" the uprisings, who had directed the fighting, and which of the fighters had been most courageous. Mapam, HaShomer HaTza'ir, and their associated kibbutz movement, HaKibbutz HaArtzi, adopted the figure of Mordechai Anielewicz, leader of the Warsaw Ghetto's Jewish Combat Organization and a member of HaShomer HaTza'ir, who was killed during the rebellion. They established a memorial to him at Kibbutz Yad Mordechai. The rival United Kibbutz Movement and its associated political party, Ahdut HaAvodah, chose as its heroes two other lead-

that sprang up throughout the country. Whatever did not emerge from all of the above, surfaced in full force in the "Greenwald trial" – commonly known as the "Kastner trial"[35] – and Kastner's murder in Tel Aviv. The impact of the Holocaust was felt by every Israeli youngster who grew up in the country in the early years of the state, when the family listened in rapt silence to the daily radio program *Searching for Lost Relatives.*

---

ers of the same uprising, Yitzhak "Antek" Zuckerman and Zivia Lubetkin, both of whom helped found one of that movement's kibbutzim, Lohamei HaGeta'ot, the name of which means "the Ghetto Fighters." In the same way other memorials for other movements were established.

35  The Kastner trial was the libel suit that the state of Israel pursued against Malkhiel Gruenwald in 1954 for publishing a pamphlet charging Israel Kastner, the press secretary of the Ministry of Commerce and Industry, of collaboration with the Nazis. Hearings were held from January 1 to October 1954 in the District Court of Jerusalem before Judge Benjamin Halevi, who published his verdict on June 22, 1955. Rudolf Kastner (1906–1957), a key member of the Aid and Rescue Committee in Hungary, was accused of collaborating with Adolf Eichmann (1906–1962) and Kurt Becher (1909–1995), two SS officers, in the course of dealing with several versions of ransom offers (which the more famous of them had labeled as "goods/trucks for blood") and his efforts to secure safe passage from Budapest to Switzerland for 1,684 Jews in what became known as the "Kastner train." The judge ruled in Gruenwald's favor, accusing Kastner of having "sold his soul to the devil." Kastner was assassinated outside his home in Tel Aviv in March 1957. Most of the decision was overturned by the Supreme Court of Israel in January 1958 in an appeal. Shmuel Tamir, a former member of the right-wing underground during the Yishuv period, IZL (Irgun Zvai Leumi), and Gruenwald's lawyer effectively succeeded in fixing the trial in the mind of the public as the "Kastner trial" (and an indictment of the ruling labor party, Mapai), rather than the "Gruenwald trial." For more, see Weitz, "The Holocaust on Trial."

A family picture, in Jerusalem, after World War II. Standing from right, the three brothers: Yonatan, Eliezer, Binyamin – Benio. Sitting first – from left – father Yitzhak, third, mother Miriam.

There could not have been a worse time, from the point of view of the family, for "forcing" the Israelis to deal with these complex and delicate issues, than the first and second decades of the young state's existence. If the father's aim was to put his son's memory to an honorable rest, he instead seeded a storm. This was a life story which encompasses the tensions and tragedies of modern Jewish history – a Jewish community torn between communism, Bundist socialism, Zionism, and ultra-Orthodoxy – while having been deeply battered by the deliberate attempt by the Nazis to eradicate it. The story of Eliezer Gruenbaum was embroiled within these varied cultural and political contexts, the heart-wrenching debates that have rested in the Jewish community in Europe and Israel from the 1930s until this day, confronting horrible dilemmas that are still causing torment.

The four narratives show why Eliezer's story provided such fertile ground for abuse and manipulation, a symbol to be exploited by all. A tragic story of life and death that still raises so many questions: Who was Leon Berger? What motivated him? Was it a deep wish to help and contribute? Was he acting only to benefit himself, or only to aid his associates? Were his actions divided? If so, did he act mostly for himself or mostly for his associates? Was he motivated by the pursuit of power? Longing for public appreciation? Fanaticism? Communist ideology? Did he hope to emulate his father? Was he competing with his father? Was it possible even to function as a public figure in those horrible camps? – as he repeatedly asked – without qualifications? Was is possible to carry out those dreadful duties and survive without those qualities? Was it possible to embody charisma, natural-born leadership, charm, while also being pitiful and ridiculous? Could courage and cowardice reside inside a person simultaneously? Was he defeated by the horrifying pressure that existed in the camps and been its victim? Has Eliezer been able to have his voice heard? Was there any chance at all – given the way historical events and the events of his life intermingled – that his voice would ever be heard? Is there any place or time when people will be historically, psychologically, and mentally ready to hear these kinds of voices? Were his claims that he was denied his glory and was left only with blood on his hands true? Could his fate have been different – given that he did what he had done – if he had not been named Gruenbaum? Was he a Shakespearian type of hero, like Macbeth – both evil and tragic, a hero and a villain, arrogant and cruel, yet courageous? Was he like an ancient Roman figure, such as the two-faced Janus, but with four or five faces? Or was he a hero from a Greek tragedy?

So, who were you, Leon Berger?[36]

*Note*: The pictures used in this article were taken from TLV Streets – בוחר ישיא (https://www.tlvstreets.com). No information

---

36　For reviews on Friling, *A Story of a Jewish Kapo*, see A. Zvielli, "The Waste and the Redemption," *Jerusalem Post Magazine*, November 7, 2014, 41; Orit Rozin, "Black and White in the Gray Zone: Where Law Ends and the Story

about the copyright holders is provided. Every effort has been made to trace the copyright holders and obtain permission to reproduce this material. Please get in touch with any information relating to this image or the rights holder(s).

Begins," Journal of Modern Jewish Studies, published online, December 11, 2015; Mark A. Mengerink, *Holocaust Genocide Studies 30.1* (2016): 134–136; Antony Polonsky, American Historical Review 121.2 (2016): 672–673; Kenneth Waltzer, Israel Studies Review 31.1 (2016): 138–141; Allan Arkush, Jewish Review of Books (2015).

# Bibliography

## Archives

Archiwum Akt Nowych (Central Archives of Modern Records), Warsaw [AAN-PPR].

Yad Vashem Archives, Jerusalem.

## General Bibliography

Avinoam, Reuven, ed. *Gevilei Esh, vol. 1.* Tel Aviv, 1962.

Azaryah, Maoz. "Mount Herzl: The Creation of Israel's National Cemetery." *Israel Studies* 1.2 (1996): 46–74.

Barnea, Nahum. "King of the Jews and His Sons." *Koteret Rashit*, December 3, 1986, 24–31.

Bartal, Israel, and Yisrael Gutman, eds. *Kiyyum ve-Shever: Yehudei Polin le-Doroteihem* [Broken chain: Polish Jewry through the ages]. Jerusalem: Merkaz Zalman Shazar, 1997.

Ben-Hanan, Uriel. "A Grandson from the War," *Hotam* (weekly supplement of *Al Hamishmar* magazine), May 12, 1989, 4–7.

Brog, Mooli. "Victims and Victors: Holocaust and Military Commemoration in Israel Collective Memory." *Israel Studies* 8.3 (2003) 65–99.

Friling, Tuvia. *Arrows in the Dark: David Ben-Gurion, the Yishuv Leadership and Rescue Attempts during the Holocaust*, Madison: University of Wisconsin Press, 2005.

––. "Contested Memory: A Story of a *Kapo* in Auschwitz – History, Memory, Politics." In *Jewish Histories of the Holocaust: New Transnational Approaches*, edited by Norman J.W. Goda, 241–250. Oxford: Berghahn Books, 2014.

––. "Introduction." *Israel Studies* (special volume: "Israelis and the Holocaust: Scars Cry Out for Healing") 14.1 (2009): v–xvii.

––. *A Story of a Jewish Kapo in Auschwitz: History, Memory and Politics of Survival.* Waltham: Brandeis University Press, 2014.

146

—. *Who Are You, Leon Berger? A Story of a Kapo in Auschwitz: History, Memory and Politics.* Tel Aviv: Resling, 2009 (in Hebrew).

Frister, Roman. *Without Compromise.* Tel Aviv: Zmora, Bitan, 1987 (in Hebrew).

Glasner-Heled, Galia, and Dan Bar-On. "Eliezer Gruenbaum: the Structuring of a Kapo's Story within the Framework of the Collective Memory of the Holocaust." *Alpayim* 27 (2004): 111–146.

Gruenbaum, Yitzhak. *Speeches in the Polish Sejm.* Edited by Mordechai Halamish. Jerusalem, 1963 (in Hebrew).

Gruenbaum, Yonatan. Unpublished manuscript.

Guterman, Alexander. *Warsaw Jewish Community between the Two World Wars: National Autonomy Enchained by Law and Reality 1917–1939.* Tel Aviv: Tel Aviv University Press, 1997 (in Hebrew).

Jerome, Jean. *Les Clandestins (1940–1944): Souvenirs d'un temoin.* Paris: Acropole, 1986.

Mark, Bernard. *Megilat Oshvits.* Tel Aviv, 1978 (in Hebrew).

—. *The Scrolls of Auschwitz.* Tel Aviv: Am 'Oved Pub. House, 1985.

Rembah, Isaac. "What of Früchtenbaum and the *Scrolls of Fire?*" [Ma leFrüchtenbaum ve le'Gville Haesh'? – המ םיובנטכורפל ], [ ?'שאה יליווג'לו ], *Herut*, September 24, 1961.

—. "When Not Fathers but Sons Eat Sour" [Banim achlu boser – סינב רסוב ולכא], *Herut*, September 10, 1961.

Stein, Sigmund. *Der birger-krig in Shpanye Zikhroynes fun a militsioner.* Paris: A. Schipper, 1961.

Tsur, Eli. *Before Darkness Fell: HaShomer HaTzair in Poland and Galicia 1930–1940.* The Ben-Gurion Research Institute, Ben-Gurion University of the Negev: Yad Yaari, Givat Haviva, 2006 (in Hebrew).

Weitz, Yechiam. "The Holocaust on Trial: The Impact of the Kastner and Eichmann Trials on Israeli Society." *Israel Studies* 1.2 (1996): 1–26.

Yablonka, Hanna. "The Development of Holocaust Consciousness in Israel: The Nuremberg, Kapos, Kastner, and Eichmann Trials." *Israel Studies* 8.3 (2003): 1–24.

Zaagsma, Gerben. "Jewish Volunteers in the Spanish Civil War: A Case Study of the Botwin Company." MA thesis, University of London, 2001.

Zait, David. *Shomer Dreams of Utopia: HaShomer HaTzair in Poland, 1921–1931*. Beer Sheeva, 2002 (in Hebrew).

Zertal, Moshe. *Den of Youth: Chapters on HaShomer HaTzair in Warsaw 1913–1943*. Tel Aviv, 1980 (in Hebrew).

# 4. View of the World from Palas Street: The Dynamics of Cultural Memory in Saul Steinberg's Representation of Interwar Bucharest

*Mihaela Gligor*

Memories are delicate and they might influence the life of people. Memories are something we share and compare and start new relationships with. Telling stories from the past is something deeply human and all cultures have this common ground. Storytelling could be the best way to keep alive the memory of our ancestors or of places we used to love. We are what we remember.

In Greek mythology, Mnemosyne (memory) was the mother of the nine Muses,[1] and thus she had complete power over time, imagination, and all cultural activities. People were always intrigued by the power and place of memory. A transdisciplinary domain of socio-human research appeared in the twentieth century, generally known as "memory studies." It is usually related to the writings of the French sociologist Maurice Halbwachs[2] and others, who contributed to the beginning of the discipline at the same time. For Halbwachs, remembering was socioculturally framed, as the individual is a social being. During the same period, Marc Bloch used the term "collective memory,"[3] and Frederick C. Bartlett established that remembering is socially framed.[4] Later, philosophers such as Henri Bergson (Maurice Halbwachs was Bergson's student at the Lycée Henri IV in Paris), psychologists such as Sigmund Freud, or writers such as Marcel Proust initiated

---

1   The nine Muses were Calliope (epic poetry), Clio (history), Euterpe (music), Erato (lyric poetry), Melpomene (tragedy), Polyhymnia (hymns), Terpsichore (dance), Thalia (comedy), and Urania (astronomy).

2   Halbwachs, *Les Cadres sociaux de la mémoire*. See also Halbwachs, *La Topographie légendaire des Évangiles en Terre Sainte*.

3   Bloch, *Feudal Society*, vol. 1, 114.

4   Bartlett, *Remembering: A Study in Experimental and Social Psychology*.

and established the theoretical discourse of the cultural roles of memory and remembrance.

An important part in the theory of cultural memory is played by the so-called "places of memory" (*les lieux de mémoire*), a term introduced by Pierre Nora.[5] These "places" do not necessary have to be physical in the geographical sense, but cultural places of a community, representing living bonds with the past.

There are many well-known and unbelievable stories of survival.[6] There are also many unknown stories. Some people had the strength to tell their story and became examples in the history books and characters in novels or movies. Other chose to live in silence, not saying a word about what happened in concentration camps or right after that. Some people transformed in works of art what they felt. Statistics are many, but the real stories are more profound and life changing. The manner in which a community relates to the past involves different actions such as connectivity, storage, retrieval, transmission, and (re)interpretation. Sharing memories is particularly important in the process that transforms the cultural type of collective memory, where past meanings and the way they shape tradition are prominent features. When consistent memory practices focus on texts, images, and rituals they result in the establishment and consolidation of a pattern that becomes relevant for the identity of that community.

---

5   Nora, *Les Lieux de mémoire.*
6   Among them, the well-known stories of two Nobel laureates: the Romanian-born Elie Wiesel (as remembered in *Night) and* Imre Kertész (as depicted in his trilogy: *Fatelessness, Fiasco and Kaddish for an Unborn Child*). See also some recent publications, including the touching story of Eva Schloss, the posthumous stepsister of Anne Frank (her *Diary* is a remarkable account of those years, and it is translated in more than 60 languages): Schloss, *After Auschwitz.* See also" Pivnik, *Survivor;* Tuszyńska, Family History of Fear. But another recently published story impressed me very much: *The Boy Who Followed His Father into Auschwitz*, by Jeremy Dronfield. "There are many Holocaust stories, but not like this one. The tale of Gustav and Fritz Kleinmann, father and son, contains elements of all the others but is quite unlike any of them" (xiii), and this because father and son lived the inferno together and they managed to stay alive. It is a remarkable story about love and survival.

The relationship between cultural memory, remembrance, and culture itself has emerged all over Europe, and the world, as an issue of interdisciplinary research. Philosophy, religious beliefs, cultural history, psychology, literature, art, or sociology, are all involved in defining and explaining what cultural memory is and why this concept is so important for the humanities. The process of remembering needs an opportunity and it is selective. "What is remembered and what is forgotten depends upon the subjective management of identity, which in turn is steered by emotions, needs, norms, and aims."[7]

Artists also tried to offer a new and interconnected explanation of what cultural memory means. Salvador Dalí's *The Persistence of Memory*, his famous painting from 1931, is one of the most acknowledged works of Surrealism. Dalí returned to the theme of this painting with *The Disintegration of the Persistence of Memory* (1954), and also produced some sculptures, like *Persistence of Memory*, *Nobility of Time*, *Profile of Time*, and *Three Dancing Watches*.

Among the stories of Jewish people who managed to escape, just in time, from the persecutions against Jews in interwar Romania, is the story of Saul Steinberg (1914–1999), who later became one of America's favorite artists. In the following pages I will focus on Steinberg's memories of "home" and how those influenced his works. My main concern is: How did he process memories of his childhood, in his drawings, later in his life? "For most of his adult life, Saul Steinberg drew maps – maps of real or imaginary locations, maps of words and of concepts. Often the maps are of actual places refracted through the artist's mental constructs."[8] *View of the World from 9th Avenue* is the most famous one, a drawing from 1976 that served as the cover for the March 29, 1976, edition of the *New Yorker*. "Saul's most famous horizon drawing became perhaps the most widely known (and widely im-

7    Schmidt, "Memory and Remembrance," 193–194.
8    Tedeschini Lalli, "Descent from Paradise," 313.

itated) cover in the history of the magazine."[9] This is a view from Manhattan of the rest of the world, showing Manhattan as the center of the world, a subject of pride for Americans. Another work, *Autogeography*, "a bird's-eye view of a green territory dotted with the names of many locales, large and small, from every corner of the world,"[10] shows his genius. But neither Manhattan, nor the green fields were the center of the world for Saul Steinberg. Romania was. Palas Street from interwar Bucharest, to be more specific.

Saul Steinberg was born on June 15, 1914, in Râmnicu Sărat, Romania, as the son of Moritz and Rosa Steinberg. His father was a printer-bookbinder who had a small business of manufacturing boxes. Details about his family can be found in the biography written by Deirdre Bair.[11] From here we learn that:

> 1907 to 1912 were the years in which the political became personal for the Steinberg family. Shortly after the first Balkan war erupted in 1907, Saul's father, Moritz, served two terms in an artillery regiment in the Romanian Army. The first time he had to impersonate his brother Martin, who had gone to Denver, so that penalties or punishment would not be inflicted on the family still in Romania; the second was under his own name. [...]
> Saul's parents came from families of Russian origins. His grandfather, Nathan Steinberg, was a sergeant-major in the Romanian Army. [...]
> His father was born in the town of Huși in 1877. [...]
> Moritz Steinberg and Roza Iancu Itic Jacobson married in Buzău on December 6, 1911. Moritz was then working as a printer and bookbinder in Râmnicu Sărat.[12]

9    Frazier, "Saul Steinberg at One Hundred."
10   Tedeschini Lalli, "Descent from Paradise," 313.
11   Bair, *Saul Steinberg*. See the entire Chapter 2.
12   Ibidem. Details about Saul Steinberg's family can be also found in Manea, "Made in Romania," first published in the *New York Review of Books*, February 10, 2000, reprinted in Manea, *The Fifth Impossibility*, 176–186. Norman

When Saul was only a few months old, his father decided to move to Bucharest. Here the family lived in a house on Strada Palas (Palas Street), "a little street completely apart from traffic."[13] As a young boy, Saul was fascinated by the life of his neighborhood. The Bucharest of his childhood was a vibrant mixture of people, cultures, languages, and religions. The city had one of the most prosperous Jewish communities. Almost 11 percent of Bucharest's population was represented by Jews in the interwar period. Most of them were artists, craftsmen, merchants, political leaders, bankers, doctors, or architects. In Saul Steinberg's neighborhood, there were sidewalk cafes, neon lights, and streets filled with cars, but also horse-drawn carts, street peddlers, and apartment courtyards teeming with life. This environment provided him access to some ethnic influences that would affect his art and establish his interest in the unique qualities of places, people, and things.

Even if life on his street was peaceful, Saul grew up in a Romania dominated by nationalism.

> Steinberg had experienced first-hand the social and urban turmoil of the Romanian capital in the aftermath of World War I. [...] [T]he Romanian capital, as well as smaller provincial towns, frequently witnessed acts of anti-Semitism and xenophobia, which led to discrimination and violence.[14]

Saul Steinberg attended high school at the Liceul Matei Basarab, which emphasized academic subjects (Greek, Latin, philosophy, and science), as well as music and art. But Romania was already by then a deeply anti-Semitic country, something he would re-

---

Manea, a Romanian writer and author of short fiction, novels, and essays about the Holocaust, and exile, a professor and writer in residence at Bard College in United States, was Saul Steinberg's friend and they shared their feelings for Romania, even if expressed in different ways.

13  Steinberg and Buzzi, *Reflections and Shadows*, 42.
14  Mihalache, "The Priest, the King and the Street Vendor," 430–431.

member with bitterness all his life. After graduation in 1932, he spent a year at the Faculty of Philosophy and Letters at the University of Bucharest,[15] before applying to the Faculty of Architecture. The Jewish quota for admission was small, and Steinberg was denied entry.

Years later, talking to his former colleague, Eugen Campus, he explained his decision to study architecture and his failed attempt at the admission exam:

> If I had declared that I wanted to dedicate myself to art, my parents would have not supported me in school. So I declared that I wanted to study architecture. My parents agreed to this serious and prestigious profession, almost on the same level with medicine. Matchmakers started to show up at our house, offering rich partners for the future architect, even agreeing to sponsor my studies for a prolonged duration. Fortunately, I did not pass the admission examination, and so I left for Milan.[16]

The fact that Saul Steinberg was a Jew had to do with his failure to pass the entrance examination. *Numerus clausus* was not introduced until 1938, but in 1933 – the very year Steinberg's application was rejected – "special entrance examinations were introduced and Jewish candidates were deliberately failed."[17] Even the few Jewish students who managed to get admitted (4 out of 160 at the School of Medicine in 1935) were subject to physical

---

15   At the Faculty of Philosophy and Letters, Saul Steinberg was a student of Nae Ionescu, the professor of the 1927 Generation that included important names, such as Mircea Eliade, Emil Cioran, and Mihail Sebastian. It's possible that Steinberg knew and participated in some cultural events organized by the Criterion Association in the early 1930s. About Criterion, see Bejan, *Intellectuals and Fascism in Interwar Romania*, 4: "For a while they [young intellectuals of interwar Bucharest] successfully balanced their social, cultural and intellectual activities and political convictions. [...] Despite its ultimate failure, the brief success of Criterion in the mid 1930s was a unique moment in Romania's tumultuous interwar period."

16   Campus, "Afinități elective," 368–369.

17   Lavi, "Romania," 341–342.

attack by fellow students and militants and were hardly able to attend classes.

It is very important to mention that by that time (1933–1935), Romania had been infected for approximately a century by anti-Semitism and xenophobia. After the revolution in 1848, the concepts of "country," "people," and "nation" set the basis for an ideology founded on the cult of native traditions and values. The peasant, with his spiritual universe, became the prototype of the Romanian. Suspicion against foreigners, justified by external dangers, was also directed at national minorities. The regime, incapable of providing for the welfare of the country, sought a scapegoat and found one in the person of the Jew, the foreigner within, who, in the opinion of the intelligentsia and the middle class, was to blame for the poverty of the entire people. In this context, the Legion of the Archangel Michael[18] had come to save Romania and make it "proud as the Holy Sun in the sky." "Romanianism" was acknowledged as the main "doctrine," and Orthodoxy became an end in itself.

Anti-Semitism in Romanian fascist ideology was particularly violent, racist, and a uniquely mass phenomenon. Jews were considered an "inferior and degenerate race" and were often blamed for the "alteration" of Romanian culture and the socioeconomic problems of the nation.[19] In this context, many young Romanian Jews emigrated to France or Italy for their studies or to find better jobs and thus carry on their lives.

---

18  The Archangel Michael Legion was constituted on June 24, 1927, by Corneliu Zelea Codreanu, who became its leader, and four others: Ioan I. Moța, Ilie Gârneață, Corneliu Georgescu, and Radu Mironovici. The Legion was a movement of a Christian type: "[O]ur purpose was to go forward, united. Going united together, with God and the righteousness of Romania before us, any destiny given to us, defeat or death, would be a blessing, and it would bear fruit for our nation" (Codreanu, *Pentru legionari*, 296).

19  For more details on those years and the problems Jews faced, see Iancu, *Evreii din România*, and Ioanid, *The Holocaust in Romania*. See also Sebastian, *Journal*.

Denaturalization was another path to the exclusion of Jews from the local economy and society: Decree Law no. 169 for the Revision of Romanian Citizenship (adopted by the Goga government on 21 January 1938), aimed at just that by denaturalizing Jews who had become citizens "illegally" in the aftermath of World War I. As a result of this legal provision, 225,222 Jews, who had enjoyed political and civil emancipation for less than two decades, lost Romanian citizenship.[20]

This increasingly anti-Semitic climate of Romania was something Saul Steinberg would remember all his life, as Norman Manea writes, coupled with an occasional expression of nostalgia for a childhood home[21] was a vehement rejection of the society, culture, and language of the country.[22]

> Anti-Semitism was one theme he did not fail to mention, as if it were an inseparable part of his native geography. He treated it with disgust, as a hideous and incurable disease or an emanation from natural waste seeping into every pore of social life; it poisoned its victims, too.[23]

This was Steinberg's own experience: "I was a college student for a year," he would recall later, "but I hardly went to school because there was an atmosphere of brutality."[24] It is an account of human cruelty, but also a testimony to the power of hope.

---

20  Ionescu, *Jewish Resistance*, 35.
21  An interesting and well-balanced analysis of Saul Steinberg's *dor* (nostalgia) toward his Romania ("contradictory manifestations of *dor*: homesickness (*dor de acasă*) and wanderlust (*dor de ducă*)," 99) comes from Andreea Margareta Mihalache, who wrote a marvelous PhD Thesis on Steinberg: "Boredom's Metamorphosis: Robert Venturi and Saul Steinberg." See the chapter "First Interlude. Boredom and *Dor*," 92–132. *Dor* is usually considered an almost untranslatable Romanian word. It always refers to something or someone truly loved.
22  For more details, see Tedeschini Lalli, "Descent from Paradise."
23  Manea, "Made in Romania," *The Fifth Impossibility*, 180.
24  Steinberg, AJC-OHL, T1 7 (tape 1, page 7), as mentioned in Tedeschini Lalli, "Descent from Paradise," 317.

The same description appears in many memoirs about those times. Here is just another one, from a Romanian Jewish student of those times, Jacob Pesate:

> There was a native fascist party in Romania; it was the Iron Guard, and from a very small unit, it became a threat to democracy. They were going around in Nazi-style uniforms and they attacked meetings of the parties who were in power. So the Iron Guard was all over the place, in small numbers but active, aggressive and mimicking the German Nazis. The leaders were sent for training in Germany and they returned with programmes which were no different from *Mein Kampf* under Hitler.[25]

In November 1933, nineteen-year-old Saul Steinberg abandoned Bucharest, a place where Jews "were usually more cosmopolitan, lured by what we could call the mirage of modern society they actually helped build."[26] He traveled to Milan and applied to the Regio Politecnico to study architecture. In his modest luggage were "a pink, green and blue box of sugary treats, and some drawings."[27] On December 16, 1933, "he enrolled in the Regio Politecnico as an architecture student, ID number 33-34/81."[28] To supplement the limited financial support he received from his parents, Saul begun to work as a cartoonist for *Bertoldo* magazine. His first cartoon was published on October 27, 1936. He soon becomes one of the paper's most popular and recognizable artists.

One of the paper's writers, Carlo Manzoni (1909–1975), a humorist, recalls his first meeting with Steinberg in these words:

25  The declaration of Jacob Pesate in Smith, *Forgotten Voices*, 37.
26  Soare, "The memory of a hurt identity," 92–109.
27  See Buzzi, "L'Architetto Steinberg," 20.
28  According to Tedeschini Lalli, "Steinberg's student identification card is among the Saul Steinberg Papers, Yale Collection of American Literature, Beinecke Rare Book and Manuscript Library, Yale University," Mss. 1053, Box 21, Folder 2353. Tedeschini Lalli, "Descent from Paradise," 318, note 18.

[He was] a young man with a blond mustache and glasses. He has a large portfolio under one arm. He puts the portfolio on the table and pulls out a paper with a drawing of a little man, a cartoon cloud exiting from his mouth: "I would like to illustrate a short story by Mosca," says the cloud. He pulls out more drawings and Guareschi looks at them and places them aside. "OK," he says, "when Mosca arrives I will show them to him. Give me your address." The young blond man says that he's studying architecture, that he lives in the student residence, and that his name is Saul Steinberg.[29]

In the spring of 1938, Saul Steinberg left *Bertoldo* for its rival, *Settebello*, where he received a place in the editorial board. In September, the first of the Mussolini regime's racial laws were promulgated, ordering the expulsion of foreign Jews; an exception is later made for university students, who can remain until they complete their degrees. Steinberg can no longer work for *Settebello*; his last cartoon there was published on September 10. The restrictive laws against Italian Jews came fast. By June 1939, Jews in all professions were banned from working for non-Jewish clients. Of course, Steinberg, as a foreign Jew,[30] could not work at all, since foreign Jews were under an expulsion order. In March 1940, Saul Steinberg passed his exams at the Politecnico and received his diploma in architecture the following month. The diploma is made out to "Saul Steinberg [...] of the Hebrew race."[31] In the same year, Steinberg's drawings are published for the first time in US periodicals: *Harper's Bazaar* (March 15), *Life* (September 27), and *Town & Country* (October), as well as the Brazilian magazine *Sombra*.

---

29  Manzoni, *Gli anni verdi del Bertoldo*, 28.

30  "Steinberg Saul of Moritz – Romanian Jew" is the heading on Steinberg's file in the papers of the Italian police in the Italian State Archives, the Archivio Centrale dello Stato (ACS), cf. Tedeschini Lalli, "Descent from Paradise," 327, note 44.

31  Ibidem, 333–334.

In 1941, like many other Jews, Saul Steinberg had a short stay in one of the concentration camps (*campi di concentramento*) set up by Mussolini to hold illegals and undesirables.

> It was a villa [Tonelli] from which you could see the sea, but you weren't allowed to go to it. The camp was small, with perhaps fifty internees: a few Jews, White Russians, gypsies, stateless persons, refugees, being held there in a fairly makeshift and human fashion as compared with the other camps. I was lucky.[32]

On July 13, 1941, after two years of frustration and fear, endless troubles, and a very long and exhausting journey, Saul Steinberg arrived in the Dominican Republic. He was among the lucky ones: between December 1, 1940 and October 15, 1941, only 210 other foreign Jews managed to leave Italy. He remained in the Dominican Republic until May 1942, when he received his US visa. In the meantime, he started to publish drawings in the *New Yorker*; the first one was published on October 25, 1941. With the US entry into World War II, in 1942, Steinberg begins to draw antifascist political cartoons. His first such work was published in the liberal New York newspaper *PM* in January. By spring, his cartoons appeared in *Liberty* and *American Mercury*.[33]

Saul Steinberg arrived in New York on July 1, 1942. At first, he supported himself with income from drawings published in the *New Yorker* and other magazines, such as *Fortune*, *Mademoiselle*, or *House Beautiful*. Very soon, he began to work for the Office of War Information, and in February 1943 he received both US citizenship and a commission in the Naval Reserve. Assigned to the intelligence services, he was sent to China, India, Algeria, and finally, in mid-1944, to Italy, having literally gone around the world from east to west in less than three years.[34]

---

32 Steinberg and Buzzi, *Reflections and Shadows*, 35.
33 For more details about his life, see Schwartz, "Chronology."
34 Idem. See also Tedeschini Lalli, "Descent from Paradise," 354.

On February 7, 1943, Saul Steinberg met fellow Romanian émigré artist Hedda Sterne,[35] who became a well-known artist in her own right. They got married in October 11, 1944. In September 1944, before going back to the OSS office in Washington, Steinberg made a short trip to Bucharest to visit his family (September 18–25); the last time he visited Romania. After settling in New York City he never returned to his homeland because there are places

> that don't belong to geography but to time. And the memory of these places of sadness, of suffering, but above all of great emotions, is spoiled by seeing them again. It's better to leave certain things in peace, just the way they are in memory: with the passage of time they become the mythology of our lives.[36]

But still, "his child self never left him, nor did his love of Elsewhere."[37] Strada Palas, the street of his childhood, remained the center of his youthful memories. He used to think very often about Bucharest, the city of his youth, and when friends announced him about their intention to visit the city, he asked for pictures of his old neighborhood or maps of Bucharest. The pictures he received from them showed him that nothing has changed on the street of his childhood, "except for some trees, which have grown taller, and a wall that's now covered with ivy. I was horrified to see an automobile in the courtyard of my house."[38] He was deeply

---

35  Hedda Sterne (Hedwig Lindenberg), artist, born August 4, 1910; died April 8, 2011. Although they separated in 1960, they remained close friends until his death in 1999. Hedda Sterne was a prolific artist whose long career intersected with some of the most important movements and figures in twentieth-century art (Hedda Sterne Foundation, "About the Artist").

36  Steinberg and Buzzi, *Reflections and Shadows*, 41.

37  Frazier, "Saul Steinberg at One Hundred."

38  Steinberg and Buzzi, *Reflections and Shadows*, 42. Steinberg knew, from his parents, that life was really hard in Romania, especially in Bucharest, during the war and immediately after. There are many important studies about those years, among them Jean Ancel, *The History of the Holocaust in Romania* (2011); Dennis Deletant, *Hitler's Forgotten Ally: Ion Antonescu and*

touched by the memory of that place. He felt joy and sorrow, in the same time, and wanted to receive a confirmation of his feelings. "To cure myself of this illness I sent two other friends to take pictures. One of them took the same pictures, but in winter with snow, which was more beautiful because the changes were less obvious."[39]

Strada Palas, as Saul Steinberg knew it, does not exist anymore. Almost the whole neighborhood was destroyed when the new Bucharest, as seen by communists, started to take shape in the 1980s. Several pictures and drawings of Palas Street survived, and they are "places of memory" that speak for themselves.[40] In this respect, "Steinberg's drawing is a critical tool revealing the city as a festival of the everyday that celebrates fragments of a personal reality, while also speaking about larger truths."[41] Writing about an exhibition dedicated to Saul Steinberg, which opened at PaceWildenstein Gallery on East 57th Street in October 1999, Marta Petreu explains his works and especially his maps: "colorful and with explanations, locking the whole globe in the rectangle of a frame and the whole biography of a person – of Steinberg's himself. [...] In Bucharest, you walk with Steinberg on Palas Street."[42]

Steinberg was present under disguise in most of his works. His country of origin was also present. "*Dor* transforms reality into an imagined reality. Animated by *dor*, Steinberg returned to his childhood homeland over and over again."[43]

---

*His Regime 1940–1944* (2006); Rebecca Haynes, *Romanian Policy towards Germany: 1936–1940* (2000).

39 Ibidem, 43.
40 A short description of the street and the area, along with some photos, can be found in Graur, "Palas."
41 Mihalache, "The Priest, the King and the Street Vendor," 434.
42 Petreu, *O zi din viața mea fără durere*, 231–233.
43 Mihalache, "Boredom's Metamorphosis," 98.

As his friends recall, most of the times,

> Saul Steinberg remembered Romania as a place of peasants in folkloric dress, mustachioed cavalry officers in parade outfits, children in school uniforms with their official numbers on their sleeves, for ease of identification and denunciation, a place where a Dadaist alloy was created out of frustration, hedonism, and grief.[44]

Steinberg first drew *Strada Palas* in 1942. It was a watercolor of the interior of his home, and it described the ten-year-old Saul in the process of observing a domestic scene.

> The artist's family is seen breakfasting at home on Strada Palas in Bucharest. Saul, ready for school in a uniform with an arm patch, [...] assumes an outsider's role. As a draftsman, too, he takes a disengaged perspective, evoking the dynamics of the household only in subtle details.[45]

It was probably drawn in the Dominican Republic,[46] while Saul Steinberg was waiting for his immigration to the United States and was deeply concerned about his family, which remained in Bucharest. This drawing appeared in the first exhibition to show Steinberg's work, held at the Wakefield Gallery, New York, in April 1943, while Saul was awaiting assignment overseas with the navy. It was the only time when this drawing was exhibited.

---

44  Manea, "Made in Romania," *The Fifth Impossibility*, 185–186.
45  Smith, *Saul Steinberg: Illuminations*, 86.
46  See Schwartz, "Chronology."

Saul Steinberg, *Strada Palas*, 1942. Ink, pencil, and watercolor on paper, 37.8 x 55.2 cm. Morgan Library & Museum, New York; Gift of The Saul Steinberg Foundation.

But there is another *Strada Palas*, from 1966, showing a parade in the 1920s Bucharest.

> In the 1966 *Strada Palas*, with its imaginary and historic characters striding together, along with apparently randomly collected architectural objects, fact and fiction are interwoven to produce a drawing that is simultaneously a mnemonic device attempting to stabilize the fluidity of memories and an eyewitness of specific historic and urban realities.[47]

In 1966, when he drew this, Saul Steinberg was 52 years old and living in the heart of New York City for more than 20 years. This *Strada Palas* is a wonderful and detailed description of a royal

---

47   Mihalache, "The Priest, the King and the Street Vendor," 427.

parade. "Parades are a recurrent motif in Steinberg's art."[48] In this case, King Ferdinand I of Romania, from the House of Hohenzollern-Sigmaringen, who ruled between 1914 and 1927, and his wife, Queen Marie, wearing crowns, jewelry, and luxurious outfits, are described in the middle of the drawing. In the second plan is Saul Steinberg's neighborhood, with simple courtyards, filled with flowers, animals, and churches.

> Starting with an Eastern Orthodox priest and ending with a Muslim street vendor, this unlikely procession speaks about the city and its inhabitants, about the ordinary and the extraordinary, the time of the everyday and the time of the festival. Royals become commoners and commoners become royals. With ruthless irony, Steinberg cuts a cross-section through the Romanian society between the two world wars.[49]

*Strada Palas* (1966) is extremely important in Saul Steinberg's intellectual legacy because it brings together myths, royalties, and the daily life of the city of Bucharest during the time of his childhood.

> While the accuracy of his memories has not faded with the passing of years and the various renditions of Palas Street are surprisingly consistent across time, each iteration brings new details that nuance the whole by offering clues for understanding larger modes of inhabitation, as well as individual and collective practices. These different drawings build upon each other and articulate a reality that is both historically documented, and imagined, highly personal, and belonging to a community.[50]

Fabulous Bucharest, transfigured by nostalgia – an image altered by the distance in time and space from the places of the interwar

---

48  Ibidem, 430.
49  Ibidem, 431.
50  Mihalache, "Boredom's Metamorphosis," 109.

Saul Steinberg, *Strada Palas*, 1966. Graphite, pen, colored inks, watercolor, gouache, colored chalks and gold enamel on paper, 58.4 x 73.7 cm; Israel Museum, Jerusalem.
Gift of the artist, through the America-Israel Cultural Foundation.
© 2020 The Saul Steinberg Foundation/Artists Rights Society (ARS), New York.

Bucharest geography – thus becomes the center of Steinberg's attention. Memories of his past often occurred in Saul Steinberg's thoughts.

> "The land of Dada," as he called Romania, reappeared more and more often in recent years, not only as "the dark land" or "the land of exile," but also as the land of his childhood, that "miraculous time" beyond recall even for a childlike artist fascinated by the magic of its set pieces and clowning.[51]

---

51  Manea, "Made in Romania," *The Fifth Impossibility*, 181.

*Strada Palas* (1966) represented Steinberg's last return to his own *illud tempus*.[52] The vivid memory of the place where he grew up and all its myths and meanings offered him a journey to the fundamental moment of beginning, and also the chance to recover something from that miraculous time of original happiness. *Strada Palas* (1966) is among Steinberg's masterpieces and offers a wonderful view of the world. His world.

> Steinberg, known to a large popular audience for his work at the *New Yorker* (he contributed 89 covers and more than 1200 inside drawings), spent a lifetime thinking with his pen, absorbing the stylistic developments of 20th-century art, and creating a spare, nervous idiom in which he could underscore the odd habits and quirks of the world we process visually.[53]

Influenced by Dada movement, Surrealism, Cubism, pop culture, and the meaningless and wonderful world around him, Saul Steinberg's varied output reflects the curiosity, humor, and open attitude of an artist trying to make sense of the chaotic postwar years.

"I don't quite belong to the art, cartoon or magazine world, so the art world doesn't quite know where to place me,"[54] he used to say. Yet, he changed the art world. Far away from Palas Street, Saul Steinberg carried all his life the place of his youth: "[I]n his last years, more and more frequent incursions into Romanian confirmed his fascination with the language and the aura of his early life."[55] The shy boy from Palas Street transformed into the cosmopolitan intellectual who found inspiration from a wide variety of sources, such as architecture, maps, children's art, callig-

---

52  "*Illud tempus*" is the Latin for "that time," a term used by Romanian-born historian of religions Mircea Eliade (1907–1986), in his book *The Sacred and the Profane* (1959), to describe the time when the world was born.

53  Kennicott, "Think You Don't Understand Art?"

54  Vanden Heuvel, "Straight from the Hand and Mouth of Steinberg," 66.

55  Manea, "Made in Romania," *The Fifth Impossibility*, 182.

raphy, postcards, rubber stamps, and underground comics, and transformed all these into masterpieces. A Romanian by birth, restless by inclination, Saul Steinberg became a recognized artist around the world. His view of the world from Palas Street became *View of the World from 9th Avenue*, a correspondence between two sacred geographies that were synonymous with his life. Saul Steinberg lived a fabulous existence, and his legacy is more than impressive.

# Bibliography

Ancel, Jean. *The History of the Holocaust in Romania*. Lincoln: Nebraska University Press, 2011.

Bair, Deirdre. *Saul Steinberg: A Biography*. Knopf Doubleday, 2012.

Bejan, Cristina A. *Intellectuals and Fascism in Interwar Romania: The Criterion Association*. Palgrave Macmillan, 2019.

Bartlett, Frederick C. *Remembering: A Study in Experimental and Social Psychology*. Cambridge: Cambridge University Press, 1932.

Bloch, Marc. *Feudal Society*, 2 vols. Chicago: University of Chicago Press, 1961.

Buzzi, Aldo. "L'Architetto Steinberg." *Domus*, October 20, 1946.

Campus, Iosef Eugen. "Afinități elective (Convorbire cu Saul Steinberg)" [Elective affinities (Conversations with Saul Steinberg)]. In *Deschizând noi orizonturi: Însemnări critice, Israel, 1960–2001* [Opening new horizons: Critical notes, Israel, 1960–2001], 2 vols., vol. 2, 368–369. Bucharest: Libra Publishing House, 2002.

Codreanu, C.Z. *Pentru legionari* [For legionnaires]. Sibiu: "Totul pentru țară," 1936.

Deletant, Dennis. *Hitler's Forgotten Ally: Ion Antonescu and His Regime 1940–1944*. Houndmills: Palgrave Macmillan, 2006.

Dronfield, Jeremy. *The Boy Who Followed His Father into Auschwitz*. London: Penguin/Michael Joseph, 2019.

Frazier, Ian. "Saul Steinberg at One Hundred." *New Yorker*, October 8, 2014. https://www.newyorker.com/culture/cultural-comment/remembering-saul-steinberg, accessed April 20, 2020.

Graur, G. "Palas – o stradă de la limita imposibilului" [Palas – A street on the edge of the impossible], *Bucureștii Vechi și Noi* [Old and new Bucharest], November 9, 2010. http://www.bucurestiivechisinoi.ro/2010/11/palas-%E2%80%93-o-strada-de-la-limita-imposibilului/, accessed April 19, 2020

Halbwachs, Maurice. *La Topographie légendaire des Évangiles en Terre Sainte: Étude de mémoire collective*. Paris: Presses Universitaires de France, 1941.

——. *Les Cadres sociaux de la mémoire.* Paris: Félix Alcan, 1925.

Haynes, Rebecca. *Romanian Policy towards Germany, 1936–1940.* London: Macmillan, 2000.

Hedda Sterne Foundation. "About the Artist," n.d. https://heddasternefoundation.org/about-the-artist, accessed April 15, 2020.

Iancu, Carol. *Evreii din România. De la emancipare la marginalizare: 1919–1938* [The Jews of Romania: From emancipation to marginalization, 1919–1938]. Bucharest: Hasefer, 2000.

Ioanid, Radu. *The Holocaust in Romania: The Destruction of Jews and Gypsies under the Antonescu Regime, 1940–1944.* Chicago: Ivan R. Dee, 1999.

Ionescu, Ștefan Cristian. *Jewish Resistance to "Romanianization," 1940–44.* London: Palgrave Macmillan, 2015.

Kennicott, Philip. "Think You Don't Understand Art? This Is the One Book You'll Need." *Washington Post*, December 14, 2018. https://www.washingtonpost.com/entertainment/museums/think-you-dont-understand-art-this-is-the-one-book-youll-need/2018/12/14/42650392-f80d-11e8-8c9a-860ce2a8148f_story.html, accessed April 2, 2020.

Lavi, Theodor. "Romania." In *Encyclopaedia Judaica*, ed. Michael Berenbaum and Fred Skolnik, 2nd ed., vol. 15, 341–342. Detroit: Macmillan Reference, 2007.

Manea, Norman. "Made in Romania." In Norman Manea, *The Fifth Impossibility: Essays on Exile and Language*, 176–186. New Haven: Yale University Press, 2012.

Manzoni, Carlo. *Gli anni verdi del Bertoldo.* Milan: Rizzoli, 1964.

Mihalache, Andreea. "The Priest, the King and the Street Vendor: Urban Allegories in Saul Steinberg's Strada Palas (1966)." *Architecture and Culture* 6.3 (2018): 423–436.

Mihalache, Andreea Margareta. 'Boredom's Metamorphosis: Robert Venturi and Saul Steinberg.' PhD thesis, Virginia Tech, 2018. https://vtechworks.lib.vt.edu/handle/10919/96190, accessed April 20, 2020.

Nora, Pierre. *Les Lieux de mémoire.* Paris: Gallimard (Bibliothèque illustrée des histoires), 3 tomes: t. 1 *La République* (1 vol., 1984), t. 2 *La Nation* (3 vol., 1986), t. 3 *Les France* (3 vol., 1992).

169

Norman, Will. *Transatlantic Aliens : Modernism, Exile, and Culture in Midcentury America*. Baltimore: Johns Hopkins University Press, 2016.

Petreu, Marta. *O zi din viața mea fără durere* [A day in my life without pain]. Iași: Polirom, 2012.

Pivnik, Sam. *Survivor: Auschwitz, the Death March and My Fight for Freedom*. London: Hodder & Stoughton, 2019.

Schloss, Eva. *After Auschwitz*. London: Hodder & Stoughton, 2019.

Schmidt, Siegfried J. "Memory and Remembrance: A Constructivist Approach." In *Cultural Memory Studies: An International and Interdisciplinary Handbook*, edited by Astrid Erll and Ansgar Nünning, 193–194. Berlin: Walter de Gruyter, 2008.

Schwartz, Sheila. "Chronology." The Saul Steinberg Foundation.

https://saulsteinbergfoundation.org/chronology/1914-yr/, accessed April 24, 2020.

Sebastian, Mihail. *Journal: 1935–1944*. Chicago: Ivan R. Dee, 2000.

Smith, Lyn. *Forgotten Voices of the Holocaust*. With a foreword by Laurence Rees. London: Ebury Press, 2006.

Smith, Joel. *Saul Steinberg*: *Illuminations*. New Haven: Yale University Press, 2006.

Smith, Lyn. *Forgotten Voices of the Holocaust*. With a foreword by Laurence Rees. London: Ebury Press, 2006.

Soare, Oana. "The Memory of a Hurt Identity: Bucharest's Jewish Sub-culture between Fiction and Non-fiction." In *Identities in-between in East-Central Europe*, edited by Jan Fellerer, Robert Pyrah, and Marius Turda, 92–109. Routledge, 2019.

Steinberg, Saul, and Buzzi, Aldo. *Reflections and Shadows*. Trans. John Shepley. New York: Random House, 2002.

Tedeschini Lalli, Mario. "Descent from Paradise: Saul Steinberg's Italian Years (1933–1941)." *Quest. Issues in Contemporary Jewish History. Journal of Fondazione CDEC* 2 (October 2011): 312–384. https://www.quest-cdecjournal.it/descent-from-paradise-saul-steinbergs-italian-years-1933-1941/, accessed April 15, 2020.

Tuszyńska, Agata. *Family History of Fear: A Memoir.* New York: Anchor Books, 2017.

Vanden Heuvel, Jean. "Straight from the Hand and Mouth of Steinberg." *Life*, December 10, 1965.

Wiesel, Elie. *Night. New York: Bantam Books, 1982.*

## 5. Traces of Survival in a World of Terror: Kathy Kacer's *Shanghai Escape*

*Arleen Ionescu*

This chapter will deal with memory and trauma studies, focusing on Kathy Kacer's *Shanghai Escape*, in an attempt to show the validity of such accounts on historical events that are usually discarded by historians and considered "fiction." I will show that nothing in the book can be considered part of the fictional realm and look for the traces of the protagonist's memories of the Shanghai Ghetto during World War II. The chapter is divided in two major parts: the first section presents the historical account of what happened in Shanghai from 1933 to the end of World War II; the second part focuses on the analysis of the book, through Sigmund Freud's concept of *Nachträglichkeit* and several other psychoanalytic theories which I relate to memory studies.

*Shanghai Ghetto: A Safe Heaven for Jewish Refugees during World War II*
Before and during World War II, when more than six million European Jews perished in concentration and death camps, the only country that saved a significant number of Jewish people fleeing from Hitler's hell in Europe was China. More precisely, Shanghai "did not enforce requirements for travel or immigration documents, because of the so-called 'International Settlement' that was established by the British and French colonial powers."[1] Shanghai offered "a safe haven for Jews at the most horrific moment in human history," as Jackie Eldan, the current Consul General of Israel in Shanghai, has declared.[22]

---

1   Li, "Synthesis and Transtextuality," 140.
2   Jackie Eldan, quoted in Wang, *Shanghai Jewish Cultural Map*, 7.

German, Austrian, Russian, Polish, and Lithuanian Jews landed in this city in several stages after 1933.3[3] The approximate number of the refugees is slightly different from one historian to another and even from one work written by a historian to another. According to Weijia Li, the approximate figure was between 17,000 and 20,000.4[4] According to Pan Guang's *The Jews in China*, between 20,000 and 25,000 Jewish people were rescued, which represents more than Canada, Australia, New Zealand, South Africa, and India saved altogether.5[5] The same historian estimates the number of the saved Jews to 30,000 in *Eternal Memories*.[6]

Adolf Hitler ascended to power as chancellor in January 1933. After the Enabling Act of 1933 passed by the Reichstag transformed the Weimar Republic into the Third Reich that was to be led by the National Socialists, the persecution of the Jewish

---

3    Although the chapter does not deal with the period before 1933, mention should be made that the first Sephardi or Baghdadi Jewish families came to Shanghai by 1862 "on the heels of the British" (see Eber, "Introduction," 6). After the turn of the century, Russian Jews fled from Russia to Harbin and then to Shanghai or directly from Vladivostok to Shanghai after the anti-Semitic pogroms of the tsarist regime, counterrevolutionary armies, and the Bolsheviks' attacks. See Wang, *Shanghai Jewish Cultural Map*, 21. According to Eber, "[t]he earliest Russian Jewish arrivals probably date from the Russo-Japanese War (1904–1905), after which Jewish conscripts who had been in the Russian army decided to remain in China. But the largest number of Russian Jews, along with some Polish Jews, arrived only after the Russian October Revolution of 1917. By the 1930s, between 6,000 and 7,000 Russian Jews were in Shanghai. Together with the Baghdadis, there were around 8,000 Jews among approximately 50,000 foreigners." While the Baghdadi families were generally affluent, the Russian-speaking Ashkenazi Jews who had fled from the civil war and revolution were less rich and "drifted south from Harbin in Heilongjiang province" (Eber, "Introduction," 7).
4    See Li, "Synthesis and Transtextuality," 140.
5    See Pan, *The Jews in China*, 113.
6    Pan, *Eternal Memories*, 3.

people started. The anti-Semitic Nuremberg Laws were passed in 1935; pogroms and the infamous Kristallnacht followed in 1938.

The following historical account is mainly based on Wang Jian's *Shanghai Jewish Cultural Map*, which offers a chronology of the waves of refugees who arrived in Shanghai from 1933 to 1945. The first German Jews (initially around twelve Jewish families comprising over one hundred people who soon increased to around 1,000 – 1,500 people) arrived in Shanghai from 1933 to the summer of 1937.[7] The efforts to welcome the "stateless Jews" continued even after the Sino-Japanese War spread to Shanghai, an event with a disastrous impact on the life of the city dwellers. The takeover of Chinese areas by the Japanese authorities and the installation of puppet governments created a vast homeless refugee population and the foreign settlements (named *gudao*) became increasingly isolated. From mid-1939 onward inflation began to soar and impacted on the lower classes, especially the poverty-stricken Chinese refugees who had crowded into Shanghai to escape from the war.[8]

However, while the Jewish community was facing such a crisis in Shanghai, Jewish people in Europe were striving to live. In 1938, Austria, which was, at that time, the home of the third-largest Jewish community in Europe, became part of Nazi Germany (through the Anschluss). The Jewish people were to be deported to Dachau and Buchenwald, so their only hope was to emigrate immediately to Shanghai, in which case they could be released.[9] News spread fast about the Chinese consul, Dr. Ho Feng Shan, and his generosity in offering them lifesaving visas. Dr. Ho (who became a "Chinese Schindler")[10] continued to offer these visas in spite of the Nazi occupiers' irritation. (They "later disposed the

---

7    See Wang, *Shanghai Jewish Cultural Map*, 22.
8    Eber, "Introduction," 9.
9    Pu and Huang, *Jewish Refugees in Shanghai*, 12.
10   Ibidem, 13. Pu and Huang compare Dr. Ho, who saved more than 4,000 Jews, to the American industrialist Oskar Schindler, who saved about 1,200 Jews and who is better known, since he became the protagonist of Steven Spielberg's film *Schindler's List*.

house of the Chinese consulate on the allegation that the house was a Jewish property"[11]). The second wave (between 21,000 and 22,000 Jewish refugees) was thus made up mainly of Austrian Jews who came mostly via Italy on ships from August 1937 to August 1939. They either remained in Shanghai or continued on to Palestine and the Philippines. The most influential Chinese newspaper, *Shun Pao*, started to make lists of the ships that arrived from Germany, Austria and Italy. They called the ships "Noah's Arks," "bearing the hope of all Jews."[12] In the long run, Dr. Ho was transferred away from Vienna by China's Ambassador Chen Jie because it was considered that he was "selling" visas, even though the latter knew very well that it was not true, but was trying not to damage the relationship between China and Germany.[13]

From August 1939 to June 1940 more Jewish families arrived in Shanghai. In August 1939 the Shanghai Municipal Council, the Conseil Municipal of the French Concession, and the Japanese leaders in Shanghai asked the Jewish refugees who had the letter "J" on their passport to apply for a permit, paying a deposit of $400 ($100 for children under thirteen). Exempted from this fee were the Jews who either had close relatives or a job in Shanghai or those who were going to marry a Shanghai resident.[14] According to Wang's account, during this period the new refugees were between 2,000 and 3,000. Around a hundred were German Jews who came to Shanghai from Hong Kong and Singapore, at that time both under British rule, after the expulsion of all German immigrants by Britain.[15]

The fourth stage, from June 1940 to June 1941, after Germany invaded the Soviet Union and Italy declared war on France and Britain, some 2,000 Jewish refugees from Poland and Lithuania

---

11  Pu and Huang, *Jewish Refugees in Shanghai*, 14.
12  Ibidem, 180.
13  Ibidem, 14.
14  Wang, *Shanghai Jewish Cultural Map*, 23.
15  Ibidem, 24.

arrived in Shanghai through Siberia to northeast China, Korea or Japan. According to Olga Barbasiewicz and Barbara Dzien-Abraham, who studied the Polish-language newspaper *Echo Szanghajskie* (Shanghai echo) and its supplement *Wiadomości* (Tidings), published in East Asia, "[s]tatistics provided by the Polish diplomatic mission identified 60 full families with both father and mother and one father with a child."[16]

In the fifth stage, from June to December 1941, around 2,000 Jewish refugees (from which 400 teachers and students from Mir Yeshiva) managed to enter Shanghai, yet after the Pacific War outbreak, "Shanghai's connection with the outside world by sea routes was cut off."[17]

Moving to Shanghai, the majority of Jewish people lived into the impoverished Hongkew (called Hongkou after 1947) District, an area people with a lower budget could afford, which was located "in the crossing zone between the Shanghai International Settlement and the Chinese Community."[18] The majority could not afford to rent houses to live by themselves but stayed in "temporarily rented or erected refugee camps with thirty to fifty people jammed in one room," or even one hundred to two hundred people in one room.[19] With the help of the Baghdadis and the American Jewish Joint Distribution Committee, they eventually managed to establish schools, set up newspapers, and even have a cultural and social life.

In July 1942 Colonel Josef Alfred Meisinger, Chief Representative of the Gestapo in Japan, known as "the Butcher of Warsaw," proposed to the Japanese authorities the "Final Solution" in Shanghai, yet, in spite of the pressures of their Nazi allies, the Japanese did not implement it. The reasons were not necessarily humanitarian but rather pragmatic. As historian Irene Eber explains in the film *Shanghai Ghetto*, the Japanese did not wish to

---

16  Barbasiewicz and Dzien-Abraham, "Remembering the Origins," 118.
17  Wang, *Shanghai Jewish Cultural Map*, 26.
18  Ibidem, 33.
19  Idem.

antagonise American Jews; in addition, the Japanese acted upon the stereotype that the "Jews are rich," "the Jews have power," "the Jews control governments."[20] According to David Kranzler, "the Japanese were very careful about being prejudiced against the Jews because they had complained about German prejudice against Asians themselves."[21] On February 18, 1943, the Japanese authorities issued a law with a view to setting up a restricted sector for stateless refugees in Hongkew, forcing them to move inside the ghetto within three months.[22] At the same time, the Jewish businessmen of British nationality, who had helped the refugees before, had become "alien enemies" and were persecuted and incarcerated in internment and concentration camps.[23] Many Chinese people who used to live in Hongkew vacated their own houses for the refugees. Chinese hospitals accepted and saved Jewish people's lives before the hospital for Jewish refugees was built.[24]

Even if the fortune of the Jewish refugees in Shanghai changed again after the attack on Pearl Harbor, when communication with the American agencies was banned, the Chinese protected their guests and never manifested "any anti-Semitic hostility" toward the ethnic Jewish people.[25] In July 1945, the Shanghai Ghetto was bombarded by the Americans and there were both Jewish and Chinese casualties. The Jewish community and the Chinese people from Hongkew went through the atrocities of the war together, "one of the positive aspects of this calamity."[26]

The Jewish community from Shanghai started to leave the city after the end of the war and the outbreak of the Chinese Civil War. As disclosed by Israel Epstein,

---

20  Eber, in Janklowicz-Mann et al., *Shanghai Ghetto*, 41:30–41:53.
21  Kranzler, in Janklowicz-Mann et al., *Shanghai Ghetto*, 42:00–42:26.
22  Pu and Huang, *Jewish Refugees in Shanghai*, 64.
23  Wang, *Shanghai Jewish Cultural Map*, 47.
24  Ibidem, 27.
25  Pu and Huang, *Jewish Refugees in Shanghai*, 258. The words belong to the mother of Ron Klinger, a boy who was born in the Shanghai Ghetto in 1941.
26  Krasno, *Once upon a Time in Shanghai*, 190.

[n]one of the European Jewish communities that arose in China in the past century were permanent. Most of those who came as refugees were, in their own eyes, transients "sitting on their suitcases" as a saying among them went, although some stayed for one or two generations.[27]

Some reunited with the survivors of the concentration camps from Europe and left for the United States, Canada, Australia, Israel, South Africa, and some Latin American countries.[28]

### Traces in Kathy Kacer's Shanghai Escape

Apart from the historical works displaying historical data, a large number of photos and a few documents from those times,[29] some of which represented the primary material of the previous section, one can add many memoirs and narratives that reveal how refugees related to the new and strange places of their arrival after having left the familiar places where they were no longer desirable: Anna Lincoln's *Escape to China (1939–1948)* (1982); Rena Krasno's *Strangers Always: A Jewish Family in Wartime Shanghai* (1992) and *Once upon a Time in Shanghai: A Jewish Woman's Journey through the 20th Century China* (2008); James R. Ross's *Escape to Shanghai: A Jewish Community in China* (1992); Ernest G. Heppner's *Shanghai Refuge: A Memoir of the World War II Jewish Ghetto* (1993); Betty Grebenschikoff's *Once My Name Was Sara: A Memoir* (1993); Claude Cornwall's *Letter from Vienna: A Daughter Uncovers Her Family's Jewish Past* (1995); W. Michael Blumenthal's *The Invisible Wall: German and Jews: A Personal Exploration* (1998); Ursula Bacon's *Shanghai Diary: A Young*

---

27 Epstein, "Preface."
28 See Wang, *Shanghai Jewish Cultural Map*, 46.
29 To these other titles can be added Kranzler, *Japanese, Nazis and Jews;* Mary Swartz and Marvin Tokayer, The Fugu Plan: *The Untold Story of Japanese and the Jews During World War II* (1978); Evelyn Pike Rubin, *Ghetto Shanghai* (1993); Yanhua Zhang and Wang Jian, *Preserving the Shanghai Ghetto: Memories of Jewish Refugees in 1940's China* (2016); Karen Shopsowitz's film *A Place to Save Your Life: The Shanghai Jews* (1994).

*Girl's Journey from Hitler's Hate to War-Torn China* (2004); Angel Wagenstein's *Farewell Shanghai* (2007); Steve Hochstadt's *Exodus to Shanghai: Stories of Escape from the Third Reich* (2012); Kathy Kacer's *Shanghai Escape* (2013) and even novels: Marion Cuba's *Shanghai Legacy* (2005); La Bei's *The Cursed Piano* (2007); Wu Lin's graphic novel *A Jewish Girl in Shanghai* (2012); Yu Qiang's *Love in Shanghai Noah's Ark* (2018). From these narratives, this chapter will focus on Kathy Kacer's *Shanghai Escape*, a book that confirms the historical account presented above, and at the same time completing it with details about the life of a Jewish family that arrived to Shanghai as part of what Wang called "the second wave" of refugees. Although the book deals with multifarious mechanisms of remembering, it cannot be strictly called a memoir, since by definition a memoir describes the experiences that the author has gone through. However, it has more historical than fictional value and cannot be discredited by historians, since, although it is not written by the Jewish girl who is a survivor of the Shanghai Ghetto and the protagonist of the book, it presents only real events as they really happened in those troubled years. Nothing is fictionalized in the sense of embellishing, ornamenting, or changing true events. This account is entrusted to another author who is a witness and who narrates the story in the third person, yet adopting the perspective of the little heroine, Lily Toufar. Lily arrived in Shanghai from Vienna and, "like thousands of other Jewish refugees, endured the difficult living conditions, dirt, disease, and death, always hopeful that the war would end and her family would still be alive."[30]

The position of the author of the book is thus what Thomas Trezise called "witnessing witnessing" (the acknowledgements in *Shanghai Escape* mentions that Lily Toufar Lash has endured the author's "endless questions and opening up" her "memory vault"[31]) as a receiver of survivor testimony yet coming not from the Holocaust but from the land of hope. Some of Lily's experi-

---

30  Kacer, *Shanghai Escape*, 3.
31  Ibidem, 243.

ences are still part of an unspeakable history whose transmission demands various forms of traumatic identification.[32] Witnesses who witness have to

> resort to conventional modes of communication in order to convey their traumatic experience to the world at large *and* to the no less forceful need for them to challenge convention so as to avoid either aestheticizing that experience or making too much sense of its senselessness.[33]

Through her narrator, the author of the book I am analyzing has to conform to the general rules that Trezise lists, following Dori Laub.[34] She must bear witness at once to witnesses and to herself; she need not only attend "to the voices of witnesses while remaining aware of her own" but also listen to other voices "with equal self-awareness. [...] Witnessing witnessing assumes a community of respondents no less than of testifying survivors."[35] *Shanghai Escape* can perhaps also be associated with what Ágnes Heller coined as "passive memory," since it is an account that lies there, at an epic distance from the main character who would otherwise have felt tempted to silence herself on the topic and to move on, leaving such precious data about the events during World War II in Shanghai unknown.[36] At the same time, such a text has to delve into "deep memory," to use Charlotte Delbo's words, that type of memory that "preserves sensations, physical imprints," "the memory of the senses."[37]

Kathy Kacer, a trained psychologist, who had worked with troubled teenagers and their families in the past, is herself the daughter of Holocaust survivors. Her mother survived by hiding,

---

32  See Trezise, *Witnessing Witnessing*, 3.
33  Ibidem, 3.
34  Trezise invokes Laub's discussion of the status of the witness, the listener, and their interaction (Laub, "Bearing Witness" and "An Event without a Witness").
35  Trezise, *Witnessing Witnessing*, 9.
36  See Heller, "Vergessen und Erinnern."
37  Delbo, *Days and Memory*, 2–3.

her father spent time in several concentration camps. Kacer has specialized in historical fiction and Holocaust fiction for children (*The Secret of Gabi's Dresser*, *The Night Spies*, *Clara's War*, *The Diary of Laura's Twin*) and has written other real stories of Holocaust survivors: *The Underground Reporters*, dealing with some Jewish children who created a newspaper during World War II; *Hiding Edith*, the story of a Jewish girl saved similarly to other hundreds of Jewish children after the Nazi invasion of France; *To Hope and Back: The Journey of the St. Louis*, which describes another act of saving Jewish children from Germany in 1939; *We Are Their Voice: Young People Respond to the Holocaust*, which gathers responses in the form of letters, essays, poems, and art by young people who hope for a future without atrocities.[38]

*Shanghai Escape* is ghetto writing and such stories generally trace the progressive deprivation of property, livelihood, personal identity, and, finally, life itself. However, the Shanghai Ghetto is the only ghetto where lives were saved. Written in the same form as Kacer's previous books, *Shanghai Escape* addresses a younger audience, and, hence, in addition to witnessing witnessing, it has to comply with a certain type of pedagogy that presupposes a "high level of sensitivity and keen awareness of the complexity of the subject matter," a moral obligation that consists in obeying several codes of practice for writing for youths and historical fiction in particular.[39]

The way the author chose to represent her subject's childhood experiences is informed by rhetorical indirection which becomes the means to navigate the disturbing landscape of Lily's memories, by returning to the child's perspective and, thus, making the story accessible to readers of a younger age not only in terms of content but also in terms of linguistic difficulty. Lily has nei-

---

38  All the information about the author is collected from her official blog: http://www.kathykacer.com/blog2/, accessed on May 13, 2020.

39  See United States Holocaust Memorial Museum, "Guidelines for Teaching about the Holocaust." See also Kokkola, *Representing the Holocaust in Children's Literature*.

ther personally seen nor experienced the Nazi genocide and so has been luckier than some of her relatives and friends. However, her story still deals with survival and inevitably frames the radical unfamiliarity of this *univers concentrationnaire* in terms of our known, familiar world. In so doing, the author domesticates Lily's memories, diminishing the horror of her story and making a few omissions, especially when the last and hardest months of survival are covered. The narrator offers very few details about Lily's life after the ghetto was bombarded by the Americans, forcing the family to move once again to the most insalubrious place they had ever lived in.

My analysis of the book will be from the perspective of memory and trauma studies. First of all, while speaking of an increasing need to memorize the place Lily grew up, a need that the little girl imposes to herself from the very beginning of the story, *Shanghai Escape* deals with repression. Sigmund Freud, the father of psychoanalysis, explained repression as a thought or memory that is so painful that the wounded unconsciously sends it to the subconscious, thus becoming unaware of its existence. Lily is yet aware of the repression that she imposes to herself consciously. Freud also spoke about conscious repression in his coauthored work with Breuer, "Case Histories." Case 3, which was investigated by Freud, mentions that Lucy R. made herself forget a traumatic event and emphasized that repression was a volitional act: "I didn't want to think of what had happened at all," she said to her psychoanalyst, who commented twice on the patient's intentionality of repressing traumatic memories: "We may observe here a deliberate repression from consciousness." "In my view this intentional repression is also the basis for the conversion, whether total or partial, of the sum of excitation."[40] Later theorists, including Anna Freud, "refined Freud's definition by stipulating that repression was necessarily an unconscious process, while deliberate or conscious avoidance of memories was termed 'suppres-

---

40 See Breuer and Freud, "Studies in Hysteria," 2: 100–101 and 102.

sion."[41] However, as John Sutton, Celia Harris, and Amanda Barnier have pointed out, Matthew Erdelyi's ambitious recent synthesis established that no clear difference between repression and suppression can be done and that it is more useful to follow Freud's definition of repression as "rejecting and keeping something out of consciousness," no matter what mechanism is involved.[42]

Irrespective of this issue, which is still a matter of controversy at present, we can remark that similarly to Freud's patient, Lily is aware of the wound of having been forced to leave her native city (even though she does not have the understanding of an adult) but consciously pushes that memory back to her subconscious from where it surges in two crucial moments, as my analysis will show.

In my investigation, I will dwell upon the way in which the narrator goes back over different traces from Lily's past. According to Roger Kennedy,

> [t]he past as we know it, then, consists of fragile enigmatic traces left by the human subject in various places – documents, oral testimony, fleeting memories, fragments of buildings. Our knowledge of the past is only ever that of knowledge of traces, or even of traces of traces.[43]

In *The Elusive Human Subject*, Roger Kennedy uses the analogy of traces left in a ploughed field to describe the complexity and elusiveness in the structure of the human subject.[44] He makes the same association in "Memory and the Unconscious," claiming that one needs to use special techniques in order

> to detect how the field was used in the past, where previous crops were made and old crops sewn, or where the field may have covered over a previous settlement. The recent

---

41   Sutton, Harris, and Barnier, "Memory and Cognition," 217.
42   See Erdelyi, "The Unified Theory of Repression"; Sutton, Harris, and Barnier, "Memory and Cognition," 216–217.
43   Kennedy, "Memory and the Unconscious," 186–187.
44   Kennedy, *The Elusive Human Subject*, 3.

activity may even bring to light traces of the past: pottery, bones, or bits of old buildings. The field is like the human subject, with crisscrossing paths and furrows, available for multiple uses, a network of traces of activity from the past and present, and holding traces of the past available to be dug up.[45]

Kennedy is, of course, indebted to Freud's *Project for a Scientific Psychology*, where the psychoanalyst described two kinds of neurons, the phi neurons, that "retain no trace," and the psi neurons, that offer "the possibility of representing memory."[46] Thus, "[m]emory is represented by the differences in facilitations between the resisting psi neurons."[47] In his investigation on how their resistance to breaching creates a difference, which can be regarded as "the true origin of memory,"[48] Kennedy is also indebted to Jacques Derrida's commentary on Freud from *Writing and Difference* that he quotes:

> We then must not say that breaching without difference is insufficient for memory; it must be stipulated that there is no pure breaching without difference. Trace as memory is not a pure breaching that might be reappropriated at any time as simple presence; it is rather the ungraspable and invisible difference between breaches.[49]

Derrida's concept of *frayage* (translated into English as "breaching") is the French translation of the German *Bahnung*, which means "facilitation" and which is "literally path-breaking, the breaking open of a path, *Bahn*."[50]

---

45 Kennedy, "Memory and the Unconscious," 187.
46 Ibidem, 187.
47 Ibidem, 188.
48 Idem.
49 Derrida, "Freud and the Scene of Writing," 252–253. In this chapter, I am using a newer edition of Derrida's Writing and Difference than Kenner used, thus the translation is different from the one he quoted.
50 Kennedy, "Memory and the Unconscious," 188.

Kennedy comments on Derrida's interpretation of Freud's major discovery of *Nachträglichkeit*, which has been translated generally as "deferred action,"[51] and on Derrida's merging difference and deferral into one word: *différance*. Kennedy's conclusions are that

> [t]he origin of memory and of the psyche as a memory in general, conscious or unconscious, can only be described by taking into account the difference between the facilitation thresholds. There is no facilitation without difference and no difference without a trace.[52]

Moreover, invoking Derrida's use of Freud's late model of the psychical apparatus as "a writing machine"[53] in order to deconstruct the traditional understanding that writing and texts represent reality, Kennedy presents Freud's "mystic writing pad" consisting of a thin protective celluloid sheath and a receptive surface of thin waxed paper that sits atop an underlying wax slab. When one lifts this covering sheet off the wax slab, the writing vanishes and one can continue writing something else on it. However, "the wax slab retains a permanent trace of what has been written, which, under a suitable light, can still be read."[54] This is exactly what Kacer's book does, writing Lily's memory and retaining the permanent traces of her journey from Vienna to Shanghai, then from one place to another in Shanghai and finally to Toronto. For Derrida, memory "is not a psychical property among others; it is the very essence of the psyche: resistance, and precisely, thereby, an opening to the effraction of the trace."[55] Moreover, going on his close reading of Freud, Derrida thinks:

---

51  Laplanche and Pontalis, *The Language of Psychoanalysis*, 111.
52  Kennedy, "Memory and the Unconscious," 188.
53  Freud, "A Note on the 'Mystic Writing-Pad.'"
54  Kennedy, "Memory and the Unconscious," 189.
55  Derrida, "Freud and the Scene of Writing," 252.

It is because breaching breaks open that Freud, in the *Project*, accords a privilege to pain. In a certain sense, there is no breaching without a beginning of pain, and "pain leaves behind it particularly rich breaches." But beyond a certain quantity, pain, the threatening origin of the psyche, must be deferred, like death, for it can ruin psychical "organization."[56]

In *Of Grammatology*, Derrida called the trace "the arche-phenomenon of 'memory,'" and mentioned that this is to be sought in the *graphie*, because it "belongs to the very movement of signification" and signification "is *a priori* written, whether inscribed or not, in one form or another, in a 'sensible' and 'spatial' element that is called 'exterior.'"[57] It is in this sense that my chapter will attempt to recall those traces, those voices to memory that Lily entrusts her narrator to write about in *Shanghai Escape*, bearing witness to what she saw.

Lily's family left Vienna on the eve of Kristallnacht (November 8, 1938), which is the starting date of the story. The omniscient third-person narrator records in a neutral style what Lily witnessed. While waiting for her husband, her mother was checking what she had packed and had to explain that they were not actually going on a holiday and why her sewing machine was more important than many of Lily's toys, which had to be left behind. The narrator's perspective is through Lily's eyes. Hearing "crashing and shattering glass from somewhere outside" and "some angry cries that rose up from the street below," Lily had no grasp of what her mum meant by "It's starting" and she went to the window to see where the noise came from. Lily "could have sworn that she heard a chorus of people shouting: 'Down with the Jews!'"[58][58] She tried to get some sense of her mother's rush to leave:

56  Ibidem, 254.
57  Derrida, *Of Grammatology*, 70.
58  Kacer, *Shanghai Escape*, 8.

*Escaping from our home? Arresting Jewish men?* Lily had little understanding of what it meant. She was too young when the laws and rules restricting the freedom of Jewish citizens had been introduced. Occasionally she overheard bits of conversations between her parents or her aunts and uncles. They talked about how Jews couldn't go to movie theaters or restaurants or the ice-cream parlor. Pop once said that Jews were being kicked on the streets and beaten in parks. For the most part it all seemed unreal to Lily; her parents had protected her from knowing about these awful things so that she wouldn't be afraid. But tonight, when she looked into her mother's face, she could see Mom's hot red cheeks, her creased brow, and the fear that glittered in her eyes, even in the darkened apartment.[59]

Apart from her actual "pain" that she needed to leave behind her dear dolls, whom she arranged on her shelf in the hope she would find them when returning, Lily did not realize the danger of Nazi persecution. Yet there is a breach in her pain. From that night on, Lily's memory has always been erased, and the narrator helps us find it in fragile and elusive traces that look like photographs of her past life. The narrator actually presents Lily's experiencing the frozen time of trauma at the moment Lily inferred that memory became vital. On the way from her apartment to the railway station, Lily screened her memory images like a film:

Lily looked around the apartment, trying to commit every detail to memory; the paintings on the walls, the clock that chimed every hour, and down the hallway, her bedroom with her feather-stuffed comforter and her dolls lined up on the shelf like obedient schoolchildren. She was determined to remember everything on the taxi ride to the train station – memorize everything about the city that she was leaving behind.[60]

59  Krasno, *Strangers Always*, 9.
60  Ibidem, 12.

While retaining all those beautiful images of her home, she repressed the horror of the other memories. There is no account of the chaos in the streets she could see from the taxi, the broken glass she must have seen on the way to the station or people being arrested on that night.

In the opening scene of the book, the reader becomes aware of the little girl's negotiating skills, when attempting to persuade her mother that her dolls were as important as the sewing machine. Lily was undoubtedly a very clever child for her age. With such great skills, she would have been able to put together the circumstances of their rushed departure from Vienna. However, there is a delay in her putting all the elements together, as she actually did not want to understand those reasons although she noticed obvious signs for fear (her parents' impatience and nervousness).

Kacer who is a trained psychologist is very well aware that her book can create a sense of *Nachträglichkeit* and looks for the traces that Lily leaves behind in order to recover the ungraspable and invisible difference between breaches and to give continuity to Lily's own story and the historical material she is using. A trained adult reader will understand that this continuity is actually "only partial and provisional," and "it is always being reorganized after the event," [61] which means it was always being deferred.

In my analysis of *Nachträglichkeit* I also resort to a psychoanalytically toned-down reading of "the return of the repressed" via Dominick LaCapra'a work, [62] where he coins the term "repetitive temporality." In LaCapra's view, we can understand events which were not available to us in the past; we can call this the belatedness of historical understanding, "bound up both with traumatic effects and with the very ability to learn from an exchange with the past."[63] In Karyn Ball's view, LaCapra's concept is essential "for emphasizing the way in which trauma operates as a kind of *affective horizon* for Holocaust historiography," which is a way of

---

61  Kennedy, "Memory and the Unconscious," 190.
62  LaCapra, *Representing the Holocaust*, 37–38.
63  Ibidem, 27.

calling "attention to the connection between trauma, ethics, and ideology in scholarly interpretations of the Holocaust."[64]

For Lily, initially Hitler and the Nazis belonged to another realm, that of ghosts, those ghosts in her Uncle Willy's stories symbolizing the anxiety belatedly triggered by Lily's traumatic experiences. Willy would always nag his niece that the ghosts would return: "'If you don't watch out, the ghosts are going to get you,'"[65] "'Maybe the ghosts'll get you at night when you're sleeping,'" "'Or they'll sneak behind you when your back is turned.'"[66] Once in Shanghai, while in the brief interlude of freedom, repressing the fear of the Nazis, Lily's impressions and past experiences are revised so as to correspond to the return of the ghosts under a different form: "Now, Willi leaned forward and whispered in Lily's ear: 'This time the ghosts are real. The Nazis may not be coming to get us. But the Japanese will!'"[67]

Freud's concept of *Nachträglichkeit* describes a complex and ambiguous temporal trajectory and has proved to be a useful model for many trauma specialists (such as, for instance, Cathy Caruth[68] or Shoshana Felman[69]) who have built the relation between memory and trauma as models of historical temporality which depart from the strictly linear.

Temporality is cyclic rather than linear in *Shanghai Escape*. Kacer makes Lily return to the repressed trauma of Kristallnacht when on December 7, 1941, she shivered in the small apartment they had not only because she was cold in an unheated apartment in the wet winter but mostly when hearing that the Japanese had just attacked Pearl Harbor: "'This is terrible,' Pop said, shaking his head from side to side. 'America will have no choice but to join the war.'"[70] Her father's gestures bring to mind a scene she

64 Ball, *Disciplining the Holocaust*, 38.
65 Kacer, *Shanghai Escape*, 18.
66 Ibidem, 19.
67 Ibidem, 20.
68 See Caruth, *Trauma;* Caruth, *Unclaimed.*
69 See Felman and Laub, *Testimony.*
70 Kacer, *Shanghai Escape*, 14.

witnessed before: "His hand was shaking, and Lily remembered another time, three years earlier, when her father looked this nervous."[71] The anxiety of her father on that night has already been inscribed in her "writing pad," although it was erased to leave space for the relatively happy moments spent with her family, the new friends she had made meanwhile; thus, what was called before "that night" gets a name:

> People were calling it *Kristallnacht*, the night of broken glass. Synagogues across Germany and Austria had been destroyed, their windows smashed and the buildings set on fire. Thousands of Jewish men, including Willi, had been arrested that night, though most were not as lucky as he had been.[72]

Lily retraces the painful memories to the moment when she had to leave Vienna: "[I]f Germany and Japan were friends, and the government of Germany was intent on torturing Jews, did that mean that the Japanese army here in Shanghai would begin to terrorize families like hers, too?"[73]

A "map of breaches," to use a Freudian term, appears in Lily's mind at the climax of terror, on the evening of February 8, 1943, when her father brought home a newspaper that stated that all stateless refugees would be forced to move in three months. This time, the ghosts that Willy had warned her about had another name: Hongkew, "the poorest part of the city,"[74] an "awful, dirty place"[75] Lily had visited with her father before. There she had met a Chinese woman with two children living in horrifying conditions:

---

71  Ibidem, 14.
72  Ibidem, 20.
73  Ibidem, 22.
74  Ibidem, 27.
75  Ibidem, 78.

All she could think about were the two little children she had met there and how hungry they were. Hongkew was a wasteland, a part of Shanghai that looked as if it had been thrown away or forgotten. Lily couldn't imagine how anyone survived in that place.[76]

The affect that attended two anterior unprocessed experiences is associated with the new piece of information that Lily's mind receives:

Pop was white, paler than the day the radio had blared the news about the bombing of Pearl Harbor, or the night they had fled Vienna. And just like he'd done on those occasions, he pulled a handkerchief from his pocket and wiped his forehead with a trembling hand.[77]

As Karyn Ball explains, when a new event is read through the previous experiences one goes through, in a Freudian paradigm, "[a]s a result of this displacement, a memory of the later episode comes to stand-in for the previous experience and its latent effects are belatedly activated by the second, which thereafter bears a double burden of cathected content."[78]

When he thought that Lily was asleep, the father continued imparting to his wife the news which was actually worse. Joseph Meisinger, the "Butcher of Warsaw" had come to Shanghai:

"I can only imagine how he got such a name. The rumors are that he's here now to deal with the Jews who managed to slip out of the Nazis' grasp in Europe. He's calling us 'the ones that got away.' There's talk that Meisinger's behind the order to move us into this ghetto."[79][79]

For fear they might be killed similarly to their relatives and friends whom they had left behind in Europe, the parents whis

76  Kacer, *Shanghai Escape*, 78–79.

77  Ibidem, 73.

78  Ball, *Disciplining the Holocaust*, 153.

79  Kacer, *Shanghai Escape*, 80.

pered about leaving Lily behind with Mother Lawler, who had offered to take her into the Missionary Home and raise her as a Catholic. Yet Lily eavesdropped on the conversation and begged her parents not to leave without her even if she knew that the word "relocated" was used by one of her mother's friends in her last letter, followed by complete silence: "They took my jewellery and the last of our money – just came and stole our things while we were forced to stand there and watch. But now we've been told that we are being relocated to a new town."[80]

Lily repressed her memories once again in an attempt not to think of what was really happening: "Lily didn't want to think about ghettos or the possibility of Nazi soldiers coming after them. She didn't want to think about being set adrift and starving in the middle of nowhere. She didn't want to think about any of this."[81] Nevertheless, from her unconscious mind where these thoughts were deliberately being blocked (one can remark the three series of "didn't want"), the conscious recalled them via a rhetorical question, "How was it possible?"[82]

Kacer's book seeks the protagonist's history of traces. The traces of Lily's memory are multiple: on the one hand, they mostly revolve around her family: her mother, a seamstress, her father, a shoemaker, who also did other odd jobs that would keep the pot boiling at the end of the day; on the other hand, the narrator gathers memories about Lily's extended family who managed to escape, with an emphasis on her favorite, Uncle Willy (the luckiest member of the family, who escaped even after being arrested by the Gestapo), her Jewish friends, Susie and Harry, and the Chinese people who suffered. Ultimately, Lily also remembers the other Jewish relatives and friends who did not make it, whose names appear on the lists of those who perished in the death camps, lists which were posted "on walls of buildings, including the synagogue" after the war was over.[83]

---

80  Ibidem, 61.
81  Ibidem, 88.
82  Idem.
83  Ibidem, 235.

As I showed in my monograph *The Memorial Ethics of Libeskind's Berlin Jewish Museum*,

> [i]n the process of witnessing and testifying, the victim needs to exchange the event mediated by memory for a consciousness of the event relating it as knowledge. Despite his/her efforts to recollect the event faithfully, the survivor is prone to omit or obliterate aspects of it that cannot be represented for, or comprehended by the listener.[84]

I had based my findings on C. Fred Alford's suggestion that events recounted by survivors could be "comparable," yet not "commensurable" with everyday events. Feeling hungry after a few hours since the previous meal cannot be compared to being hungry continuously from the lack of food in the ghetto.[85] As in other memoirs of survivors, ordinary words such as *hunger* and *fear* fall short when used to depict the extraordinary circumstances Lily lived through. She felt hungry almost every day in Hongkew, which made her look thinner and diminished her physical powers. Her stomach felt "empty from early morning until bedtime."[86] The narrator recounts how Lily emptied four out of the six bottles of milk she was supposed to take home, expecting punishment from her mother, who, however, did not say a word about that incident.[87] Lily experienced hunger even on the day when her family gathered together after a long time for a big feast with a piece of meat that her mother had brought from the convent, which was stolen by a cat directly from the boiling pot before they could eat it. In addition to hunger, closeness to death, and annihilation could be brought on by getting sick with dysentery from the poisonous bacteria "in the water that flowed from the pipes of Hongkew"[88] (which was the reason why Lily's

---

84  Ionescu, *The Memorial Ethics*, 18.
85  Alford, *After the Holocaust*, 68.
86  Kacer, *Shanghai Escape*, 138.
87  Ibidem, 146–147.
88  Ibidem, 130.

mother always purified the water by adding drops of bleach that she had brought home whenever she was allowed to get out of the ghetto). Lily had to let go of fear when she was injured and Dr. Didner had to sew some stitches to close a cut in her head without any pain killers, since these were not available[89] or when her Uncle Willy was in a coma for days after "some jagged wires had cut deeply" into his leg and there was no medication to stop the infection.[90] Lily's fear took on hyperbolic proportions when her mother was slapped across the face by a Japanese soldier as she could not provide him with her documents fast enough.[91] Lily's fear turned into terror when she saw in the newspaper images of the victims whom the Russians had found in Auschwitz, "ghost-like men, women, and children with sticks for arms and legs," with faces that looked "so thin and shrunken that they almost didn't look human."[92]

> It was terrifying enough to *hear* the news on the radio of thousands and even millions of Jews being killed in these death camps. But to *see* the faces of those who had been held captive, filled Lily with such dread that her knees went weak, and her head began to spin.[93]

Lily's eyes also witnessed grim images, "scenes of the crime," the terror of the Japanese actions against the Chinese people. The narrator reports on the Japanese authorities' brutality and also shows how Lily avoided "an explicit confrontation" with what she perceived as atrocious:

> Lily felt so sad to see elderly Chinese men and women bow to the gruff Japanese soldiers who barked orders at them and forced them to open their packages. She longed to help. She wanted to cry out to the soldiers and say, "Stop

---

89 Ibidem, 185–187.
90 Ibidem, 216
91 Ibidem, 171.
92 Ibidem, 182.
93 Idem.

hurting those people. They aren't doing anything to you!" And yet she knew that there was nothing she could do, just as the Chinese citizens had no choice but to submit to these inspections.[94]

As Lily advanced in her new life in Hongkew, she had learned to master her fears of mice and bugs and, in a world in which she witnessed the obliteration of individuals every day and in which death was always present, her fear of death. After the bombs fell in the ghetto, Lily testified on the death of a Chinese girl. The testimony is composed of traumatic visual images: "The girl's arms and legs were twisted at awkward angles. The child's head was completely severed from her body and lay to one side, as if had been tossed there like a forgotten ball. Flies were already beginning to gather on the remains."[95] The narrator seems to suggest that soon there would be no trace of the unimportant existence of the child, yet Lily's memories of the poor torn body will remain.

The story of atrocity and survival ends with an account of the Japanese surrender that Lily's mind records in the most minute details, bringing to mind the same process of remembering as a series of photographic traces from the beginning of the book:

Lily gazed long and hard at the growing crowd of people. Aside from the fact that everyone looked so happy, it was hard, at first, to notice anything different. And then it hit her. There were no Japanese police patrolling on the streets of Hongkew, demanding to see identification papers. There was no guard at the end of East Yuhang Road, keeping people from walking where they wanted. The barbed wire that had blockaded the end of the street was gone![96] The

94  Ibidem, 46–47.

95  Ibidem, 178.

96  Another witness who lived as a child in Hongkew, Alfred Kohn, testifies that "[t]he Ghetto did not have a wall around it. [...] [T]his side of the street was the Ghetto, the other side was not the Ghetto" (Janklowicz-Mann et al., *Shanghai Ghetto*, 01:13:15–01:13.20).

open road practically called out to Lily and all the Jewish refugees of Hongkew, beckoning them to leave the ghetto and cross into the free part of Shanghai for the first time in years. And when Lily looked around, she realized that the Japanese flag no longer flew from every lamppost and every building. The flags, along with the Japanese patrols and barricades, had all disappeared.[97]

With this image, Lily and her parents leave the place that saved them. Memories of terror inscribed in "the writing machine" give way to the hope of a better future.

## Concluding Remarks

The purpose of this chapter was both to give an account on the Shanghai Ghetto and to offer a glimpse into the life of the Jewish refugees by focusing on Kathy Kacer's *Shanghai Escape*. The book was analyzed through an interdisciplinary approach that combines psychoanalysis, memory and trauma studies in order to explore the traces of the protagonist's memory. In a permanent search for the traces of survival in a world of terror, I insisted on the way Lily repressed her memories but also learned to master her fears and managed to do her duty as a witness, also offering the reader a glimmer of hope at the end of the story.

## Acknowledgement:

Research supported by the Program for Professor of Special Appointment (Eastern Scholar) at Shanghai Institutions of Higher Learning. This chapter is also part of the research for the Double First-Class Project "China's Politics of Hospitality: The Shanghai Jewish Community during WW2," School of Foreign Languages, Shanghai Jiao Tong University, project manager Professor Arleen Ionescu.

---

97  Kacer, *Shanghai Escape*, 230–231.

# Bibliography

Alford, C. Fred. *After the Holocaust: The Book of Job, Primo Levi, and the Path to Affliction*. Cambridge: Cambridge University Press, 2009.

Bacon, Ursula. *Shanghai Diary: A Young Girl's Journey from Hitler's Hate to War-Torn China*. Milwaukie, OR: M Press, 2004.

Ball, Karyn. *Disciplining the Holocaust*. Albany: State University of New York Press, 2008.

Barbasiewicz, Olga, and Barbara Dzien-Abraham. "Remembering the Origins: Everyday Life of Polish Jewish Refugees' Children in Shanghai under Japanese Occupation." *Maska: Magazyn antropolog-iczno-społeczno-kulturowy* 40.4 (2018): 115–130.

Bei, La. *The Cursed Piano: A Novel*. Translated by Howard Goldblatt and Sylvia Li-chun Lin. South San Francisco, CA: Sinomedia International Group, China Books, 2007.

Blumenthal, W. Michael. *The Invisible Wall: German and Jews: A Personal Exploration*. Washington, DC: Counterpoint, 1998.

Breuer, Joseph, and Sigmund Freud. "Studies in Hysteria" (1895), "Case Histories." Freud, "Case 3: Miss Lucy R., Age 30." In *The Standard Edition of the Complete Psychological Works of Sigmund Freud*, edited by James Strachey et al., 24 vols., vol. 2, 20–163. London: Hogarth Press and Institute of Psychoanalysis, 1953–1974.

Caruth, Cathy, ed. *Trauma: Explorations in Memory*. Baltimore: The Johns Hopkins University Press, 1995.

––. *Unclaimed Experience: Trauma, Narrative, and History*. Baltimore: The Johns Hopkins University Press, 1996.

Cornwall, Claude. *Letter from Vienna: A Daughter Uncovers Her Family's Jewish Past*. Foreword by Raul Hilberg. Vancouver: Douglas & McIntyre, 1995.

Cuba, Marion. *Shanghai Legacy*. New York: Celadon Books, 2005.

Delbo, Charlotte. *Days and Memory*. Translated by Rosette Lamont. Marlboro, VT: The Marlboro Press, 1990.

Derrida, Jacques. "Freud and the Scene of Writing." In Jacques Derrida, *Writing and Difference*. Translated, with an introduction and additional notes by Alan Bass, 246–291. London: Routledge, 2005.

——. *Of Grammatology*. Translated by Gayatri Chakravorty Spivak. Corrected edition. Baltimore: The Johns Hopkins University Press, 1997.

Eber, Irene. "Introduction." In *Voices from Shanghai: Jewish Exiles in Wartime China*, edited and translated by Irene Eber, 1–28. Chicago: University of Chicago Press, 2008.

Epstein, Israel. "Preface." In Guang Pan, *The Jews in China*. Beijing: China Intercontinental Press, 2015.

Erdelyi, Matthew H. "The Unified Theory of Repression." *Behavioral and Brain Sciences* 29 (2006): 499–511.

Felman, Shoshana, and Dori Laub, eds. *Testimony: Crises of Witnessing in Literature, Psychoanalysis, and History*. New York: Routledge, 1992.

Freud, Sigmund. "A Note on the 'Mystic Writing-Pad'" (1925). In *The Standard Edition of the Complete Psychological Works of Sigmund Freud*, edited by James Strachey et al., 24 vols., vol. 19, 227–234. London: Hogarth Press and Institute of Psychoanalysis, 1953–1974.

Grebenschikoff, Betty. *Once My Name Was Sara: A Memoir*. Ventnor, NJ: Original Seven Publishing Company, 1993.

United States Holocaust Memorial Museum. "Guidelines for Teaching about the Holocaust." N.d. https://www.ushmm.org/teach/fundamentals/guidelines-for-teaching-the-holocaust, accessed May 13, 2020.

Heller, Ágnes. "Vergessen und Erinnern: Vom Sinn der Sinnlosigkeit." *Sinn und Form* 53.2 (2001): 149–160.

Heppner, Ernest G. *Shanghai Refuge: A Memoir of the World War II Jewish Ghetto*. Lincoln: University of Nebraska Press, 1993.

Hochstadt, Steve. *Exodus to Shanghai: Stories of Escape from the Third Reich*. New York: Palgrave, 2012.

Ionescu, Arleen. *The Memorial Ethics of Libeskind's Berlin Jewish Museum*. London: Palgrave Macmillan, 2017.

Janklowicz-Mann, Dana, Amir Mann, Martin Landau, and Sujin Nam. 2002. *Shanghai Ghetto*. Film. Rebel Child Production. DVD. New York: Docurama, 2004.

Kacer, Kathy. Author's official website. http://www.kathykacer.com/blog2/, accessed May 13, 2020.

——. *Shanghai Escape*. Toronto: Second Story Press, 2013.

Kennedy, Roger. *The Elusive Human Subject*. London: Free Association Books, 1998.

——. "Memory and the Unconscious." In *Memory: Histories, Theories, Debates*, edited by Susannah Radstone and Bill Schwarz, 179–197. New York: Fordham University Press, 2010.

Kokkola, Lydia. *Representing the Holocaust in Children's Literature*. New York: Routledge, 2003.

Kranzler, David. *Japanese, Nazis and Jews: The Jewish Refugee Community of Shanghai, 1938–1945*. Hoboken, NJ: Ktav Publishing House, 1976.

Krasno, Rena. *Once upon a Time in Shanghai: A Jewish Woman's Journey through the 20th Century China*. Beijing: China Intercontinental Press, 2008.

——. *Strangers Always: A Jewish Family in Wartime Shanghai*. Berkeley, CA: Pacific View Press, 1992.

LaCapra, Dominick. *Representing the Holocaust: History, Theory, Trauma*. Ithaca, NY: Cornell University Press, 1994.

Laplanche, J., and J.-B. Pontalis. *The Language of Psychoanalysis*. Introduction by Daniel Lagache. Translated by Donald Nicholson-Smith. London: Karnac Books, 1988.

Laub, Dori. "Bearing Witness, or the Vicissitudes of Listening." In *Testimony: Crises of Witnessing in Literature, Psychoanalysis, and History*, edited by Shoshana Felman and Dori Laub, 57–74. New York: Routledge, 1992.

——. "An Event without a Witness: Truth, Testimony and Survival." In *Testimony: Crises of Witnessing in Literature, Psychoanalysis, and History*, edited by Shoshana Felman and Dori Laub, 75–92. New York: Routledge, 1992.

Li, Weijia. "Synthesis and Transtextuality: The Jewish Reinvention of Chinese Mythical Stories in 'Shanghai Ghetto.'" In *Dimensions of Story-*

*telling in German Literature and Beyond: For Once, Telling It All from the Beginning*, edited by Kristy R. Boney and Jennifer Marston William, 140–151. Rochester: Boydell & Brewer, 2018.

Lincoln, Anna. *Escape to China (1939–1948)*. New York: Manyland Books, 1982.

Pan, Guang. *Eternal Memories: The Jews in Shanghai*. Shanghai: Shanghai Brilliant Publishing House, 2015.

—. *The Jews in China*. Beijing: China Intercontinental Press, 2015.

Pu, Zukang, and Xie'an Huang, eds. *Jewish Refugees in Shanghai: 26 Stories of Jewish Refugees in Shanghai during World War II*. Shanghai: Shanghai Jiao Tong University Press, 2016.

Qiang, Yu. *Love in Shanghai Noah's Ark*. Translated by Huang Fuhai. Shanghai: Shanghai People's Fine Arts Publishing House, 2018.

Ross, James R. *Escape to Shanghai: A Jewish Community in China*. New York: The Free Press 1992.

Rubin, Evelyn Pike. *Ghetto Shanghai*. New York: Shengold Publishers, 1993.

Shopsowitz, Karen. *A Place to Save Your Life: The Shanghai Jews*. Film. New York: Filmakers Library, 1994.

Sutton, John, Celia B. Harris, and Amanda J. Barnier. "Memory and Cognition." In *Memory: Histories, Theories, Debates*, edited by Susannah Radstone and Bill Schwarz, 209–226. New York: Fordham University Press, 2010.

Swartz, Mary, and Marvin Tokayer. *Fugu Plan: Untold Story of The Japanese and the Jews during World War II*. London: Paddington Press, 1978.

Trezise, Thomas. *Witnessing Witnessing: On the Reception of Holocaust Survivor Testimony*. New York: Fordham University Press, 2013.

Wagenstein, Angel. *Farewell, Shanghai*. Translated by Elizabeth Frank and Deliana Simeonova. New York: Handsel Books, 2007.

Wang, Jian. *Shanghai Jewish Cultural Map*. Translated by Fang Shengquan, Shi Fengjie, and Jiang Lina, revised by Zhu Jisong. Shanghai: Shanghai Brilliant Publishing House, 2013.

Wu, Lin. *A Jewish Girl in Shanghai* [Youtai nü hai zai Shanghai]. Shanghai: Shanghai wen yi chu ban she, 2012.

Zhang, Yanhua, and Wang Jian. *Preserving the Shanghai Ghetto: Memories of Jewish Refugees in 1940's China*. Translated by Emrie Tomaiko. Encino, CA: Bridge 21 Publications, 2016.

## 6. Between Memory and Memoralization Policies: How Romanian Children Jewish Survivors Living in Israel Remember the Holocaust

*Eugenia Mihalcea*

The first to be sentenced to death in the Nazi extermination camps were the children. Specifically, those under the age of fifteen who were not fit to work were sent to gas chambers right from their descent from the train. It is estimated that over 1.5 million children were killed in this way.[1] They were Jewish children (1.2 million), but also Roma, institutionalized children, or children with various disabilities. In comparison to adults, who survived by 33%, the number of children who remained alive after the end of the war is much lower – only 6 to 11% of those who had been deported.[2]

They were the first to be killed and the last to testify about their lives during the Holocaust. Only in the last decades has a new interest concerning the experiences of Jewish children emerged in academia, especially in the fields of psychology and sociology.[3] Scholars are engaged in researching what children survivors remember, how trauma affected their lives in terms of their future development, and how they changed their stories over time.

Sharon Kangisser-Cohen, for example, researched the transformations that appear in survivors' testimonies, analyzing the interviews given by Jewish Holocaust survivors immediately after the end of the war and testimonies of the same people recorded

---

1   Benjamin, Florian, and Ciuciu, *Cum a fost Posibil?*, 157.
2   Center for Advanced Holocaust Studies, *Children and the Holocaust*, i.
3   Specifically, research into the experiences of surviving Jewish children began in the 1980s. Among the first to work in this area were Judith and Milton Kestenberg, who started interviewing Jewish children survivors from all over Europe and created an archive of over 1,400 testimonies. The researchers analyzed the interviews and explained, among other topics, how experiencing the Holocaust as children influenced their adult lives (Kestenberg and Brenner, *The Last Witness*).

many years later. The author argues that survivors changed their stories, because the individual memory is in a continuous negotiation and dialogue in time, influenced by the sociopolitical context in which the interviewees lived.[4] According to Kangisser-Cohen, the factors that influence the individual memory are internal survivors' markers, such as age and emotional state at the time of the interview, and the impact of other remembrance episodes on the understanding and interpretation of these events in their personal past.[5] Her findings are valuable when talking about Holocaust survivors' memories in general and about children survivors' memories in particular. There is but one additional element that needs to be taken into account when analyzing children survivors' testimonies: by the time they were interviewed for the first time (1980s – 1990s), they were distanced chronologically and also spatially from the event.

For example, Jewish children survivors repatriated to Romania from Transnistria (orphans or with parents) immigrated to Israel in large numbers. At the moment of their first interviews they were distanced in time and space from the events. Moreover, they grew up in a different country, in a different environment, in a different society, speaking a different language, developing a different identity.

In this context, we ask these questions: How do they recall the Holocaust? How do they choose to talk about Transnistria? How do they identify as survivors of the Holocaust?

I argue that the way children Holocaust survivors from Transnistria talk about their experiences and about themselves as survivors of the Holocaust is essential for understanding if and how their stories are influenced by the dominant Israeli narrative about the Holocaust to which they were exposed during adulthood. In my approach I follow Barbara A. Misztal in saying that memory is individually constructed, but also socially influenced by the national dominant discourse in a country.[6]

---

4    Kangisser-Cohen, *Testimony and Time.*
5    Ibidem, 17.
6    Misztal, "Memory and Democracy."

It should be noted that the present study is based on testimonies of children survivors who were deported to Transnistria during the Holocaust, but who were no longer children by the time they first testified. Consequently, their testimonies must be viewed in the light of the fact that their perception of their own past is in close connection with their experiences over the years.

In order to show that I analyzed children survivors' testimonies using narrative qualitative research of content, I addressed narrative research, as defined by Lieblich, Tuval-Mashiach, and Zilber, following both the memories of the testimony and how the narrative is built.[7]

Thus, I studied the interviews looking for prior-defined themes: silence and remembering after the war, the way they identify themselves as Holocaust survivors, and the influence of the Israeli narrative on their stories.

The interviews with children Holocaust survivors from Transnistria are part of the Kestenberg Archive.[8] Dr. Judith S. Kestenberg began the project of interviewing children survivors of the Holocaust as well as Nazi children in 1981 with her husband, Milton Kestenberg. The Kestenberg family, as well as many associates, traveled all over the world, interviewing more than 1,400 children. Interviews were recorded in audio to keep the interviewees confidential. For the same reason, interviewees are only given their first names or initials.

This project – having as main purpose a psychological analysis – not only recorded past events, but also explored childhood and postwar years. The interviewers, together with the interviewees, tried to integrate memories and experiences into a coherent, chronological narrative. Interviews have taken place in various countries, including Israel.

---

7    Lieblich, Tuval-Mashiach, and Zilber, *Narrative Research*, 2.
8    The archive was in the custody of the Oral History Division, the Avraham Harman Institute of Contemporary Jewry, the Hebrew University of Jerusalem. Now it is to be found at the National Library of Israel.

For this chapter I chose seven interviews with survivors who were children in Transnistria, who immigrated to Israel shortly after the war, and who were living in Israel at the time of the interviews.[9] All interviews are conducted between 1983 and 1984.

The choice of interviews with survivors who immigrated and lived in Israel is essential to this research, as my aim is to examine the extent to which survivors have been influenced in their testimonies by the collective memory of the society in question, as well as by the various groups they have been part of.

*"Society Is Like the Woman in Ephesus, Who prefers to Hang the Dead to Save the Living."*[10]

The above comparison was used by Maurice Halbwachs to explain how societies defend their citizens by removing the memory of the dead so that the ones still living can continue their lives. We can understand, exploiting the same pattern, how the Israeli society reacted when, between 1948 and 1960, 1.2 million emigrants had been absorbed – half of them survivors of the Holocaust.[11]

Researchers who explained the attitude of the Israeli society toward the survivors and the stages of Holocaust memorialization in Israel state that the Holocaust entered the collective consciousness of the Israeli society only in 1961, along with the Eichmann trial. First of all, the trial was based on testimonies – survivors were given the chance to speak. Second, the whole country witnessed the trial that had been broadcast through all means of communication.

However, before that, between 1945 and 1948, was a period marked by great diplomatic and military efforts for the development of the state of Israel. In this context, most survivors who had come before or even during those years to Israel wanted to be

---

9   All analyzed interviews were in English. For the research I used transcripts of the interviews.

10  Halbwachs, *On Collective Memory*, 74.

11  Yablonka, "Holocaust Survivors in Israel," 186.

actively involved: "[T]he most obvious evidence of this desire was the high rate of survivors' participation in the War of Independence."[12] Therefore, survivors' testimonies often include a passage, more or less, about their participation in the War of Independence. This demonstrates, according to Hanna Yablonka, the two worlds in which survivors lived in Israel between 1945 and 1948: on the one hand, Israeli society forced them to engage in a rapid, participatory integration, and, on the other hand, their memories of the Holocaust were still very alive in their minds.[13]

Between 1949 and 1959, ten years following the War of Independence and the establishment of the state of Israel, survivors' immigration and integration occupied a central place in their lives.[14] From the desire to integrate, some survivors had the number that was tattooed on their arms at Auschwitz removed. Their decision was the consequence of the fact that society, both directly and indirectly, accused them of having passively accepted their fate during the Holocaust.[15]

The accusations against the survivors have had a double effect, as Sharon Kangisser-Cohen explains: on the one hand, they have led to the creation of a negative stereotype in the society about the survivors, and, on the other hand, they produced a "conspiracy of silence": a silence imposed by society, and, at the same time, self-imposed.[16] Survivors decided to forget the Holocaust experiences for fear that memories would degrade their future. Moreover, they thought silence would protect their children from pain and ensure them a normal life.[17]

Only after the Eichmann trial did Israeli society become more aware about the past it had ignored and survivors begin to speak, to tell their stories to students, soldiers, and so on. However, "the

---

12  Ibidem, 192.
13  Ibidem, 192.
14  Ibidem, 193.
15  Kidron, "Embracing the Lived Memory."
16  Kangisser-Cohen, "Finding Their Voices," 24–25.
17  Ibidem, 26.

Holocaust was still presented in general terms: six million Jews, Auschwitz, Majdanek, Treblinka; therefore, the dominant voices were of those survivors who were imprisoned in these camps."[18]

Thus, we can say that survivors began to speak publicly about what had happened only 20 to 30 years after the end of the war. At the same time, it is important to point out the nuance highlighted by Kangisser-Cohen – namely, that the "witness age" did not mean the same for all survivors. Transnistria, for example, was not one of the very well known locations in the story of the Holocaust (such as Auschwitz). Consequently, Romanian Jewish survivors were not interviewed about their experiences in the first place.

*Remembering Their Past, Living the Present*
The seven survivors – whose testimonies represent the case study in this chapter – immigrated to Israel in the early postwar years. Five of them had lost both parents, one was fatherless, and another child was repatriated with the transport of orphans, although he had parents. Nearly everyone arrived in Israel between 1944 and 1946.

CW[19] was born in Chernivtsi in 1933. Because her mother died at birth, she was raised by her grandparents. In 1940, the Russians seized part of the family house, and her uncles (whom she believed to be her brothers) were taken into the Russian Army. In 1941, the street on which she lived was part of the Chernivtsi Ghetto. She was deported with her grandparents to Transnistria: they went by train to Atachi, Moghilev, and then to Kopaigorod. CW recalls that she saw how the soldiers broke the heads of some Jews who could not walk and that many people fell into the water and drowned at the crossing of the Dniester River. In Kopaigorod, they were taken to a nearby forest, where the grandparents died of typhus. After their death, CW was taken by the Jewish community and sent to live with a Bessarabian family. Due to the

---

18   Ibidem, 34.
19   Interview no. (257) 28–14, from the Kestenberg Archive.

worsening of the living conditions in the village, CW was later sent to the orphanage in Kopaigorod.

An aunt helped her leave with the transport of orphans to Romania. She arrived in Bucharest, and from there to Israel, in 1946. With the support of Youth Aliyah, CW studied and became a teacher. She worked as a teacher for disadvantaged children in Tel Aviv.

ZH[20] was born in Siret, Bucovina, in 1930. He moved with his family to Adâncata, where they lived until 1940. In 1940, when the Russians began to nationalize their properties, ZH's family – parents and an older sister named Tova – moved to Chernivtsi. In 1941, ZH's family was imprisoned in the Chernivtsi Ghetto, and in December deported to Transnistria. They went by train to Mărculeşti and further on foot to Berşad. They lived in a small kitchen in the house of some locals, for a fee. The parents got sick and died, and the two brothers were kicked out. ZH worked for the peasants in the village to support himself. He then went to the Balta orphanage, and there he worked in a factory.

In 1944 he was repatriated and went to Iaşi, Bârlad, and finally to Bucharest. From Bucharest he was taken by the Russians to Odessa, along with eighteen other children. He obtained a permit to travel to Chernivtsi, where he lived with an aunt and started trading in the market to survive. ZH joined a Zionist organization and immigrated to Israel. He married in 1959, worked in construction, and has three children.

SP[21] was born in Cluj in 1933. The family – two parents, SP and a younger sister – was deported in 1942 from Vatra Dornei. They arrived in Atachi, and then in Palanca. The family survived by selling their personal items for food, but also by stealing from the surrounding fields. In 1943, when the Red Cross organized a transport of orphans to be repatriated to Romania, the parents sent the two girls with this transport. In Romania they lived with a relative, and then were sent to an orphanage in Buzău. After

---

20  Interview no. (257) 27–24, from the Kestenberg Archive.
21  Interview no. (257) 27–42, from the Kestenberg Archive.

being released from Transnistria, the parents came to Bucharest and found the girls. The family moved back to Cluj where they stayed until 1960, when they immigrated to Israel. SP married in 1959.

MW[22] was born in 1927 in the village of Berhomet, near Chernivtsi. When MW was four, the family moved to Chernivtsi, then to Bucharest, and then back to Chernivtsi. In October 1941, MW and her family were deported to Transnistria. They went by train, then on foot, crossed the Dniester River, and were interned in a stable. Her parents died of typhus. The two girls were moved to the Berșad orphanage, where MW's sister died. MW was helped by a relative in the hospital and left with a transport to Romania. She arrived in Iași, at an orphanage, along with several children, including her future husband. She immigrated to Israel in 1944 and married in 1947. In Israel, she attended an agricultural school for two years, but did not practice. She had two children.

MS[23] was born in 1928 in Rădăuți, Bucovina, in a well-placed family. Because of their communist sympathies they moved to Chernivtsi. In 1941 they were deported to Transnistria.

MS remembers that many people died on the road. His family found a living space for which they paid with the things they had with them. Due to worsening conditions, MS's mother committed suicide. A few months later, his father got sick with typhus and died.

He remained alone at the age of thirteen, with his younger sister. They were moved to the Berșad orphanage. A few months later they were transferred to another orphanage in Balta, where his sister fell ill and died. In 1944, with the support of the Jewish community and the Red Cross, he was repatriated with other orphaned children. He arrived in Iași, then in Bucharest, from where he immigrated to Israel, in 1944. In 1948 he entered the

---

22 Interview no. (257) 28–15, from the Kestenberg Archive.
23 Interview no. (257) 28–3, from the Kestenberg Archive.

army. MS worked in the army until 1972. He organized several meetings with children from the orphanage in Balta.

KL[24] was born in Bessarabia in 1930. When she was five, her family moved to Chernivtsi. They were deported to Transnistria by train, and then by boats across the Dniester River and further to Moghilev. In the first year of the deportation, her father died of typhus. Toward the end of the war, KL and an older sister were sent to Romania with a transport of orphaned children. In Romania, the two sisters were separated and lived with different families. In 1945, they immigrated to Israel with Youth Aliyah. In Israel, KL studied, became a teacher, and in 1948 wanted to participate in the War of Independence, but was not allowed. She wrote poetry in Yiddish about what had happened in Transnistria, but never published it.

YF[25] was born in Soljenitz, Bucovina, in 1923. He was the only child of the family. In 1941, the family was deported by train to Berşad. YF remembers that many people died along the way, including his relatives. After his parents died, YF was helped by an acquaintance who offered him food. When the Berşad orphanage was established, YF was moved there. In 1944, YF and other orphans were repatriated to Romania. They arrived in Iaşi, and later were adopted by Jewish families. Because the Russians were advancing to Iaşi, YF and his friends decided to leave for Bucharest. In November 1944 they boarded a ship in Constanţa, arriving in Israel at the Atlit detainee camp. He participated in the War of Independence, and then worked for five years in the army. He met his wife shortly after immigration and had two children.

*A Conspiracy of Silence*

> So I learned the silence. It was not easy to remain silent. But it was the best way for all of us. [...] Over time, I hid the miserable traces of suffering. I grew up like a kibbutz boy. Bronze, strong, involved in everyday activities.[26]

---

24 Interview no. (257) 27–30, from the Kestenberg Archive.
25 Interview no. (257) 40–58, from the Kestenberg Archive.
26 Appelfeld, "The Awakening," 149–150.

The testimonies presented in this article were recorded in 1983 – 1984. In those years, interviews were given mostly by adult survivors who were at the age of retiring. The way they perceived their own achievements in life had a great influence on the tone of the testimonies.[27] This was also the period when children survivors started being interviewed. At the time of the interview they had already been living in Israel for 30 to 40 years, had had families, and worked for the state. Their experiences of immigration occupy an important place in their narratives.

For example, CW remembers that after she arrived in the camp in Israel she was very busy studying and engaging in various activities, "as life in an institution." She says she was in a room with children from Tehran who had their own problems. That's why CW says she did not have anyone to talk to: "I thought my problem was just mine."

KL, who arrived in Israel in 1945, says the integration process was difficult: "Everyone went to work and build." She attended a seminar and studied, but although she feels professionally fulfilled now, she states that in the years after immigration she felt very lonely. For ZH, doing well in Israel occupied the first place in his daily concerns. He says that after completing his service in the army he was in a difficult position, because there were no jobs and he did not have enough training to get one. ZH had many temporary jobs, studied in the construction field, and then began to get work. Only afterward did he marry and have a family.

"Past images have mixed up with my new life – I've become an adult," says MW. Shortly after arriving in Israel, the War of Independence began, and there were other concerns. The army was the main concern for MS, too, who joined in 1948, but remained in various positions until 1972. He retired with the rank of major. "I was happy in the army. […] The army was my home," says MS.

Although after immigration there was a time when survivors were concerned about their new lives and not about the past, re

---

27  Wieviorka, *The Era of the Witness*, 138.

search shows that Israeli society did not encourage them to speak. "You always had that feeling you cannot say. If you say, you're unhappy, and if you do not want to feel unhappy, shut up," KL says. Even more than being silent, she repressed any sign that would have identified her as a survivor of the Holocaust. KL says she wrote poetry in Yiddish, but she was worried that someone might see it and because of this she throws it away: "To write in Yiddish [...] in general, Sabra was the ideal."

KL says that immediately after the war survivors' testimonies did not occupy a central place on the public agenda in Israel. Moreover, after the establishment of the state and the War of Independence, a new type of person was desired: the Israeli, a person who was supposed to be the antithesis of the passive Jew of the diaspora, the victim of the Holocaust.[28]

Apart from the silence imposed by society, there were two trends in the attitude of families toward survivors: encouraging or discouraging them to talk. MW says that she talked from the beginning about what had happened because her husband was a survivor, too. However, she did not want to tell her children too much because she thought it was her past and her concern:

> What is inside me is enough. [...] We both talked to our children about our experiences, but only if the situation demanded. I never asked them to sit down and listen. I would tell them, if they did not eat, how we were looking for garbage, hoping to find a potato shell to eat. Some children ask to be told, my own, no.

Similarly, ZH recalls his experience with his children. He says he just reminds them that it is important to value what they have: independence, freedom, the fact that people can defend themselves. ZH states that he could not tell the children more about the experience in Transnistria because it was very difficult to talk about it.

---

28 Kidron, "Embracing the Lived Memory."

Also for YF it was easier to recall small events from the camp, for example, how to run with legs wrapped in material. He avoided, however, giving details about what had been done to them.

For CW the silence was imposed by her husband. When witnesses began to testify because they wanted to be financially compensated by Germany, CW's husband told her she did not need the money. Her attitude, supplemented by fear of talking, led to silence.

All the examples presented above show that in many situations the attitude of Israeli society marked the survivors' decision to be silent. However, there is no pattern concerning the silence imposed or self-imposed. Survivors from Transnistria fall into the more general picture of the Holocaust survivor. Their voices had not been heard in the first place because of the silence imposed by society; it was self-imposed our of fear or because of the attitude of their family members.

*Transnistria versus Auschwitz*

At the time of the interviews the survivors had been living in Israel for 30 to 40 years, all the time being exposed to the different Israeli discourses about the Holocaust. This exposure sometimes created complementary and at other times conflicting narratives in their testimonies. For example, when asked how her father looked after Transnistria, MW says: "We all looked like people in Auschwitz or Treblinka. My husband remembers me when I was 16. All our hair had been cut off to prevent infestation with lice, I had 18 kilos." She also stresses that their experience, as survivors from Transnistria, was different: "Our family was kept together but we experienced the death of each member of our family, right alongside of us. In the other camps people were led away, to gas chambers or to be shot and there were no witnesses."

The same struggle we can see in MS's testimony. When asked by the interviewer if he was in a ghetto or not, he replies: "But all Transnistria was a big concentration camp. What I mean, the

Jews of.... I mean the Gentiles lived outside and the Jews inside the ghetto.... A concentration camp in a ghetto, but not the same as in Germany with barbed wire, this was not the same."

At the end of the interview, suddenly KL asks: "What else do you want to hear? I do not have stories like others do who survived the camps. Stories like that I do not have."

The Holocaust in Romania had a few local characteristics. In August 1941, the territory of Transnistria was created and placed under Romanian administration. The Romanian authorities, the allies of Nazi Germany, deported Jews from Bessarabia, Bukovina, and northern Moldova there and evacuated and killed local Jews. Around 150,000 Romanian Jews out of the country's 756,930 were sent across the Dniester River in a massive wave of deportations that started in the autumn of 1941.[29] They died mainly of starvation, cold, and diseases. They were not gassed; they were not put into camps like in Poland, but scattered all over Transnistria in improvised spaces – former factories, schools, and even in forests under the clear sky. Between 280,000 and 380,000 Romanian and local Jews died there.[30]

Children survivors of the Holocaust from Transnistria immigrated to Israel in great numbers in the first years after the war. They were encouraged to integrate as soon as possible into Israeli society.[31] They had to adopt a new ideology, to become accustomed to a new environment, to learn a new language and a new way of dressing, to forget everything about their previous life in Europe. Otherwise, they would have been considered outsiders.[32]

---

29  According to the national census of Greater Romania from 1930, the Jews were 4.2% of the local population in the country, with the biggest percentage in Bessarabia and Bukovina (Friling et al., *International Commission*, 7).
30  Friling et al., *International Commission*.
31  Ofer, "Mending the Body," 129.
32  Ibidem, 151.

This is exactly what Aharon Appelfeld recalls:

> What could we do, 12-, 13-year-old boys with so many memories of death? To tell them? To outsource them? To bring them back to memory? [...] External questions were meaningless. There were questions that were incomprehensible, questions from this world that had nothing to do with the world we came from. [...] So I learned the silence. It was not easy to shut up. But it was a good way for us to go further.[33]

## Conclusion

Survivors who immigrated to Israel immediately after World War II were preoccupied with restoring their lives and becoming Israelis. At the same time, the past was not forgotten, but was kept somewhere in their minds until a trigger made them speak. For most of them, the trigger occurred in the 1980s, when Israeli society was not only willing to listen, but also eager to integrate their stories into the educational system and in school text books. (The Holocaust became a mandatory subject to be taught in high school in 1980.) In that period survivors were at the heart of Holocaust research, as well as a mandatory presence in public spaces, ceremonies, and schools.

However, even after the voices of the survivors began to be heard, the symbols that penetrated the collective memory were set: six million Jews killed, Auschwitz, Majdanek, Treblinka, the Nazi criminals. Consequently, the survivors recall these symbols, because the ghettos and camps formed in Transnistria do not fit into the Auschwitz or Treblinka narrative. As the witnesses say, they lived in forests, in local houses, in former factory buildings, kolkhozes.

For survivors, Transnistria is an unknown, a foreign space, but also the room or forest where they lived for many years with their families. In order to understand the "meaning that people give to

---

33  Appelfeld, "The Awakening," 149–150.

space and place in the Holocaust,"[34] we will not refer to Transnistria as the territory of about 40,000 kilometers where ghettos and camps were organized.

CW, for example, who was born in Chernivtsi in 1933, says she remembers very little about her hometown. Instead, the street where she lived, the house where she grew up, every piece of furniture in the apartment, is still alive in her memory. For her, the ghetto was not a shocking experience, on the one hand, because the street where her family lived was included in the ghetto and so they did not have to move, and, on the other hand, because, as she says: "We did not understand anything from the war."

CW was deported by train with her family. She says that they waited a long time at the train station; after that they were put in a cattle car and taken in an unknown direction. She does not know where they were taken, that she "does not remember places," but after descending from the train they walked through fields and mud. Space becomes concrete, as Tim Cole explains, only when it is associated with a negative event during the Holocaust.[35] For CW, this event represents the death of her grandparents, in a forest near Kopaigorod. But even in this case, the space has no concreteness. She does not remember where her relatives were buried, but only that they slept among the trees and that many of the deportees died there.

Like CW, ZH says that they went to Transnistria by train, to an "unknown" place, taken from their homes, "from a specific place, to the unknown." For him, the moment of departure was marked by the fact that his father read at the very beginning a passage from the Torah called *Lech-Lecha* (You will leave), a coincidence that stuck with him.

SP remembers Transnistria in a similar manner. In fact, she does not even mention the name of the territory where the Jews were deported to, but only says that after a few days spent in the open air in the Chernivtsi Ghetto they were put on the cat-

34 Knowles, Cole, and Giordano, *Geographies of the Holocaust*, 13.
35 Ibidem.

tle train a taken to a "big water." The Dniester becomes a turning point in SP's story, because when she crossed the river she witnessed scenes of violence: soldiers snatching jewelry from a neighbor's hand, but also because she was in the same group of deportees with the mentally ill from Chernivtsi. About the Cariere de Piatră place, where she stayed until 1943, she does not give details, but only says that it was a terrible place, due to lack of food, hygiene, and disease.

For MW, the place where they were deported to, which he describes as a very distant territory, "already in Russia," a long way away, was, in the end, the stable where they crowded in among the straw in order not to be cold and where both of his parents died.

We also find the feeling of the unknown in KL's testimony. She says that after crossing the Dniester, she began to feel that there was a war. But it is not the river itself that represents the boundary between this world and the different world into which KL passed, but what she experienced there: the cold, the lack of a home, the people who spoke an unfamiliar language. "The smells were terrible everywhere" is a phrase that KL repeats several times in the interview when referring to the space where she lived in Transnistria.

Other Holocaust survivors in Transnistria, in an attempt to help the interviewer better visualize those places described them to be beyond human imagination and compare them to the extermination or transit camps emblematic of the Holocaust. Moreover, the experience of deportation was, for most of them, akin to a death march because they were strolling between different places in Transnistria. They saw many people who died on the road, parents and relatives who died of illness. In fact, although of the seven interviewed six are orphans, no parent was shot. They all died from illness, lack of hygiene, or starvation.

The specificity of the Transnistrian Holocaust is evident in survivors' testimonies: they walked and walked, from one camp to another and they were often moved to other localities after their parents died.

According to Sharon Kangisser-Cohen: "death marches are remembered as chaotic, periods of extreme physical suffering, cold, improper clothing and lack of food."[36] And in the case of the survivors from Transnistria, for whom the experience of deportation meant especially a continuous death march, the memories are very vivid, not necessarily because they are fixed in time and space, but simply because they are related to extreme physical suffering. "The concentration camp system involved a routine in which survivors could expect to have certain basics: food, work, sleep. [...] Death marches had no routine, and victims could not expect to receive food or sleep"[37]

The only places that the survivors remember in more detail are the orphanages where they all ended up, whether they lost both parents, a single parent, or were sent to the orphanage by their parents out of a desire to save them from Transnistria. Consequently, the survivors from Transnistria appropriated different symbols in their testimonies as a way to integrate their stories into the generalized Israeli narrative of that time.

---

36 Kangisser-Cohen, *Testimony and Time*, 53.
37 Ibidem.

# Bibliography

Alexander, Jeffrey C. *Remembering the Holocaust: A Debate*. Oxford: Oxford University Press, 2009.

Appelfeld, Aharon. "The Awakening." In *Holocaust Remembrance: The Shapes of Memory*, edited by Geoffrey H. Hartman, 149–152. Cambridge: Blackwell, 1994.

Benjamin, Lya, Alexandru Florian, and Anca Ciuciu. *Cum a fost posibil? Evreii din România în perioada Holocaustului*. [How was it possible? The Jews in Romania during Holocaust]. Bucharest: Editura Institutului Național pentru Studierea Holocaustului din România "Elie Wiesel," 2007.

Center for Advanced Holocaust Studies, ed. *Children and the Holocaust: Symposium Presentations*. Washington, DC: United States Holocaust Memorial Museum, 2004.

Ciuciu, Anca. "Children of the Holocaust: Orphans of Transnistria." In *Holocaustul la periferie* [The Holocaust on the periphery], edited by Wolfgang Benz and Brigitte Mihok, 157. Bucharest: Cartier, 2010.

Friedman, Philip. "Problems of Research on the European Jewish Catastrophe." *Yad Vashem Studies on the European Jewish Catastrophe and Resistance* 3 (1959): 25–39.

Friling, Tuvia, et al. *International Commission on the Holocaust in Romania (ICHR). Final Report*. Iași: Polirom, 2005.

Gouri, Haim. "Facing the Glass Booth." In *Holocaust Remembrance: The Shapes of Memory*, edited by Geoffrey H. Hartman, 153–160. Cambridge: Blackwell, 1994.

Halbwachs, Maurice. *On Collective Memory*. Chicago: University of Chicago Press, 1992.

Ioanid, Radu. "The Destruction and Rescue of Jewish Children in Bessarabia, Bukovina and Transnistria." In *Children and the Holocaust: Symposium Presentations*, edited by Center for Advanced Holocaust Studies, 77–92. Washington, DC: United States Holocaust Memorial Museum, 2004.

Kangisser-Cohen, Sharon. "Finding their Voices: The Life Stories of Child Survivors of the Holocaust in Israel." PhD dissertation, Hebrew University of Jerusalem, 2003.

———. *Testimony and Time: Holocaust Survivors Remember.* Jerusalem: Yad Vashem, 2014.

Kestenberg, Judith S., and Ira Brenner. *The Last Witness: The Child Survivor of the Holocaust.* Washington, DC: American Psychiatric Press, 1996.

Kidron, Carol A. "Embracing the Lived Memory of Genocide: Holocaust Survivor and Descendant Renegade Memory Work at the House of Being." *American Ethnologist* 37.3 (2010): 429–451.

Knowles, Anne Kelly, Tim Cole, and Alberto Giordano, *Geographies of the Holocaust.* Bloomington: Indiana University Press, 2014.

Levy, Daniel, and Natan Sznaider. "Memory Unbound: The Holocaust and the Formation of Cosmopolitan Memory." *European Journal of Social Theory* 5.1 (2002): 87–106.

Lieblich, Amia, Rivka Tuval-Mashiach, and Tamar Zilber. *Narrative Research: Reading, Analysis and Interpretation.* London: Sage Publications, 1998.

Lomsky-Feder, Edna. "Life Stories, War and Veterans: On the Social Distribution of Memories." *Ethos* 32.1 (2004): 1–28.

Misztal, Barbara A. "Memory and Democracy." *American Behavioral Scientist* 48 (2005): 1320–1338.

Ofer, Dalia. "Mending the Body, Mending the Soul: Members of Youth Aliyah Take a Look at Themselves and at Others." In *Holocaust Survivors: Resettlement, Memories, Identities,* edited by Dalia Ofer, Françoise S. Ouzan, and Judy Tydor Baumel-Schwartz, 128–164. New York: Berghahn Books, 2012.

———. "The Past That Does Not Pass: Israelis and Holocaust Memory." *Israel Studies* 14.1 (2009): 1–35.

Shapira, Anita. "The Holocaust: Private Memories, Public Memory." *Jewish Social Studies* 4.2 (1998): 40–58.

Wieviorka, Annette. *The Era of the Witness*. Ithaca: Cornell University Press, 2006.

Yablonka, Hanna. "Holocaust Survivors in Israel: Time for an Initial Taking of Stock." In *Holocaust Survivors: Resettlement, Memories, Identities*, edited by Dalia Ofer, Françoise S. Ouzan, and Judy Tydor Baumel-Schwartz, 184–206. New York: Berghahn Books, 2012.

## Interviews

Kestenberg Archive:

Interview no. (257) 27–30.
Interview no. (257) 27–24.
Interview no. (257) 27–42.
Interview no. (257) 28–14.
Interview no. (257) 28–15.
Interview no. (257) 28–3.
Interview no. (257) 40–58.

# 7. Vapniarka: Personal Memories from the "Camp of Death"

*Olga Ştefan*

The Holocaust has of course been a topic that has generated enormous amounts of research, focusing primarily on the crimes of Nazi Germany. Much less attention has been dedicated to the killing fields of Transnistria, or the Transnistrian Governorate, a Romanian-administered territory between the Dniester River and the Southern Bug River (not to be confused with the contemporary region of the same name), conquered by Romania and Germany during Operation Barbarossa, launched against the Soviet Union on June 22, 1941.[1] Here, between 1941 and 1944, more than 300,000 Romanian and Ukrainian Jews were killed[2] through starvation, sickness, cold, and the "Holocaust by bullets," a term coined by Patrick Debois.[3]

In the first few weeks of the occupation, mostly Romanian troops shot thousands of Jews in villages, towns, and cities, then ghettoized the survivors. Romanian authorities began the deportations of Jews from Bessarabia, Bukovina, and Romania's Old Kingdom to concentration camps and ghettos in Transnistria in late August 1941. Mass shootings occurred in some areas, particularly the concentration camps of Bogdanovka, Domanevka,

---

1   There are a few studies on the deportations of Jews and Roma by the Antonescu regime to Transnistria, some of which have also been translated into English. These include Ioanid, *The Holocaust in Romania;* Dumitru, *The State, Antisemitism;* Ancel, *Transnistria.* However, the present chapter does not draw from these sources, but rather from the personal testimonies, autobiographies, and oral histories cited.

2   There is no consensus on the exact number of Jews killed. Some, like Jean Ancel, say between 250,000–300,000, the Wiesel commission claims 280,000–380,000, while others claim the figure to be much higher, reaching over 400,000. If we add Roma casualties, the number can very well be much higher still.

3   Debois, *Holocaust by Bullets.*

and Akhmetchetka, in the fall and winter of 1941 after some survivors of the Odessa massacre, carried out by Romanian troops, were deported there. All the camps and ghettos in Transnistria fell under the authority of the Marshal Antonescu-appointed governor, Gheorghe Alexianu, with the exception of one: Vapniarka, a concentration camp three kilometers away from the eponymous small village on the Odessa-Lviv train line. From fall 1941 until August 1942, 1,000 survivors of the Odessa massacre and deportees from Bessarabia and Bukovina were imprisoned there, of whom the majority died of typhus. A few hundred Jews survived, but were shot later during transfer. Starting in September 1942, the camp was designated a political prisoner camp, and authority was transferred from the Transnistria Governorate to the Ministry of Internal Affairs in Bucharest.

The particular conditions in this camp, its special status, the prisoners' unique organizational strategy that led to their survival, the diverse makeup of the prisoners, the complex, sometimes conflicting representations of life and events within the camp, and the instrumentalization of the fate of this camp and its prisoners by the communist regime in postwar Romania make it an extremely interesting case study, yet one that has really not been undertaken until now.[4] In this text, and in future examinations, the Vapniarka concentration camp is analyzed through the subjective prism of the survivors, including their journals, books, recorded testimonies, and artistic objects. The material we present here is by no means exhaustive but it does employ lesser or entirely unknown works.

4    Shapiro, "*Vapniarka*," relies on information found in the archive of the International Tracing Service (now known as the Arolsen Archives-International Center on Nazi Persecution), in Bad Arolsen, Germany. While I also draw from the few documents found in this archive, namely those of Dr. Arthur Kessler, these documents came to me directly from the family. The remainder of this chapter draws from sources not included in the archive.

## First Impressions of Vapniarka

Almost all accounts of the first contact with Vapniarka attest to the greeting that the commandant of the camp, Colonel Murgescu, uttered to the newly arrived deportees, one that remained etched in their memories as an omen of what was to come.

Nathan Simon, one of the earliest detainees to be hospitalized in the camp (with lower-body paralysis), even titled his 1993 autobiography after a fragment of this greeting, which he recalls as, "You entered the camp on two legs, but should you ever get out you will crawl on all fours."[5] Yehiel Benditer wrote his study on Vapniarka two years later, in 1995, drawing on historical documents and personal testimonies of survivors, but does not refer directly to his own recollections, preferring to present a more objective perspective. On the topic of the notorious greeting, he cites Matatias Carp's *The Black Book* from 1945, echoing Simon's version.[6] Geza Kornish, whose short autobiographical notes were published even later than Benditer's and Simon's, in 2000, agrees with them.[7]

Sergiu Lezea, who had not been a detainee in Vapniarka but rather used survivors' testimonies to compose a self-proclaimed "literary treatment" of the camp which was published in 1945, also reports a similar expression.[8] Aurel Baranga's report about the camps in Transnistria was also based on testimonies and some documents, but not on his personal experience It was published as a book in 1946. He dedicates one chapter to Vapniarka

---

5  Simon, "… *auf allen Vieren werdet ihr hinauskriechen.*" All translations from this publication included in this text are made by Olga Ştefan from the original German. This book is part of the archive of *The Future of Memory* (https://www.thefutureofmemory.ro/).

6  Benditer, *Vapniarca.* All translations from this publication included in this text are made by Olga Ştefan from the original Romanian. Book is part of the archive of *The Future of Memory.*

7  Kornish, Überlebt durch Solidarität.

8  Lezea, *Vapniarca.* All translations from this publication included in this text are made by Olga Ştefan from the original Romanian. Book is part of the archive of *The Future of Memory.*

and quotes Murgescu, who in this version was pointing to the cemetery and stating, "See what is here and know what is awaiting you. This is how you will get out of here, or on all fours."[9] Dr. Arthur Kessler, the head of the camp medical staff, in his unpublished memoirs written in the 1960s but based on notes that he kept during his captivity,[10] echoes Baranga's version, with some variations, quoting Murgescu, "On the slope behind the grave you can see the grave of 550 people who were in the camp before you. They died of typhoid. Try to do better if you can."[11] M. Rudich, who also published his account of Transnistria in 1945, dedicating a chapter to Vapniarka, and like Baranga and Lezea, basing the work on testimonies of survivors, claims Murgescu expressed himself similarly to Simon's and Benditer's renditions.[12] Only Adalbert Rosinger and Simion Bughici, who never managed to publish their memoirs during their lifetimes, never address this detail. Both men, along with Yehiel Benditer, Nathan Simon, and Gabriel Cohen, had been deported to Vapniarka as political prisoners from inside Romania: Rosinger, Bughici, Benditer, and Cohen came from the Târgu Jiu camp, while Simon came from the Văcărești prison. Rosinger had been involved in various left-wing activities before and during the war, but left the party in 1934 due to his dissatisfaction with the leadership and its attitudes, continuing his involvement in antifascist resistance through other channels,[13] Benditer was also jailed for antifascist activities but had not been a member of the communist party, while Simion Bughici was an enthusiastic member of the party and later, in the early 1950s, became the Minister of

9   Baranga, *Ninge peste Ukraina*. All translations from this publication included in this text are made by Olga Ștefan from the original Romanian. Book is part of the archive of *The Future of Memory*.

10  Kessler, "Ein Arzt im Lager."

11  Spitzer, "Solidarity and Suffering."

12  Rudich, *La Braț cu MOARTEA*.

13  Interview with Veronica Rosenberg, Rosinger's daughter, made by Olga Ștefan and included in her film *Gestures of Resistance* (2019) as part of *The Future of Memory* platform (https://www.thefutureofmemory.ro/).

Foreign Affairs. Gabriel Cohen had joined the party from its beginning in 1921, and was the printer and designer of the illegal *Scînteia*, the official party newspaper, from 1931 to 1933.[14]

The accounts of Vapniarka published after 1989, or those not published at all (including that of Simion Bughici[15]), underline the fact that the deportees from the Old Kingdom and Northern Transylvania were all Jewish, mostly nonpolitical, despite the stated goal of the Antonescu regime to target communists specifically. Kornish, who himself had been imprisoned for antifascist activity in Timișoara, insists on the point that "[d]eportations were aimed exclusively at Jews, and not only communist ones but also those considered to be sympathizers. More than 60% of the Vapniarka camp inmates had never had anything to do with communism."[16] Lezea and Baranga, on the other hand, in works published by communist presses immediately after the war, speak only of "political detainees" and "antifascists" making up the camp population, almost never mentioning the word "Jewish," while Rudich, whose book appeared through an independent publisher in 1945, highlights the specific nature of the crimes of the Antonescu regime committed against the Jewish population. The camp itself is described by almost all in the exact same way:

> Kornish: The camp was secured by triple-wire fences. Inside, there were three single-story main buildings and some other small buildings, which were used as kitchens and for other purposes. The women were accommodated in the first building, the men in the second building and in the third building.[17]

---

14  Interview with Ella Roizman, Cohen's daughter, made by Olga Ștefan and included in her film *Gestures of Resistance* (2019) as part of *The Future of Memory* platform (https://www.thefutureofmemory.ro/).
15  Bughici, unpublished memoir.
16  Kornish, Überlebt durch Solidarität.
17  Ibidem.

Benditer: The camp was located in the destroyed buildings of a former military school built by the Soviets, situated near a forest, which extended alongside the railway line. [...] The camp was surrounded by three rows
of barbed wire and guard towers every 50 m. In front of
the three pavilions for the detainees, there was beaten
ground that served as space for roll call. On the other side
of the ground were two other smaller buildings which
in the past had contained the kitchen and mess hall, the
laundry, and showers.[18]

Rosinger: The large buildings at the edge of town, which
had belonged to the Soviet Army, and in front of the
buildings there was a huge plateau of a few hectares
where we could walk during the day. The entire camp
was surrounded by a triple fence of barbed wire. On one
end of the camp there was a large latrine in an open field.
We men were sent to the second pavilion. On the ground
floor, in a large open room, where I, too, was placed,
there were 320 internees, while on the first floor also
about that number. At both ends of the building were
separate rooms, smaller, where only 2 to 5 people were
accommodated in each.[19][19]

In one of the extremely expressionistic wood engravings made
by Aurel Mărculescu (Aron Marcovici, b. 1901, Piatra Neamț-d.
September 1947) in the camp itself, the architecture of the barracks is depicted as long and rectangular, with two floors and ten
window frames on the length of each floor, and five on the width.
On the grounds in front of the barracks, a cripple and two other
dark human forms appear hunched over and seem to be moving
with difficulty. An emaciated, hollow-eyed half of a face, rem-
iniscent of that in Edvard Munch's *The Scream*, peeks out from

18 Benditer, *Vapniarca*, 20.
19 Rosinger, unpublished memoir, chap. 7. All translations from this text included here are made by Olga Ștefan from the original Romanian.

the bottom of the work. The barbed wire fence, as well as a guard post, is visible behind the barracks. No words can really capture human suffering like a few simple, twisted lines.

Image part of *The Future of Memory* archive
(https://www.thefutureofmemory.ro/).

A maquette made by Avi Solomovici years after the war represents the three camp barracks as having eight windows on the length of each floor, rather than Mărculescu's ten, and three on the width. There are seven watchtowers, as well as a guard post on the ground. The maquette even contains miniature detainees walking on the grounds in front of the barracks, some with sticks, others carrying heavy objects, yet another similarity to Mărculescu's print. There are two small buildings facing the barracks, on the other side of the grounds. The latrine is depicted as an area next to one of these two buildings surrounded by straw.

The living conditions were execrable and entirely inhuman. There were no windows to keep the harsh cold air from entering the buildings, the roof was in many areas caved in, and there were no bed frames.

229

The maquette of Vapniarka concentration camp[20]

---

20 *A Model of the Vapniarka Camp, Transnistria*. Catalog no. 51307. Ghetto Fighters House Archives. https://www.infocenters.co.il/gfh/notebook_ext. asp?book=114713&lang=eng, accessed April 9, 2020.

Kornish: The rooms were cold, there were no beds or bunks, we slept on the concrete floor on a thin layer of straw and we were freezing. Most of us had caught colds. We put on everything we possessed to protect ourselves against the cold. We suffered constantly from weak bladders and, because we were not allowed to use the latrine, a barrel was placed in the dormitory where more than a hundred men could go to relieve themselves. In the mornings, those on duty had to drag the barrel and its contents to the latrine, empty it out and clean it. I was not spared this task, either.[21]

## Number and Affiliation of the Prisoners

If the details describing the camp and the "welcome" received by the detainees is similar in almost all accounts, then the first point of divergence that we encounter among them is the number and affiliation of the prisoners.

Rosinger: Arriving at the camp, we were able to see how our convoy grew to about 1,100 people, all of them Jews. Attaching to our group other groups of deportees along the way, our convoy came to consist of three groups. It consisted of: a first group of 420 former inmates in Târgu Jiu; a second group of 60–70 people, Jewish detainees in Romanian prisons, primarily in Caransebeş, who were there to execute their sentences for communist activity; and a third group – of about 600 people – arrested from their homes in various cities to be deported, being suspected of supporting the anti-Hitler struggle.[22]

Kornish: It should be mentioned that there were three categories of prisoners among the Jews deported on our transport to Vapniarka. There were the Jews who had not been

---

21  Kornish, Überlebt durch Solidarität.
22  Rosinger, unpublished memoir, chap. 7.

previously arrested (550 of them), others who came from the Târgu Jiu camp (406 internees), and a third group who had been detained at Caransebeş jail (85 prisoners). It is important to mention this, because their differing states of health were later to have serious repercussions.[23]

Benditer: During the second part of September 1942, a total of 1,201 Jews were deported to Vapniarka from the various regions of the Old Romanian Kingdom and Transylvania. Of these deportees, 407 were from the detention camp in the former jail of Târgu Jiu, 72 were transferred from the Caransebeş prison, and 722 had been randomly taken from their homes in various Romanian cities. There was also a group of Christian Romanians, charged and convicted for criminal offences. However, the non-Jewish detainees in the camp never exceeded 10 percent of the total number of detainees.[24]

Dr. Arthur Kessler: On September 16, 1942, a group of 1,200 people was brought to Vapniarka. [...] From this group, 80 were from a jail in Romania. There they had a very difficult prison regime, with poor conditions of food, clothing, and movement. Six hundred came from a concentration camp in Romania and had been for the most part in forced labor building a tunnel. They were also subjected to poor food and living conditions. Over 500 were arrested from their homes. [...] In the Vapniarka camp, at this time, there were already 150 Ukrainians and Russians, a small number of which were war prisoners, a larger number were inhabitants of the region, as the camp was also being used as a jail.[25]

---

23  Kornish, Überlebt *durch Solidarität*.
24  Benditer, "Cattle Fodder for the Victims."
25  Kessler, "Lathyrismus." All translations from this publication included in this text are made by Olga Ştefan.

Nathan Simon: Our transport was composed of 90 political prisoners, 450 from the Târgu Jiu camp, and 570 deported from their homes in Romania. All together we were 1,110 Jews, of which a few hundred were women and some children.[26]

Also in the three books published immediately after the war, the numbers vary. Rudich mentions 1,300 people, Baranga 1,200, and Lezea writes of "more than a thousand." In his telling, Rudich describes an episode that does not appear in any other account: he claims that, "[d]ivided into two convoys, [...] the people sent to Vapniarka were to be shot and thrown into common graves upon arrival. The order was badly implemented. So instead of the first convoy, the other was executed at Mostovoi-Berezovka."[27]

*Work*
The work details were supposed to be organized by the official Jewish Committee, but Rosinger specifies, as we will see later on, that in fact the division of labor was influenced, if not entirely determined, by the clandestine communist collective.

Benditer: The governor of Transnistria responsible for supplying the camps aimed, on the one hand, to facilitate the extermination of the detainees and, on the other, to increase his profits. He presented a petition to the ministry in November 1942 proposing that the "Jews" in Vapniarka be used for a variety of labor projects: "By so doing," he claimed, "the camp would be less congested, food for labor would be ensured and the risk of outbreak of epidemics would be diminished." The work projects were not too far from the camp. The prisoners were taken into the forest to chop wood, to the train station to stack or to load wood, and to unload coal and other materials from trains. Sometimes, the prisoners in these work teams managed to ob-

26  Simon, "... *auf allen Vieren werdet ihr hinauskriechen*," 64.
27  Rudich, *La Braţ cu MOARTEA*, 87.

tain a piece of bread, a potato, or some other food, which they clandestinely brought into the camp in order to help the old, the sick, and those incapable of work. Since there was a complete lack of sugar in the camp, the heaps of beets from the fields near the train station were regarded as "manna from heaven." Sometimes soldiers would pretend not to notice when the teams returned from work with a few beets. They were cut into slices, fried, and distributed first to the sick and, if some were left, only then to others.[28]

Kornish: Work at the railway station created an opportunity for us to send news out, thus breaking the silence about life in the Vapniarka camp. People outside found out about our fate, and this was very important. [...] The men who had been ordered to the train station to unload coal, including myself, tried especially to "make friends" with the guards (most of them were police reserves). Our approach was based on the idea of achieving solidarity between internees and guards, and this political work really bore fruit later on.[29]

Nathan Simon: The market was held two to three times per week (in town). Once I arrived there, I would get a half a loaf of bread, 150 grams of bacon, and a liter of milk, which I drank straight out of the bucket. A potato sack weighing 60 kilograms was placed on my back, and then I would walk back to the camp with it.[30]

*Food and Lathyrism*
The specificity of Vapniarka, besides its status as a political prisoner camp, was Colonel Murgescu's scheme of exterminating the prisoners slowly by providing them with toxic feed as food. How-

---

28  Benditer, "Cattle Fodder for the Victims."
29  Kornish, Überlebt durch Solidarität.
30  Simon, *"… auf allen Vieren werdet ihr hinauskriechen,"* 74.

ever, this fit perfectly within the scope of the "final solution" of the Antonescu regime that resulted in the death of hundreds of thousands of Jews in Transnistria and the occupied territories under Romanian administration. In the case of Vapniarka, Murgescu's policy turned out to indeed have devastating and permanent effects on the camp population, although most prisoners survived due to the extraordinary solidarity they practiced, which we will address later in more detail. Dr. Kessler tells that the Ukrainian prisoners that had been in Vapniarka already since May 1942 were receiving 200 grams of peas per day and 200 grams of bread until the arrival of the Jews on September 16, and thereafter all detainees started to receive 400 grams of peas per day and the same 200 grams of bread, a detail that affected the rapidity with which the Jewish detainees developed symptoms.[31] The first case of paralysis was a Ukrainian in November, a full five months after arrival, while the first Jewish case was in December, only a month and a half after arrival. In early January, Dr. Kessler determined that the specific species of the peas eaten by the inmates was *Lathyrus sativus*, which in "quantities over 300 grams per day" caused various damaging symptoms, in many cases leading to spastic paralysis in the lower part of the body. By May 1943, over 800 of the 1,400 prisoners (mostly Jews and a few Ukrainian Christians)[32] of the camp showed varying degrees of lathyrism, a neurological disease caused by eating the peas. Most of the more severe cases were young Jewish males brought to Vapniarka from Romania's prisons as Dr. Kessler and Geza Kornish mention earlier. They

---

31  Kessler, "Lathyrismus."
32  The numbers I cite above are based on Dr. Kessler's notes, see footnote 62. However, documents from May 5, 1943, show that the number of detainees at Vapniarka was 1,312, among whom 1,092 were Jews and 198 Christian. The other 22 were considered criminals and were Christians. Among the Jews, 835 were men, 136 were women, and 5 were children (Arhivelor Naționale Istorice Centrale, fond Ministerul de Interne, pachetul 91, fila 569, p. 445).

had been made more vulnerable by the harsh conditions they had been subjected to before.

The lathyrism at Vapniarka, like many of the other episodes discussed here, is addressed with more or less attention and detail by each one of our references, depending on their personal relation to it and their storytelling goal. Dr. Kessler, being the head doctor in charge of the infirmary, and the one to discover the source of the inmates' illnesses, logically dedicates the majority of his memoirs to the topic, detailing the symptoms, attempted treatments, and steps taken to change the diet of the internees. He later wrote additional medical texts solely on the analysis of the disease.

> Dr. Kessler: A delegation goes to the commanding officer on duty, Captain Burădescu. We are three physicians and I am elected as spokesman. In a serious manner I describe the desperate situation, hundreds of completely or partially paralyzed [prisoners], lame and helpless, with room temperatures below zero degrees Celsius, without a bed, bag of straw, blankets during the heavy Russian winter, terrible hunger, softened through unpalatable bread and occasional supplements of meat from a fallen horse. I explain to him that we are prisoners in a camp during wartime, that we may possibly be killed by bombing raids or epidemics, but that it is against international law and the duty of a state to poison us on purpose. There are already 120 completely lame and another 1,000 on their way. The cause is the toxic pea food. This diet has to be stopped immediately and another form of nutrition to be introduced. Medical help, medicines, transfer to hospitals for the most severe cases is immediately necessary. He listens calmly with a pinched face and finally replies briefly, "How do you know that we are interested in keeping you alive?" End of conversation.[33]

---

33  Kessler, "Ein Arzt im Lager."

Out of the seven pages dedicated to Vapniarka in Rudich's book, only one paragraph mentions the paralysis that affected more than half of the internees, leaving room for short report on the other events in the camp. Baranga, however, in his six-page chapter on Vapniarka, makes the source of the paralysis and the impact on the detainees a recurring theme, emphasizing the heroic feats of the "antifascist collective" to counter it. Lezea mentions the epidemic but he dedicates most of his book to political conversations among detainees. Nathan Simon, being one of the earliest affected by the paralysis, unsurprisingly devotes long passages to the manifestations of the illness and his state of mind, as well as descriptions of the great deeds of Dr. Kessler, who cared for him in the hospital, not to mention that his book is in fact dedicated to the doctor. Simion Bughici's 31-page typed memoirs refer to the food and its effects on the population on one page. Dr. Kessler's name however, does not appear at all, but was only added as a handwritten note on the back of a page at a later date.

> Bughici: Later it became clear that the paralysis was caused by the peas, which were criminally given to us as our daily ration. [...] Our reaction was violent. We refused the food, we demanded medical expertise and chemical analysis of the pea fodder, we sent protests to the governor of Transnistria, to the Interior Ministry, and the Red Cross. We requested an inquiry and the punishment of the guilty.[34]

Throughout his text, Bughici uses the abstract "we" pronoun when referring to any actions taken in the camp, especially those that improved conditions for the population, thus including himself in all life-saving decisions, even when those were clearly the actions of others, as evidenced by various documents and Dr. Kessler's memoirs. In Vapniarka, Bughici was a member of the official Jewish Committee, composed of individuals from a variety of backgrounds and political leanings, "as the majority [of

---

34  Bughici, unpublished memoir.

the camp population] had no political allegiances at all."[35] He and Ștefan Voicu (Aurel Rottenberg, whose 1980 memoirs we do not consult here) were both communist activists who had come from the Târgu Jiu camp, as mentioned before.

However, in Benditer's book, a six-page chapter and another twelve-page chapter describe in great detail the food, the intention of the commander to exterminate the detainees, the trajectory from the beginning of the illness and the development of its many symptoms, the attempts made primarily by the medical staff headed by Dr. Kessler – whose name is also absent from the accounts of Baranga, Rodich, and Lezea – to help the detainees by writing official memoranda to the camp commander,[36] and the acts of resistance that were organized in order to change camp policy. These will be presented later.

> Benditer: The Ministry of Internal Affairs intended to cause a gradual extermination of the detainees through the accumulation of toxins in the body. [...] Alarmed by the proportions and severity of the illnesses, the doctors addressed memoranda and reports directly to the commander of the camp, and insisted that the Jewish Committee also formulate urgent requests to be sent to the commander in order to squelch the wave of sickness. [...] All the requests were rejected with the exception of the opening of a canteen where certain products, like potatoes, grain, or milk, could be purchased at high prices.[37]37

> Kornish: We remembered what they had clearly told us when we arrived at the camp and we demanded that Colo-

---

35  Benditer, "Cattle Fodder for the Victims."

36  "The doctors in Vapniarka themselves sent the results to the Romanian authorities in two memoranda, the first on January 20, 1943, and the second on March 8, 1943. Until the first report was sent, 66 prisoners suffered from paralysis of the lower body, and more than 400 presented symptoms of advanced paralysis" (Obidin, "Holocaustul în România").

37  Benditer, "Cattle Fodder for the Victims."

nel Murgescu, the camp commander, immediately replace the forage peas, which were poisoning us, with healthy food. [...] There was great panic in the camp, but Colonel Murgescu refused our request. After that, our internal leadership ordered all internees to a meeting in Pavilion II and the doctors demanded that we refuse to accept and consume these poisonous peas, because we would otherwise die a slow but certain death.[38]

*Organization, Solidarity, and Resistance in the Camp*

The elements that all the testimonies we reference highlight to varying degrees are the excellent organizational strategies of the camp leadership, the discipline, and particularly the solidarity practiced among the prisoners. The organization and solidarity were credited with the elimination of the typhus epidemic and with improving the living conditions of the prisoners, leading to a very high survival rate. Although several of the survivors died in the years following the war, only about 25 (23 Jews and about 2 Ukrainians) died in captivity from September 1942 to December 1943.[39] What not all agree on is whether these three survival strategies derived from the specific communist modes of organizing, if they were an inherent aspect of Jewish mutual aid as seen in other ghettos and throughout Jewish history, or if they resulted from the very special makeup of the prisoner population, composed of many doctors, intellectuals, and educated political prisoners with previous experience, used to implementing strict discipline.

Immediately after arriving in the camp, the inmates nominated their own leadership, the official Jewish Committee composed of Emanuil Vinea, Paul Dascălu, the lawyer Burger, Rado Alexandru, Simion Bughici, Paul Donath, and, according to Bughici, also Ernestina Orenstein (later married to Stoica Chivu). Her name is not mentioned by any of the other authors. As throughout the

38  Kornish, Überlebt durch Solidarität.
39  Obidin, "Holocaustul în România."

other spaces of forced confinement for Jews in Transnistria, there were no officially appointed *kapos*. The Jewish Committee of Vapniarka divided the inmates into groups of a hundred, each represented by a spokesperson, and those groups further divided into ten groups of ten.[40] Each decimal division had what was called an accountant responsible for food distribution and a hygiene supervisor. Besides being part of the Jewish Committee, Bughici was also a spokesperson for a group of a hundred on the ground floor of Pavilion II. In parallel to this official Jewish Committee there was a clandestine communist collective that operated in the shadows. Some of the testimonies also point to abuses committed in the camp by this clandestine communist collective.

> Benditer: Among those who arrived from the detention camp in Târgu Jiu was a core of action-oriented and decisive people. As a first objective, they decided to take action to change the system to select group chiefs. [...] There were many intellectuals and well-known leaders among the deportees, including former colleagues of the officers. [...] The commandant and his officers were interested in maintaining order in the camp, especially since they feared that an outbreak of epidemic diseases would endanger the troops lodged in the vicinity of the camp. [...] The most important step in the development of solidarity was the grouping of detainees by their former place of domicile in Romania. The biggest and wealthiest communities came from Arad, Timișoara, and Bucharest. Following in size and wealth were the communities from the counties of Moldova: Iași, Bacău, Botoșani, and Buhuși. The most destitute were those from Dorohoi, Bessarabia, and Bucovina. Accepted by the commanding officers as traditional forms of community organization among Jews, the communi-

---

40  Some say that this division was initiated by the Jewish Committee, others say by the clandestine communist collective while Dr. Kessler claims it was the doctors who suggested it.

ties were able to help each other as much as possible under the circumstances. The wealthier ones assisted those from Moldova, Bucovina, and Bessarabia. Groups for the care of the sick were organized within each community. Notwithstanding differences of opinion, in all instances where there was a threat to the detainees, the communities acted with firm unity in order to alleviate the danger. In order to reduce typhoid fever as well as other epidemic diseases, the camp's sanitary conditions and hygiene had to be strictly observed. [...] As a result, many epidemics were avoided and the number of sick did not increase considerably.[41]

Rosinger: Those who came from prisons and from Târgu Jiu, who had an experience of organizing life in difficult conditions, formed the nucleus that took over the leadership of our life inside the camp, they being used with collective discipline. As among us were people with various professions – doctors, pharmacists, engineers, tinsmiths, plumbers, carpenters, and various other craftsmen – it was not too difficult for us to make the camp livable in a relatively short time. After many discussions, the commandant provided us with old planks and nails, dismantling the floors of other buildings, so that bunk beds were made. The water pipe was repaired, the kitchen was put into operation, and an oven for killing parasites was made, and in six to eight months we also had a shower room, which was a great achievement.[42]

Kornish: From day one, life in the camp was coordinated by the leadership of an illegal organization. All those who were seen as reliable and who had proven this through their previous activities were part of this organization. I was accepted into the organization after a few days. [...] The pos-

41  Benditer, "Cattle Fodder for the Victims."
42  Rosinger, unpublished memoir, chap. 7.

sibility of a typhus epidemic was the biggest danger, apart from political and administrative arbitrariness. [...] Every morning before getting up, the internees' shirts and undergarments were checked for lice, as they spread the disease. [...] In the beginning, the lice had to be squashed between the fingernails. Later, when we had managed to convince the camp commanders that even their staff, their guards etc., would not be spared the disease, they installed an oven where the lice could be destroyed at high temperatures. Every item of clothing was taken to this parasite-extermination chamber as soon as one single louse was discovered. [...] Our illegal leadership placed a lot of importance on hygiene. Even if someone had only one spare shirt, it had to be clean at all times. This measure also forced us to preserve our self-respect, not to neglect ourselves, and not to resign ourselves to our fate. [...] The food was handed over to the organization and distributed among all the members several times per week as additional nutrition. These portions were called "*chaluk*," a term that originated at the Doftana jail. Nobody was excluded from this economic community. Nonmembers of the collective could also participate, as long as they agreed to the conditions. Anyone who gave something to the collective was allowed to keep a portion separate from the "*chaluk*" as a bonus. This also strengthened solidarity.[43]

Dr. Kessler: Life in the camp develops with timetable and division of labor. A guiding hand can be felt. It is not us nor any of our acquaintances. But it is there. Each hundred-strong contingent has its meal apportioned. They are all of the same cut, as are the contingent leaders. Section leaders are two advocates, of the indifferent type, but they are advised what to do and say. By whom are they advised?

---

43 Kornish, *Überlebt durch Solidarität*.

And about March 1943, he writes,

> Self-help is active. Two communities, Arad and Timișoara, send plenty of valuable food, also blankets, padding, clothes, and some of it reaches us and provides tangible relief.[44]

Gabriel Cohen's drawings, which he, like Mărculescu, made in the camp, are mere sketches, unsophisticated and stylistically akin to caricatures, but they bear witness and document the events and people of Vapniarka. This one illustrates the hygiene team's fight against exanthematic typhus.

Part of *The Future of Memory* archive (https://www.thefutureofmemory.ro/).

The clandestine communist collective was led by Lazăr Grinberg and Bernath Andrei (Bondy), who had been members of the Central Committee of the Antifascist Front and which was, in fact, directed by the Communist Party. Nathan Simon main-

---

44  Kessler, "Ein Arzt im Lager."

tains that the two men conceived and implemented the following points as necessities for the camp population's survival:

- Discipline and unity among all prisoners
- Destruction of the lice for the elimination of typhoid
- Struggle against hunger
- Organize the prisoners in such a way that whatever provoca tion made by the camp administration would be withstood by them
- Win sympathy of the camp commander
- Receive as many information as possible from the camp commander
- Achieve connection with the outside and Romania
- Prepare for even more extreme situations[45]

Rosinger, however, saw the clandestine communist collective very differently from his fellow inmates.

> Rosinger: If the ordinary members of the communist col-
> lective really had a hard time, the leadership of the col-
> lective, the party hierarchy, the party members brought
> from prisons, had remarkably better living conditions than
> the mass of the deportees. They sat in their small room,
> separate, because the many small rooms at the ends of
> the pavilions were all reserved for the leadership. In the
> small rooms, living conditions were incomparably better.
> [...] The policy of the camp collective leadership, both in
> Vapniarka and in Târgu Jiu, was a pyramidal policy. The
> lower layer was formed by ordinary internees and the mid-
> dle layer was made up of simple members of the collective,
> the enthusiasts who served those in the top layer, the party
> aristocracy. The upper party cadres had to be protected and
> spared, so they were given the lighter work and the heav-

---

45 [45] Simon, *"... auf allen Vieren werdet ihr hinauskriechen,"* 66.

ier work remained the task of the middle and lower layers of the pyramid. Members of the leadership worked at tailoring, rope making, and other crafts in Târgu Jiu and at easier work in Vapniarka, while ordinary laborers were sent to hard labor. At Vapniarka, those who had money could always buy food – milk, potatoes, bacon, butter, bread, fruit – from the Ukrainians and even from the camp canteen. [...] The leadership of the group had brought considerable funds with them from Târgu Jiu, so they had sufficient resources for supplies. [...] It sometimes happened that someonewould be harshly beaten by the leadership, for example, once Varadi Andrei, an honest old revolutionary activist with a critical spirit, not to mention some recalcitrants, who were also brought to order, not by persuasion, but by beatings. Nothing could have happened without the approval of the leadership of the collective.[46]

In his book, Benditer engages Rosinger's statement directly, and states the following:

Rosinger grossly exaggerates when he writes that anyone who had money in Vapniarka could purchase food at the canteen or from the Ukrainians. [...] Like in many camps and ghettos, those who had money could improve their personal situation. In Vapniarka, those who didn't have money to procure a little extra food were forced to nourish themselves solely with poisonous pea fodder.[47]

Marcel Roman, however, agrees with Rosinger's assessment of the collective's privileged position in the camp:

[A]t the head of the clandestine leadership [of the collective] were those whose principle was based on the leading role of the "conscious minority" but who, fighting the principle of petty bourgeois egalitarianism, organized their

---

46  Rosinger, unpublished memoir, chap. 7.
47  Benditer, *Vapniarca*, 45.

own life on the principle of "ruling elites," reserving for the group at the top of this pyramid as many rights as possible, which brought them closer to a normal life, their only deprivation being the lack of freedom, apart from the danger of being killed, a danger that afflicted us all.[48]

## Hunger Strike and Changing Politics in Romania
As Bughici and Kornish attest above, radical organized resistance against the attempts of the camp officials to exterminate the detainees started once the source of the paralysis and the other symptoms of lathyrism were established. It was in fact the medical staff, including Dr. Moritz and Dr. Kessler, who recommended that the Jewish Committee convince everyone to stop eating the peas until the camp officials change the diet.

> Benditer: [A]n intense educational campaign was started to alert people to the dangerous effects of this food. People were advised to refuse the daily rations that were made available to them. At the same time, an appeal was made to the wealthier communities to share the little food they had saved. Many opened their little boxes, where they had stored the food they had received from home, or had bought at the canteen. [A more lenient camp commander would occasionally allow a small canteen to function.] They gave some of this food to the sick in the infirmary. Similarly, those who worked outside the camp, at times when this was allowed, brought back and shared some of the food, which they had obtained at their places of work. Thus, the deportees were able to refuse eating the peas. For about three weeks, they were able to withstand their hunger pains. The strike culminated when people refused to allow the food to be brought in through the camp gate.[49]

---

48  *Buletinul Vapniarca.* Translation made by Olga Ştefan.
49  Benditer, "Cattle Fodder for the Victims."

Dr. Kessler on the other hand, characterizes it as: "The majority of the peas returned to the kitchen, no strike, but abstinence to the extreme."[50]

> Kornish: We did not go to work the following days, and the strike lasted three weeks. During this period, they gave us a daily ration of 200 grams of bread and 200 grams of dried apples and pears, which we used to make tea. For two days, they withdrew the bread, which was full of straw. The sacks of forage peas were thrown out over the fence. [...] No shots were fired, either, and finally they gave us potatoes, as well as horsemeat twice a week. [...] Protests by the Jewish community in Bucharest also contributed to a change in our diet. Following these events, Colonel Murgescu was replaced. [...] This is how the outcome of our hunger strike should be perceived, and to emphasize this claim I quote Colonel Murgescu's answer to a relevant question by Dr Kessler, the undisputed leader of approximately 20 deported doctors: "What makes you think the survival of your people means anything to us?"[51]

In describing the meeting between the camp commandant and the medical team, Kornish and Dr. Kessler conflict. Dr. Kessler stated that he had the conversation with Burădescu, not Murgescu.

As Benditer recounts, the camp was visited by Governor Gheorghe Alexianu on January 4, 1943. He "met with several deportees from Vapniarka, former law school colleagues from Chernovtsy, and promised that he would allow parcels with medication sent from Romania to be received in the camp,"[52] then, in the following weeks, the camp was inspected by several medical commissions from Romania. Continuous appeals were being made by the camp's medical staff, the Jewish Committee, and through the

---

50  Rosinger, unpublished memoir, chap. 7.
51  Kornish, Überlebt durch Solidarität.
52  Benditer, *Vapniarca*, 51.

illicit messages sent by members of the work details, as Kornish attests, through the Romanian guards at the train station on behalf of the prisoners.[53]

On January 23, 1943, Murgescu received an order from the Ministry of Internal Affairs to change the inmates' diet but despite this improvement, his adjunct commander, Captain Popescu, continued to impose harsh punishments and restrictions on the camp population. According to Benditer, Popescu was replaced on February 4, 1943, by Colonel Popovici, who was much more humane toward the detainees and even carried messages and goods back and forth from the camp and Bucharest. Shortly after this upswing in camp life, Colonel Popovici was caught acting as a courier and was almost court-martialed.[54]

> Rosinger: Of course, this improvement in our regime was in large part the result of the military disaster suffered by the Hitler bloc in Stalingrad.

> Kornish: The political situation probably contributed to his [Popovici's] sympathetic attitude, because news was now arriving from the front about setbacks of the German Army.

Colonel Popovici was replaced by Captain Burădescu, a painter known as a Gestapo agent who was even more brutal than Murgescu and Popescu toward the detainees.[55] One of the first episodes that took place during this period, which left an impression on many, was Burădescu's attempt to discover the clandestine leadership of the camp and those who passed messages about camp conditions to the Red Cross. Each one of our survivors describes

---

53  See Obidin, "Holocaustul în România." After receiving the first memo on January 20, 1943, the doctor responsible for Vapniarka, Lieutenant Colonel Gheorghe Tătăranu, ordered that the pea fodder be taken out of the detainees' diet.

54  Benditer, *Vapniarca*, 51.

55  Ibidem, 57.

this event completely differently, with the exception of Kornish and Bughici, who do not mention it at all.

> Benditer: One such agent of Burădescu was a beautiful Ukrainian, whom, it is believed, had contact with the Gestapo. She even managed to win over the trust of one of the lawyers in the leadership of the committee. But she was ultimately discovered, isolated, and boycotted before she could provoke any damage to the internees. She disappeared quickly and without a trace from the camp.[56]

> Nathan Simon: A young Ukrainian was brought in with visible signs of torture on her body. Her name was Vera and was thought to have been a partisan. Because she was so beautiful it was not surprising that the men tried to get to know her. Our good Dascălu was the lucky one with whom she entered into a relationship, and it seemed like real love was growing. And as suddenly as she appeared, Vera disappeared. Then it was all clear that she must have been an agent of the Gestapo, who had the mission to penetrate the leadership of the collective. [...] Dascălu was removed from his post and now had to deal with the responsibility for the appalling consequences of his failure.[57]

However, Rosinger, as we saw earlier, perceived the leadership of the clandestine communist collective as abusers of their position. He even tells us the fate of the two culprits after the war, something that none of the other accounts venture to do. This becomes another substantiating argument in his judgment of the collective's behavior, and his indictment of the party when it came to power after the war. He recalls the event thus:

> Immediately, it was revealed that she was Russian from Bessarabia, her name was Vera Isacenco, and her internment

---

56   Ibidem.
57   Simon, "... *auf allen Vieren werdet ihr hinauskriechen*," 59.

took place by order of the Inspectorate of Gendarmerie of Tiraspol. [...] Bernath Andrei entrusted Paul Dascălu, also part of the leadership, with the task of approaching the new internee in order to "unscramble" her and bring her closer to the collective, so that the leadership would be informed of her true intentions. [...] Given that we are all human, that Dascălu himself has been imprisoned for almost two years, plus Vera's charm, it is not hard to imagine that an intimate relationship was established between the two beings under the conditions of the months of the Transnistrian camp. [...] The fact is that the information gathered by Dascălu, concerning Vera and transmitted to the party, did not satisfy Bernath Andrei and thus Dascălu came to be suspected by the party of informing Vera in their hours of intimacy. Dascălu was unmasked as a traitor and was cruelly beaten by Bernath Andrei with his own hands in front of the internees. [...] I want to also note that immediately after liberation in 1944, Dascălu was arrested and spent many years in jail during the height of the socialist era. [...] As for Vera Isacenco, after liberation, the Romanian authorities turned her over to the Soviets, who freed Vera, finding her innocent.[58]

Later, on May 1, Burădescu attempted to stage a pogrom against the Jewish detainees by inciting the Ukrainians against them, and then using the general chaos that ensued as an excuse to order his soldiers to fire upon the Jews. Miraculously, the soldiers refused and instead fired into the air. In Bughici's notes, we do not find any mention of Vera, and this attack was, according to him, carried out by common criminals from the Jilava prison in Romania, not Ukrainians. A significant section in his writings details his interactions with these Romanians from Jilava – who made up the last lot to be deported to Vapniarka in 1943 – and his

---

58  Rosinger, unpublished memoir, chap. 7.

decisive action and success in convincing them to stop fighting. The soldiers' refusal to fire does not feature anywhere in his text.

## Culture in the Camp

Culture was a very important aspect of camp life and seen as one way for the detainees to resist the inhumanity they were experiencing: to boost morale and the will to live, and to avoid sinking into despair. Starting around the Jewish holidays in December 1942, lectures on various topics began to be held regularly, even in the most adverse conditions. Skits, performances, and musical recitals also took place.

> Benditer: In the evenings, after the barracks were locked, the windows were covered with blankets. Not a trace of light could be seen from the faint glow of the pieces of wood that the deportees had placed on the burning coals. By this pale light, they gathered together group by group, sitting on the low wooden bunks and on the floor, listening to lectures, poetry, or prose.[59]

> Lezea: This spring [referring to 1943] the flowers of our labor bloomed in the workshops: the wonderful exhibition organized in the large salon on the first floor where the women reside. Practical objects and even small art pieces made of wood or metal, wood engravings, small paintings, and local sketches by visual artists lit up the otherwise barbed-wired sky of Vapniarka.[60]

> Kornish: Some totally unexpected cultural activities took place in the camp while Colonel Popovici was in command. The internees produced a variety of craftworks, which were displayed at a camp exhibition. The commander and some officers visited the exhibition and had to acknowledge that there were many talented Jews. There was also a perfor-

59  Benditer, "Cattle Fodder for the Victims."
60  Lezea, *Vapniarca*, 90.

mance with singing, violin, dancing, and gymnastics. [...] Later, after a radio had been smuggled into the camp, we were briefed about the latest news on a daily basis. It worked like this: a single intermediary went for a walk in the courtyard with one collective member, let's say me, and delivered, e.g., five news items. I had to memorize them exactly in order to convey them one by one to several others who were also walking in the courtyard. News from the front was inconspicuously conveyed to nonmembers as well. This also strengthened solidarity and sometimes also boosted morale.[61]

## Liberation

On March 6, 1943, a commission was sent to Vapniarka to select the Jews who had been sent to the camp erroneously. From among the 554 files of Jews arrested from their homes, 427 were determined to not have valid cases for detention, among them Aurel Mărculescu. Although they were to be freed, the commission recommended they be sent to other ghettos first (Olgopol, Savrani, and Golta). The transfer of this group to the respective ghettos began in late May 1943. In June 1943, Captain Burădescu was replaced by Lieutenant Colonel Sabin Motora. Like Popovici before him, the prisoners appreciated Motora for his humanity and support. In the first days of October 1943, an order came to transfer to Rîbnița 54 political prisoners who had come to Vapniarka from the Caransebeș and Văcărești jails and who had not finished their sentences.[62]

---

61 Kornish, Überlebt *durch Solidarität*.

62 Benditer writes that it was Burădescu in fact who proposed to the 2nd Regiment of Internment that the detainees from Romania's prisons that had not finished their sentences at Vapniarka should be sent to another prison in Transnistria. This was approved and only months later the order came, when Motora was already commander. See Benditer, *Vapniarca*, 68.

## The Remaining Detainees

The internees from Caransebeş and Văcăreşti who had finished their sentences were left behind. Those that were transferred to Ribnita were massacred by retreating SS troops on March 17, 1944, among them Lazăr Grinberg and Bernath Andrei, the leaders of the clandestine communist collective in Vapniarka. Only three survived the Ribnita massacre, one of them Matei Gall, who's published memoirs are not cited here. On October 14, 1943, the Vapniarka concentration camp administration received the order to evacuate the entire camp. The buildings were disassembled and the materials loaded on freight cars, and the detainees boarded on a train toward Grosulovo, where the 564 Jewish deportees would remain until March 10, 1944, when they received the order to return to Romania. They were then taken to Târgu Jiu camp, where the majority remained until Romania's liberation on August 23, 1944. It was on this day that the country officially turned its arms against Nazi Germanyand King Mihai arrested Marshal Ion Antonescu.

Benditer: They [people in the convoy] were marched in the direction of Tiraspol. Before giving the order to move on, Colonel Motora addressed the troops with the following words: "It is not your responsibility to watch them, but to protect them." The gendarmes were instructed to avoid the heavily traveled roads so that there was less of a chance of encountering withdrawing troops, especially the German units. [...] Suddenly, behind a curve in the road on a hill, stood a group of Vlasovs. Fully armed, pointing automatic weapons, they were waiting for the convoy. They motioned to the accompanying soldiers to step aside yelling, "Jid caput" ("Death to the Kikes"). To reinforce the intimidation, they fired several shots in the air. At that moment, Colonel Motora's car arrived on the scene. [...] He motioned to the Vlasovs to stop shooting. Then, he ordered the soldiers to close ranks around the convoy and march faster to leave the danger zone as soon as possible. Once again, the lives of 450 deportees were saved by the energetic intervention of Colonel Motora. [...] After several hours of negotiations with the bridge commander, permission was given to allow the group from Grosulovo to cross the bridge. Thus, at midnight of March 13, 1944, the deportees reached the western shore of the Dniester at Tighina.[63]

Kornish: Colonel Sabin Motora was the last commander of the Vapniarka camp and later commander of the Grosulovo camp. Thanks to his efforts in March 1944, the inmates had a last-minute chance to cross the Dniestr River and to reach the Romanian side alive, thus escaping certain death. In his testimony about the Vapniarka concentration camp, Nathan Simon described this odyssey in great detail. During the last phase of the escape from Transnistria, Colonel Motora apparently gave the following order to the guards: "You must not guard the internees, you must protect them!" And, indeed, his courageous actions prevented an attack by Vlasov's troops. This was an extremely courageous deed. Colonel Hristache Popovici's humane behavior should be mentioned once more at this point. Both of the above-mentioned commanders acted in an unselfish manner and endangered their own freedom, perhaps even their lives, to save the internees. Their actions deserve special appreciation.[64]

*Conclusions*

Due to its special status as a camp for political prisoners, and because several survivors later became important members of the communist apparat, Vapniarka remained the emblem of what the communist regime called the "antifascist struggle." The term for

---

63   Benditer, *Vapniarca*, 85.
64   Kornish, Überlebt durch Solidarität.

the victims of fascism that was generally used by communists was "antifascist," thus masking the ethnic character of Romanian fascist persecution against Jewish and Roma targets. But if we understand "antifascist" to refer to one engaged in action against the fascist terror and not just anyone on the receiving end of it, then the reality of the camp's population was otherwise: the majority of the prisoners were not even politically inclined and numerous internees were even religious. And while the communist rhetoric after the war in Romania preferred to sublimate ethnic minorities into one national construct of the "Romanian people," one cannot forget that the "Christian" communists that were incarcerated in the country's political prisons did not get deported, only Jews did. So Vapniarka, despite its very diverse population, and its designation as a camp for political prisoners, was just another Jewish camp in Transnistria with a regime of extermination.[65]

Each of the works we reference reveals the tendency to infuse history with one's own subjectivity. Of course, the majority are memoirs or art objects that inherently aim to reveal personal experience, not only historical fact, which is instead sometimes manipulated or altered to ensure that the author's narrational agenda prevails. In others, the ideological frame within which they operate is very clear. The language used by Sergiu Lezea is typical of the stilted expressions and slogans popular in the communist press, as is Aurel Baranga's. Despite a radical ideological turn in Eastern European countries and an unfettered "anticommunism" that unfortunately often took the form of right-wing nationalism, the works published after 1990 manage to maintain a balance and not condemn the communist activists of the war period even when rightly criticizing the postwar regime. Benditer merely disregards the clandestine communist collective's particular communist principles and does not make much fuss of their

---

65  In November 1943, from a total of 1,312 detainees, 619 were communists (ArhiveleNaționale Istorice Centrale, fond Ministerul de Interne, pachetul 91, fila 569, p. 445). This statistic conflicts with the testimonies mentioned in this study, which puts that number lower.

impact on the manifestation of solidarity in the camp. Instead, he accentuates the extraordinary efforts of the doctors and nurses, the typical forms of Jewish self-organization and mutual aid, as well as the prisoners' discipline. Geza Kornish's memoirs are highly influenced by both Nathan Simon's and Yehiel Benditer's, whom he also cites, but while acknowledging the crimes committed by the communist regimes until 1990, he doesn't waver in commending primarily the clandestine communist collective, of which he was part, for saving the lives of the inmates. Bughici paints a picture in which the only heroes were the members of the collective and does not mention the doctors' names at all, effectively erasing them from history, while Rosinger condemns the collective for abuses and totalitarian tactics. It is important to note that Rosinger was tried and sentenced to eight years in prison within the Foreign Trade political trials of the early 1960s, which targeted Jews, and his memoirs, like Bughici's, were written in the 1970s, in his case after being released from prison. Along with Benditer's, the most reliable testimony in our view is Dr. Kessler's unpublished memoir due to his concurrent recording in his notebook of the events as they happened, although some details seem to contradict others' accounts at times. More research and cross-referencing personal testimonies with documents is necessary and is forthcoming in future research.

What we do not get from these memoirs is a clear picture of the friendships that were made, and the interactions among people. The respective names of those we cite here, especially those that had spent time at Târgu Jiu together, do not appear in the works by the others, except in a few instances. Bughici is mentioned only briefly by Rosinger, while Rosinger is not at all by Bughici, in this case due to political motives. Benditer does not mention Bughici at all, for example, and Geza Kornish is entirely absent from all testimonies. Aurel Mărculescu and Gabriel Cohen are only mentioned by name in Benditer's work, without any discussion about personal interactions with them.

While personal experience and political beliefs informed the storytelling and the narrative thread in all works, including Benditer's, despite his ambitions to present a more objective picture, what resounds from all the authors is that the camp population was saved from epidemic diseases and certain death only through discipline, solidarity, and efficient internal organization. While not all our references attribute these strategies to the clandestine communist collective, some placing more weight on existing traditions of Jewish mutual aid, the actions of the medical staff or of the Jewish Committee with its diverse representatives, it is without question that only through solidarity and its practical implementation were the majority of the internees able to survive. This should be a lesson to us now, when the economic crisis propelled by the COVID-19 pandemic exposes the profound inequities in our society and the corruption of the political class in many countries whose policies during this time, even more than before, were guided almost entirely by self-interest. What the case of Vapniarka demonstrates is that our hope, too, like that of the prisoners in the camp, lies in a more equitable distribution of resources and a collective response toward supporting the weak in our society, a contemporary form of solidarity that must function in the interest of the majority, not only of the privileged few.

# Bibliography

## Archives

ArhiveleNaționale Istorice Centrale (Bucharest), fond Ministerul de Interne.

## General Bibliography

Ancel, Jean. *Transnistria, 1941–1942: The Romanian Mass Murder Campaigns*. Tel Aviv: Goldstein-Goren Research Center, Tel Aviv University, 2003.

Baranga, Aurel. *Ninge Peste Ukraina*. Bucharest: Editura Scînteia, 1946.

Benditer, Yehiel. "Cattle Fodder for the Victims." Translated by Felicia (Steigman) Carmelly. In *The Nizkor Project: Shattered! 50 Years of Silence: History and Voices of the Tragedy in Romania and Transnistria: Part Two: Personal Testimonies*, 1991–2012. http://www.nizkor.com/hweb/people/c/carmelly-felicia/benditer-ihiel.html, accessed April 9, 2020.

Benditer, Yehiel. *Vapniarca: lagărele Vapniarca și Grosulovo, închisoarea Ribnița, ghetourile Olgopol, Savrani, Tridubi, Crivoi-Ozero și Trihati*. Tel Aviv: Anaïs, 1995.

Bughici, Simon. Unpublished memoir, 1975.

*Buletinul Vapniarca*, June-December 1978.

Desbois, Patrick. *Holocaust by Bullets: A Priest's Journey to Uncover the Truth behind the Murder of 1.5 Million Jews*. New York: St. Martin's, 2008.

Dumitru, Diana. *The State, Antisemitism, and Collaboration in the Holocaust: The Borderlands of Romania and the Soviet Union*. Cambridge: Cambridge University Press, 2016.

*The Future of Memory*: https://www.thefutureofmemory.ro/.

Kessler, Arthur. "Ein Arzt im Lager – A Camp Physician: Excerpts of Arthur Kessler's Memoirs Relating to the Epidemic of Neurolathyrism in Camp Vapniarka, Transnistria." *CCDN (Cassava Cyanide Diseases & Neurolathyrism) Network News* 25 (June 2015), 3–10. https://www.

researchgate.net/publication/280316680_Translation_of_Ein_Arzt_im_Lager_-_A_camp_physician_-_by_Arthur_Kessler, accessed April 9, 2020.

Kessler, A. "Lathyrismus." *Monatsschrift für Psychiatrie und Neurologie* 113.6 (1947): 345–375.

Kornish, Geza. Überlebt durch Solidarität – *KZ Wapniarka, Ghetto Olgopol in Transnistrien, Arbeitslager in Rumänien*. Konstanz: Hartung-Gorre Verlag, 2004. Translated as Geza Kornis, *Survival through Solidarity: Vapniarka Concentration Camp, Olgopol Ghetto in Transnistria, Labour Camp in Romania: A Contemporary Eyewitness Report*. http://www.bjt2006.org/GK01.html, accessed April 9, 2020.

Lezea, Sergiu. *Vapniarca*. Bucharest: Editura Tiparnița, 1945.

Obidin, Y. "Holocaustul în România." *Războiul Pentru Trecut*/Война за Прошлое [The war for the past], October 18, 2015. https://razboiulpentrutrecut.wordpress.com/2015/10/18/holocaustul-in-romania/, accessed May 17, 2020.

Rosinger, Adalbert. Unpublished memoir, 1978.

Rudich, M. *La Braț cu MOARTEA, vedenii din Transnistria*. Biblioteca Hehault, 1945.

Shapiro, Paul A.. "Vapniarka: The Archive of the International Tracing Service and the Holocaust in the East." *Holocaust and Genocide Studies* 27.1 (2013): 114–137.

Simon, Nathan. *"... auf allen Vieren werdet ihr hinauskriechen": Ein Zeugenbricht aus dem KZ Wapniarka*. Berlin: Institut Kirche und Judentum, 1994.

Spitzer, Leo. "Solidarity and Suffering: Lager Vapniarka among the Camps of Transnistria." In *Witnessing Unbound: Holocaust Representation and the Origins of Memory*, edited by Henri Listiger Thaler, 105–130. Detroit: Wayne State University Press, 2017.

Thaler, Henri Listiger. *Witnessing Unbound: Holocaust Representation and the Origins of Memory*. Detroit: Wayne State University Press, 2017.

# Afterword: The Time of Terror, the Time of Remembrance

*Przemysław Urbańczyk*

This volume surpasses traditional approaches to the Holocaust by its ambition to operate a perspective, which is substantially broadened by inclusion of rarely recalled histories, applying rare points of view, or showing people rarely consociated with the horrors of that time. These atypical aspects offer a reader of this collection of essays an insight into that wrong-headed reality where life was valued very little.

*Memories of Terror: Essays on Recent Histories* is edited by Mihaela Gligor, who managed to persuade a group of interesting scholars to undertake a joint effort of reporting the results of their individual studies. They present both various examples of victimization and persecution of Jews during World War II as well as stories which reveal the post-Holocaust life of survivors. Obviously, they are not comparable but equally fascinating as pictures of "second lives" randomly given to some people who were thus unwillingly "nominated" witnesses or even guardians of the remembrance of unimaginable tragedies.

Besides Mihaela Gligor, who initiated this project, the book includes texts written by two other former fellows of the Polish Institute of Advanced Studies. Katharina Friedla, who discusses the life of religious Polish Jews who spent the war in the militantly atheistic Soviet Union. Based on various testimonies, diaries, and interviews, she shows the endurance of people desperately struggling for their collective identity. Tuvia Friling investigates the mystery of Eliezer Gruenbaum – a Jewish activist whose life was ineffaceably stained by his service as a kapo in Auschwitz. This story, which offers no final answer and no conclusive judgment, illustrates very well the kinds of unsolvable dilemmas which some people were faced with.

The book is strongly "Romanian" in its selection of subjects, which is not a drawback but, just opposite – an asset. For this inclination turns our attention to the area, events, and people who are not often included in the discussion of the atrocities to which the Jews were subject during World War II: the phenomenon of stigmatization applied to Jews expelled to the enclave of Transnistria (by Sonia Catrina); the personal story of Saul Steinberg who had to leave Europe for America (by Mihaela Gligor); the tragic fate of Romanian Jewish children (by Eugenia Mihalcea), or the relatively little known story of Transnistria where c. 380,000 Romanian Jews were exterminated (by Olga Ştefan). All these chapters create a new vision of the suffering nation (the Jews). The story about the Shanghai Getto (by Arleen Ionescu) is also touching.

My personally preferable chapter is Mihaela Gligor's analysis of how Saul Steinberg "processed" traumatic memories of his childhood and juvenility in Europe. My once favorite artist, whose intriguing drawings were reproduced in the 1960s and 1970s by the legendary Polish journal Przekrój, is shown here with a face different than the one would expect of this often sarcastic observer of "civilized" people – sometimes puckishly hidden in cats and dogs.

*

Such a collection of painful memories of the long departed past inevitably provokes not only historical reflections but also current reactions regarding the necessity of remembrance. The only answer to the recurring question "How long and how much shall we recall the atrocities of the Holocaust?" is "Enough" – long enough to make sure that these painful memories will make humanity resistant to the temptation to solve socioeconomic and political problems by implementation of an organized massive sweeping away of people defined as collective enemies.

Our naïve hope that the danger of the reappearance of massive deadly terror has been ultimately removed during the moral "enlightenment" of the post-World War II period eventually fell in ruin during the ethnic cleansing in Rwanda (1994) and the wars inflicted at the end of the twentieth century by the collapse of

Yugoslavia. Those horrific explosions of politically steered cruelty showed that "civilized" standards only superficially cover the primitive attitudes which, in specific circumstances, easily re-emerge from the pits where they seemed to be buried and terminally sealed.

When confronted with such a volume as this one, we have to reconsider our self-complacency and think of the measures necessary to remove stigmatization appealing to racial, religious, ethnic, or other collective imputations. Educational strategies which promote a culture of a "permanent" dialogue based on tolerant respect should be in the focus of politicians who seriously preplan socially sustainable future.

Warsaw, May 28, 2020

## About the Authors

Professor **Raphael Vago** is a Senior Lecturer and Senior Research Fellow, Department of History, Tel Aviv University, The Stephen Roth Institute for the Study of Contemporary Antisemitism and Racism and the Cummings Center for Russian and East European Studies.
E-mail: vago@tauex.tau.ac.il

**Sonia Catrina** is an Associate Researcher with the Elie Wiesel National Institute for the Study of the Holocaust in Romania, and her research interests relate to Holocaust "memoryscapes" in non-Western societies.
E-mail: soniacatrina@gmail.com

**Katharina Friedla** holds a PhD from the Department of History and Jewish History, University of Basel, Switzerland. In recent years she has been working as researcher, translator, and scientific advisor for many institutions in Germany, Israel, and Poland. She has published several books and articles on Jews in Germany, Poland, and the USSR before, during, and in the aftermath of World War II.
E-mail: katharina-friedla@web.de

**Tuvia Friling** is a Professor and a Senior Researcher at the Ben-Gurion Research Institute and the Ben-Gurion University of the Negev, Israel.
E-mail: friling@bgu.ac.il

**Mihaela Gligor** is a researcher in the Philosophy of Culture at the Romanian Academy Cluj-Napoca, "George Barițiu" History Institute, Department of Socio-Human Research, and Associate Professor at Faculty of History and Philosophy, Babeș-Bolyai University Cluj-Napoca, Romania.
E-mail: mihaelagligor@gmail.com

**Arleen Ionescu** is Professor of English Literature and Critical Theory at Shanghai Jiao Tong University, School of Foreign Languages, Department of English.
E-mail: anionescu@sjtu.edu.cn

**Eugenia Mihalcea** is a PhD student at Weiss-Livnat International Multi-Disciplinary Center for Holocaust Studies, Education and Commemoration, University of Haifa, Israel. This chapter is a part of the MA thesis she wrote during her fellowship at the Hebrew University of Jerusalem.
E-mail: eugenia.mihalcea@gmail.com

**Olga Ștefan** was born in Romania, raised in Chicago, and currently lives in Zürich. She is an independent researcher, curator, and documentary filmmaker. Her art projects and writing can be found at https://olgaistefan.wordpress.com/, while *The Future of Memory* platform and respective films can be found at https://www.thefutureofmemory.ro/.
E-mail: olgastefanconsulting@yahoo.com

**Przemysław Urbańczyk**, Full Professor at the Institute of Archaeology and Ethnology (Polish Academy of Sciences) and at the Institute of Archaeology (Cardinal Stefan Wyszynski University), is also the Director of the Polish Institute of Advanced Studies in Warsaw.
E-mail: uprzemek1@poczta.onet.pl

Lightning Source UK Ltd.
Milton Keynes UK
UKHW010642140121
377037UK00002B/552